MW00897015

Growing Up in Pensacola II

Personal Essays

by Charlie Davis

Edited by
Sandra Lockney Davis

1

Copyright 2016 by Charles Eugene Davis

ALL RIGHTS RESERVED. THIS BOOK, OR PARTS THEREOF, MAY
NOT BE REPRODUCED IN ANY FORM WITHOUT PERMISSION
FROM THE AUTHOR

Printed by CreateSpace

LIBRARY OF CONGRESS CATALOG CARD NUMBER: pending
ISBN 978-1511731249
First Printing: 2016
PRINTED IN THE UNITED STATES OF AMERICA

Front Cover

Ora Wills, Aunt Jenny Hudgens, & Doris Cannon **Aunt Jenny's Swimmin' Hole**	Dickie Davis **5 Flags Speedway**	Herbert Lockwood **Pensacola Boxers & Golden Gloves**	Bill Pennewill **The USS** *Pennewill*
Joe Tarbuck **The Judge**	**Jerry Maygarden**	Capt. Shirley Brown **The Brown Family & Boats**	Charlie Evans **My Friend Charlie**
Norman Redding **My Brother In Law in Raiford Prison**	Frank Davis with BoSpot & Cricket **Hunting**	**Gordon Towne**	E. W. Hopkins **Hopkins Boarding House, Hoppy's and the Hopkins Family**
Alan McMillan	Capt. Sydney Clopton **The Ten Kids**	**John E. Frenkel, Sr**	**Eugene Rasponi**

**Other Books by
Charlie & Sandra Davis**

Growing Up In Pensacola

They also Serve

**So, What's a Nice Girl Like You Doing in a Place Like This?
Seoul To Saigon**

Preface

This sequel, *Growing up in Pensacola II,* like Volume I, is about local people I've known at some point during my eighty-four years as a Pensacola native. It was not my plan to write a sequel when I finished the first book in 2009, but sales were much greater than expected, and requests for the book continue today. I was humbled and pleased by the number of requests for the book, and invitations to give book talks at local organizations, and book stores.

The structure of *Growing Up In Pensacola II is* the same as the first book, consisting of separate chapters on individuals and groups of interest, as well as distinguished leaders in various fields, like sports, radio, military, banking, politics, commercial fishing, the maritime industry, educators, schools, judges and others. As in the first volume, every story is supported by pictures and illustrations, the most difficult and time consuming part of producing a book of this nature, but they unquestionably enhance the stories.

Pensacola has a rich history, and although I'm not a historian, I believe my coverage of people, places and things, gives a personal touch to the historical significance of the time period involved. I hope you enjoy reading these stories as much as I enjoyed writing them.

Charlie Davis
Gulf Breeze, Florida

Acknowledgments

This book would still be in the writing and rewriting stage without the advice and encouragement from my fellow writers in the Critique Group of the West Florida Literary Federation. I am deeply grateful to Ron Tew, Patty Damm, Linda Miragliotta and Jack Beverly for their honest critique of every word, sentence, paragraph I wrote, rewrote and rewrote again while completing this second volume.

I am also grateful to the many individuals who responded to my requests for information and pictures. Also, to those who submitted to interviews in person or via telephone or emails. It would have been impossible to complete the chapters without their individual help and suggestions.

I wish to thank fellow members of Gulf Coast Authors, an organization of local published writers, for the comradery and encouragement I've received from the many talented professionals of various genres. Gulf Coast Authors' books are available at many festivals throughout Northwest Florida, South Alabama, their website, www.gulfcoastauthor.com and www.amazon.com.

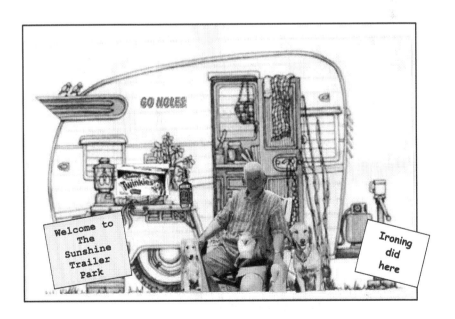

A simple thanks to my wonderful wife, Dr. Sandra Lockney Davis, is not enough. She labored weeks and months to prepare this manuscript for publication, which was no easy task. Her knowledge of the technology required to scan photos, insert the many pictures, place captions, format the manuscript and deal directly with the printer, was invaluable. I couldn't have done it without her.

A few years ago, my son, Frank Davis, jokingly commented, "If it wasn't for Sandra, Dad would be living in the Sunshine Trailer Park living on Twinkies." Frankly, I don't disagree with his humorous observation and I tell her often, "If you leave me, I'm going with you."

TABLE OF CONTENTS

CONTENTS

TABLE OF CONTENTS (con't)

CONTENTS:

1

Alan McMillan

Alan McMillan

$\mathbf{A}$lan McMillan is currently the Commodore of the Pensacola Yacht Club, but that's not why I chose to write about him, although that's quite an accomplishment and honor in itself. I've known Alan and his family for many years. We were neighbors, and I was his and his brother Neil's scoutmaster back in the late 1950's. I didn't see Alan again until after he retired and moved home. However, I was kept informed about his progress and whereabouts through occasional contacts with his family and relatives.

It was only a few months after the United States entered WWII, shortly after my two older brothers, several of Alan's uncles and thousands of other local young men volunteered for military service, our neighborhood welcomed a newborn resident. He was Alan C. McMillan, born on April 1, 1942. Today, he is considerably older and has probably been the butt of

"April Fool" jokes at least seventy-four times. I'm pleased and honored to write about Alan and his accomplishments, not just because he is a product of my old neighborhood, but because he's a local, nice guy who did well. His story isn't about a kid growing up in poverty with holes in his underwear and accustomed to wearing hand-me-downs, but it is about a kid who grew up in an average neighborhood to become a success on his own. Alan arrived in this world with good family genes, but before writing about his achievements, I thought the reader would be interested in knowing where those genes came from.

Van, Angus, Jr., Alan, Virginia, and Neil McMillan

A look back through Alan and his sibling's maternal heritage shows their grandmother, Eva Gonzalez Sheppard, was a direct descendent of Don Manuel Gonzalez and Marianna Bonifay, both of whom received land grants from the King of Spain in the 1700s. They and their descendants are the subjects of many books and papers about their part in the history of Pensacola. Don Manuel Gonzalez was a former Spanish soldier who took part of his pay in the form of a land grant, which included all of present day East Pensacola Heights. Don Manuel married Maria Louisa Bonifay, the daughter of Joseph and Marianna Pingrew Bonifay, Alan and his sibling's 4th great grandmother. *

11

The Sheppard Family:
Sitting L to R: Dudley, Mary, Eva, Laurie, Oscar and Evelyn
Standing: Alan, Lucy, Nixon, Virginia, and Frank

Their maternal grandfather, Oscar N. Sheppard, arrived in Pensacola in the late 1800s from Panama City. Recently, while my wife and I were having lunch with Alan, he related a humorous story about one of his ancestors on the Sheppard's side of the family. He said it was known that a grandfather, many generations back, was a General during the American Civil War, or the "War of Yankee Aggression," as it is referred to by some of my "Red Neck" friends. He related how it was always a source of pride for his relatives, a traditional Southern family, to brag about having an ancestor who was a general in the Confederate Army. This great source of family pride continued for years. Recently, papers were obtained when a distant relative died who had researched the family history. The papers verified their grandfather, their object of admiration, was indeed a general during the Civil War—in the Union Army.

The McMillan family, Angus Murphy McMillan and Virginia Sheppard McMillan, along with their children, Angus, Jr., Neil, Alan, Virginia and Van, lived across the street from us on Gonzalez Street (originally 7th Street). On one end was the Oscar and Eva Gonzalez Sheppard home (Virginia's parents) at the corner of Bayou Boulevard and Gonzalez Street. On the other end was the home of Ms. Hela Gonzalez

Maguire and her brother, Oscar A. Gonzalez, Mrs. Sheppard's siblings. So, the McMillan kids had their Grandparents and aunts and uncles on one side and their great aunt and great uncle on the other. Recently, Alan acknowledged how fortunate he and his siblings were to have had their grandparents, aunts and uncles living so close. It must have been a great arrangement, because most of us kids had to go on trips, long trips for some of us, to see our grandparents, aunts and uncles.

I suspect that whenever members of the McMillan and Sheppard family got together, whether in their homes or on the patio under the large oaks that surrounded the Sheppard house, the conversation would have eventually turned to sailing. It's no wonder that sailing was, and still is their passion, since Oscar Sheppard, their patriarch, was a 1908 charter member of the Pensacola Yacht Club (PYC), and a member of the 1920 PYC crew that won the first Lipton Cup race, held on Lake Pontchartrain.

In her book, *History of the Southern Yacht Club*, Flora K. Scheib wrote, "The first skipperette regatta was held in 1921 in the recently acquired Fish Class Sloops" and "Another expert skipperette was Mrs. Angus McMillan" (Alan's mother). In 1964, Alan Sheppard, a prominent Pensacola Attorney, Alan's uncle and namesake, was the commodore of the Pensacola Yacht Club. The following year, he became the commodore of the Gulf Yachting Association. The late Angus McMillan, Alan's father, won more than his share of sailing trophies, some of which are currently on display at the PYC.

Alan & Eileen Sheppard with Alan & Gloria McMillan

Alan's paternal grandfather, Angus Murphy McMillan, was a prominent Escambia County official and businessman. Although born in

Santa Rosa County in 1864, he lived the majority of his life in Escambia County where he and wife, Mattie Pou McMillan, raised their six children. In his long political career, he was first elected as the Escambia County Tax Assessor at age 28, and subsequently elected as the Clerk of the Circuit Court, and prior to his retirement in 1909, he served as the Clerk of the Court of Record. After retirement, he entered the real estate business with partner, C. N. McClure. Angus Murphy McMillan died in 1919.

So, Alan is the product of an impressive gene pool, which helps to explain his successes. As for his educational background, he graduated from Pensacola's Catholic High School, and received his Associate's Degree from Pensacola Junior College, now Pensacola State College, in 1963. He earned his B.S. Degree from the University of Florida in 1966 and his M.A. Degree from the University of West Georgia in 1980. He also completed a Senior Executive Fellowship at Harvard University in 1980.

Following his graduation from the University of Florida in 1966, Alan began his career in the Federal Government at Eglin Air Force Base. It was during the years at Eglin, living in Ft. Walton Beach his first son, Alan, Jr. and daughter, Susan, were born. Four years later he moved to Atlanta to join the U. S, Department of Labor as the Regional Human Resources Director, later serving as the Regional Administrator for the Occupational Safety and Health Administration (OSHA) in both the Chicago and Atlanta Regions. While living in Atlanta, Alan's second son, Preston, was born.

Alan traveled extensively, but he made time for his family. He said:

> One of the joys of being a dad was getting involved in my children's activities and particularly sports." His son, Alan, Jr. loved soccer, so Alan got dragged into coaching, a sport he didn't grow up with and really didn't understand, but he did it anyhow. He ended up loving both the sport and coaching the kids. Looking back on those times, Alan said, "They won many championships, and I remember feeling like I was Vince Lombardi.

Hannah, Gloria, Kyle, P. J., Alan, Alan, Jr. & Preston

14

Alan (far left) with former Illinois Governor Rod Blagojevich, and then, Senator Barack Obama.

Alan (far right) meeting with Crown Prince of Baharain, the Minister of Energy and CEO of BAPCO

Alan with Al Gore and Senator Tim Johnson

15

Alan with Secretary of Transportation, Federico Pena

With the President of the AFL/CIO, Richard L. Trumka

With the Korean CEO of Samsung

With the German CEO of Mercedes Benz, Dieter Zetsche

In 1987 Alan and family moved to Washington, D.C., when he was named Acting Assistant Secretary of Labor for Mine Safety and Health (MSHA); in 1988, he was appointed Deputy Assistant Secretary of Labor for the Employment Standards Administration. It was a big change from Atlanta to the nation's capital. Alan described the transition in a recent email:

Alan in
Washington, D. C.

Of course, I got a lesson in big time politics. My first boss in D C during the Reagan Administration was Secretary of Labor, Bill Brock. He was a terrific Secretary and had already served as a Congressman and Senator from Tennessee and later would serve as Chairman of the Republican Party. In my first week as Acting Assistant Secretary for MSHA, he took me to a private introduction meeting with Senator Ted Kennedy, who was a Majority Chairman for the Democrats. Those two political opposites had worked together for years, usually arguing the issues but in private treated each other with the friendship and respect one would expect from old friends and close collogues. Quite the opposite view one would get from reading the Washington Post. Like that occasion there were probably several dozen other times, many of which when I was testifying before Congress that I asked myself, "What's a kid from Pensacola doing here?"

The *Finesse*

In Washington D.C., he was a sailor away from home without a boat, but he remedied that situation. While home on a visit, he purchased a 38 ft. sailboat from his brother, Neil who operated a Hunter Sailboat dealership. He and his crew raced it on the Chesapeake Bay and started winning races. One such race was the Maryland Governor's Cup, with over two-hundred boats. It was an important race, and probably with Alan's encouragement, five crewmembers from Pensacola joined him on his boat, *Finesse,* for the race. Alan and his crew won in their class.

17

Standing: Neil, Neil, Jr., Alan,
Sitting: Stuart & Andrew

From 1989 to 1992, Alan served as Deputy Assistant Secretary of Labor and Acting Assistant Secretary for OSHA, where he was responsible for day-to-day OSHA operations, safety and health standards and directing OSHA's nationwide enforcement responsibilities. In 1990, President George H. W. Bush awarded him the Presidential Award for Distinguished Executive Service, the Federal Government's highest award for Senior Executives.

During his time in Washington D. C., Alan often met with visitors from home. He describes one such visit:

It was great to have many family, friends and visitors from Pensacola come to Washington, especially when Gloria and I could host them. When the Pensacola play, *Seaplane,* played at the Kennedy Center, an entire delegation from Pensacola came to D C, we proudly participated with our hometown delegation.

In October, 1992, Alan joined the Los Alamos National Laboratory in New Mexico, where he led the organization's safety, health, and occupational medicine activities. He later assumed the position of Deputy Director of the Laboratory's Environmental, Safety, Health and Quality programs.

From 2001 until his retirement in 2008, Alan served as the President and Chief Executive Officer of the National Safety Council, the nation's largest not-for-profit safety and health advocacy organization. Prior to becoming President, he served for six years as the Executive Vice President and Chief Operating Officer. At retirement, he had more than forty years of government and private sector safety, health and environmental experience.

Alan's career required much travel, nationally and throughout the world, but in 2008, he said:

Finally, it's retirement to my hometown of Pensacola with Gloria Quinn McMillan, my wife of thirty-three years. Now we get to spend time with our ten grandchildren and our great- granddaughter.

Gloria & Alan enjoying retirement

Reflecting on his past, he recently wrote:

> As I look back over the years, I never had a bad job, perhaps a few bad days here and there, but mostly blessed by opportunity and good fortune. The best of my life came from the family and the values of growing up in Pensacola surrounded by lots of aunts and uncles, thirty-two cousins, brothers, sisters and grandparents; going to Sacred Heart grade school, Pensacola Catholic High and Pensacola Junior college; being a newspaper boy together with other East Pensacola Heights kids like Leon Pyle, Victor and Micky Mabire; and swimming and waterskiing on Bayou Texar, diving off the Bayou Bridge, and trying to stay out of trouble.

Since Alan retired, and returned home, he served as President of the Star Lake Homeowner's Association; Commodore of the Pensacola Yacht Club; a member of the Board of Directors of WSRE; chaired the 2010 Escambia County Administrator Candidate Review Committee, and served on the 2013/14 committee; a member of the Mass Transit Advisory Committee; and Vice Chair of the Restore Act Advisory Committee to the Escambia County Board of County Commissioners.

The old adage, "If you want something done, give it to a busy person," is applicable to Alan McMillan, or maybe he's simply a glutton for punishment. Perhaps it's a little bit of both, but either way, it's obvious he doesn't mind taking on responsibility. He will soon wind up three years as Commodore of Pensacola Yacht Club, and then what? Stay home and prune his camellias? I doubt it. It will be interesting to see. As with all the essays in this book, it is always interesting to become reacquainted with old friends in the process of writing their story, and then experience the joy of sharing it with readers.

*Source of material about Don Manuel Gonzalez and Marianna Bonifay from paper written by Virginia McMillan Poffenberger.

Alan & Gloria enjoying their family: "3 Kids, 10 Grandkids and 1 Great Granddaughter

Alan & Gloria with Christie Hankins, President of the
Camelia Club

Grandson Austin, Alan and Alan, Jr.

Alan & Gloria aboard the *Finesse*

Alan, Alan Jr. Preston & Susan

Alan with granddaughter, Lauren McMillan at her
University of Georgia graduation

Neil & Susan (Owsley) McMillan

Gloria & Alan at a Commodore's Ball

Alan & Gloria with Alan Sheppard and his daughter, Kateri Gamburger at a Commodore's Ball

Granddaughter, Emily Gray christens another *Finesse*

Alan & Gloria

Alan & Gloria with her parents, Carl & Skip Quinn, and her brother, Anthony Quinn

Alan with Chase Elliott at 5 Flags Speedway

The PYC Championship Crew:
Carlos Melville, Neil McMillan, LeAnn Pickering, Andrew McMillan, Alan McMillan, Darrell Harrison and David Richards

55th Reunion of Catholic High School Class of 1960

2

Aunt Jenny's Swimmin' Hole

1948. Ora Wills, "Aunt Jenny" Janie Hudgens (Ora's great-grandmother) and Doris Cannon (Ora's Aunt)

Of the many swimming holes around Pensacola, a particular favorite of folks who lived in the Brent area, north of town, was "Aunt Jenny's Hole," a wide spot in Carpenter's Creek. I grew up hearing about the popular swimming spot from my older brothers and their friends, although it was also referred to as "Jenny's Hole," and "Hudgins Hole." It seems those Brent kids had as much fun at their swimming hole as we did at ours on Bayou Texar in East Pensacola Heights. Aunt Jenny's Hole provided a place for families and friends to socialize, swim, cool off on a hot summer day and relax. Its location on ten acres owned by a black family during the time that segregation was the law of the

24

land, made it unique because the visitors who used the swimming hole were white.

It's unknown when residents in the Brent area began using that section of Carpenter's Creek for swimming and washing their clothes, but it was probably long before 1902, when Fred Hudgins, a black man from Alabama, purchased the ten acres from the Blackmon family. It was through his property that the creek flowed and, although "Aunt Jenny's Hole" no longer exists, its prior location on a current map of Pensacola would place it south of Bayou Boulevard, between North 9th Avenue and Davis Highway, southwest of Sacred Heart Hospital. At Fred Hudgins death, the property passed to his wife, Janie (Jenny) Hudgins, the legendary "Aunt Jenny," after whom the swimming hole was named. Jenny's daughter, Minnie and son-in-law, Sim Dawson, raised four children on the ten acres. The Hudgins-Dawson family was the only black family in the

Ora Dawson Wills

Ora's daughter, Angela Kyle Wills

neighborhood. One of their daughters was the mother of Ora Dawson Wills, a retired English teacher, writer and poet, who currently lives on the remaining two acres of the family's original estate.

Ora Will's mother died in an automobile accident on Davis Highway, a few blocks from their home on the ten acres, when Ora was a small child. Consequently, she was raised by her great-grandmother, Janie Hudgins ("Aunt Jenny"), and her grandmother, Minnie Dawson, whom Ora called "Mama," and refers to her as Mama in her many writings. An aunt, Doris Cannon, Minnie Dawson's other daughter, also lived in the family home, and was like a mother to Ora during her early childhood. "Aunt

Jenny" died in 1948, and Ora's grandfather, Sim Dawson, died in 1963. Her grandmother, (Mama) died in 1989.

1940's. Minnie Dawson, Ora's Grandmother, and Doris Cannon's Mother

1960's. Sim Dawson, Ora's Grandfather

The Brent area was considered "way out in the country" when I was a kid. I grew up in East Pensacola Heights, but was born in Brent in 1932, not far from Aunt Jenny's Hole. My older brothers and cousins used to frequent the swimming hole, but we moved into town when I was a young child. I recall the mentioning of Aunt Jenny's Hole in a lot of the conversations at family gatherings, as many of my relatives lived in the Brent area. I had never been to the well-known location until, as a teenager in the late 1940s, I rode my Cushman scooter to a wooded area off 9th Avenue during hunting season and shot my first mallard duck in a wide section of Carpenter's Creek. That part of North 9th Avenue at the time was undeveloped and far outside the city limits, and it was sometime later I learned that where I shot the duck was actually Aunt Jenny's Hole. This was years prior to the development of the area, such as Sacred Heart Hospital, Cordova Mall and Albertson's grocery store. As the crow flies, it's not very far from 9th avenue to Davis Highway. Frankly, I should be thankful that Ora's grandfather, Sim Dawson, didn't catch me hunting on his property.

In one of Ora's published works, she explains, "People took their Saturday night baths in the creek, washed their clothes, and baptized converts." She includes personal memoirs written by two of her childhood

26

friends, Joy Martin Newsom and Virginia Garrison Saunders, who grew up in the same neighborhood:

Joy describes Aunt Jenny's Hole as "black like coffee on the deep end and the color of tea at the shallow end." She and her brother, Bubba Martin, learned to swim when her mother "dropped" them near the deep end with instructions to "swim," which they obviously did. Joy wrote: "That began a magic summer, and in fact, a magic childhood. As we got older, bolder, and better swimmers, Mother would let us go to the creek by ourselves." Joy relates an incident when mutual friends of ours, Gilbert Barrow and Bobby Rawson, aware she was afraid of snakes, decided to dropa live snake down her back while at the swimming hole.

I had heard stories about the "shoot-the-chute" someone had installed at the swimming hole, which was a cable threaded through a short pipe, and stretched from the top of a pine tree to v-shaped stumps on the opposite side of the creek. "The object," Joy said, "was to let go of the pipe midway over the creek. Some showoffs would do flips and all kinds of crazy things as they let go of the pipe." She wrote how the real daredevils would delay letting go of the pipe before falling into the creek, and how Frank "Blackie" Jernigan waited too long to let go and "ended up with his head lodged between the v-shaped stumps, bleeding like a stuck pig, his scalp lacerated from ear to ear." Joy writes about her last attempt to visit Jenny's Hole sometime in the late 1960s. She "was devastated to find that Springdale Subdivision had been built, and Jenny's Hole was just a memory." She concluded with, "It was a magic time for all of us, thanks to the kindness and tolerance of two black ladies who never complained about the herd of kids that seemed to descend on them every spring, summer and fall. Thanks from all of us."

Virginia lived about a half mile from the creek, and writes, "Some of my happiest memories are of going to the creek, commonly called 'Jenny's Hole.'" She recalled how her entire family spent time at the creek, especially on hot summer days, that it was not uncommon to discover boys skinny dipping at the swimming hole, and how she considered Ora's mother, Minnie, "special" and "the best cook in the world." Virginia wrote, "Some of my favorite memories of Oree are sitting with her family on their front porch in the late summer evenings. Her Papa, Sim, would put old rags in a dish and set them on fire. He believed the smoke would drive the mosquitoes away," and "during these times, Sim and Minnie would tell ghost stories." She wrote the following about the namesake of the

27

swimming hole: "Aunt Jenny was Oree's great-grandmother. She was a formidable lady that I remember being a little scared of. She didn't mind telling me to go home when it was supper time. Any time she got tired of me hanging around she would say, somewhat gruffly, 'Ginny, go home!' I would run home and not go back until the next day." Virginia concludes her story with, "Minnie, Sim, Aunt Jenny and Oree will always be in my mind and heart and a wonderful part of my growing up. I am grateful to my heavenly Father for allowing us to get to know them."

The death of Ora's mother was a tragedy, not only for Ora, but for the family and friends. Unfortunately, tragedy was not a stranger to the Hudgens-Dawson family, because Ora's uncle, Sim and Minnie's twenty year old son, William Dawson, was murdered near the homestead in 1934, about a year before Ora's mother died in the accident. William's death was no accident. His father, Sim, found him, lying in a path with his hands tied behind his back, dead. He was shot in the back and left to die. The murder, no different than a lynching, was minimally investigated and remains unsolved. Sim Dawson knew in his heart the men who murdered his son were white, not black, according to Ora. "Blacks in those days didn't tie up and shoot people, they used a knife," she explained. Sim Dawson knew that whites in the Brent neighborhood knew who killed his son, and on one occasion a white man he knew well, came to him intending to tell him who the murderers were, but changed his mind and walked away.

There can be no greater pain for a parent than to lose a child, but to have a child murdered, and never know who did it, or why, but know that there are some who do know but won't reveal the answers, must have been unbearable for Sim and Minnie Dawson and their family. What is truly remarkable and heartwarming is the fact that despite their loss and its circumstances the Hudgens-Dawson family did not turn their hurt and bitterness against their neighbors or the community. They were generous to a fault, and "Aunt Jenny's Hole" was shared with their friends and their friends and became a legend.

Ora   captures the pain and anger her grandparents felt after William's death in a long poem she published, entitled "1934" Following are two excerpts from her poem:

> Mama suppressed
> the pain
> too numbed
> to hate

28

and early in the morning
or in the heat of noon
washing and ironing the clothes
came to understand
that the guilt that
stained them
stained her
stained all,
the memory stayed
and before she died
she prowled the dark house
at midnight
vomiting chunks of grief
a half-century old
"Dey killed my chile,
killed 'im dead
Lawd Jesus
killed 'im dead

Papa held the
pain
and it festered
he hated the men who
 robbed him
of his brightest son
hated the white grinning faces
"Don' trust 'um,"
he said it a thousand times
"William, he come back to
the house, from the creek.
went up the road
I found 'im layin' dere,
hans behin' 'is back
Dey killed 'im dead."

3

Beach Buggies

A drive on Santa Rosa Island, to the east or west, is always nostalgic for me. As I recall, during the early post World War II years, all of Santa Rosa Island was a desolate place, no houses, just the Casino and the pier along the emerald waters of the Gulf of Mexico, separated by squeaky, sugar white sand. The area, including the two structures, was a tiny part of the island known to the world as Pensacola Beach. The old quarantine station on the north side of the island, and west of the bridge, later became the "Fish Hatchery," but, today it is occupied by the U. S. Environmental Protection Agency. Fort Pickens, at the western end of the island, where Pensacola Bay flows into the Gulf of Mexico, may just as well have been hundreds of miles away because there were no roads leading west or east from the Casino and pier area. Once people arrived at the small, paved parking area on the island they were stuck, as there was no other place to go. If they drove onto the beautiful, soft, white sand, they would be stuck, literally, which, by the way, brings me to my point. The island, then and

W. A. "Bill" Davis taking his sons for a ride in his beach buggy.

perhaps for the next twenty plus years was a Mecca for beach buggy owners, their families, their friends and their "new-found friends."

The wonderful stripped down beach buggies came in all sizes, makes and models, and opened up a new frontier for the avid fishermen, crabbers, swimmers, sunbathers, and explorers. Every self-respecting "local yokel" wanted to own a beach buggy, searched the junk yards and used car lots for old clunkers with good engines, then bought or borrowed a cutting torch, and the frenzy began.

The vehicle of choice for most would-be beach buggy owners was a Model-A Ford, and there were still a few around back in the 40s and 50s. In my previous book, Growing Up In Pensacola, I wrote about the first beach buggy I had ever seen. It was built from a Model-A Ford, and traveled on the soft sand on both sides of the island with ease.[1] A wide variety of other vehicles were converted into beach buggies. The basic requirement, other than a good running engine, was wide tires and the lightest weight possible. Much was stripped or cut away, usually down to the chassis, leaving the bumpers, gas tank, lights, windshield and seats. It was an open air affair, complete with weather and mosquitoes. Some preferred light weight pickup trucks with wide tires and low air pressure, which helped with maneuvering in the soft beach sand. Others employed more imagination and craftsmanship, as did, Jack Watson, an avid diver and fisherman, who took a large truck, cut it down to its chassis and added a full protective canopy over

31

a flat bed. For comfort, he furnished the "family beach buggy" with a table, chairs, and a "potty" for Mom and the kids. His family traveled all over the beach in the sheltered beach buggy, rain or shine. They were often seen fishing and crabbing from the old bridge in the comforts of home on their modified pick-up truck.

Ralph Atwell

In the early 1950's, the Mosquito and Rodent Control Division of the Escambia County Health Department constructed a small cabin several miles east of the paved road on Pensacola Beach. Access to the cabin was either by boat, four-wheel drive vehicles, or beach buggies. On Wednesday nights, employees of the Mosquito and Rodent Control and their friends would gather at the little building, which was fully equipped with a bathroom and kitchen, for what eventually became known as the "Wednesday Night Fish and Grits Club."[2] On each Wednesday afternoon the road along Pensacola Beach looked like a convention of beach buggy owners heading east in the direction of the "Mosquito Control Shack." By dark, enough fish had been caught, cleaned and ready to fry. While enjoying the delicious meal of fried fish and hushpuppies, and other delicacies, such as "mountain oysters," occasionally brought by a local veterinarian, the well fed crowd discussed local politics and other forms of gossip. An important part of the evening was the Wednesday Night Fights on T.V., and to make it interesting each person put his money in the pot prior to the scheduled bout. After the fights and the bets settled, the participants began to leave. To the island's menagerie of animals, whose habitat had been invaded by noisy creatures, machines and smells, the parade of lights and sounds from the beach buggies must have been a frightening experience for them. However, a quiet quickly returned among the sand dunes for the remainder of the night, marking the end of a great evening of camaraderie, fellowship and lies.

In the mid-1950s, while home from F.S.U. for the weekend, I borrowed my Brother Bob Davis' beach buggy, which he had only recently completed. When my roommate, Ralph Atwell[3] and I were driving across the bay bridge toward the beach, part of the front bumper fell off and damaged an oncoming vehicle. It later cost us $70.00 to get the lady's auto repaired. At the beach, we enjoyed driving all over the island, putting Brother Bob's machine to the test. It performed well. However, in my

32

exuberance I drove a bit too close to the water, and a wave caught us, causing the little beach buggy to jerk sharply to the left, into the water. The spray from the water, killed the engine, and I was unable to restart it. People on the beach helped us attempt to pull it back from the water, but to no avail. By the time I got a wrecker out to the beach, the beach buggy had settled down in the sand too far, and the operator's attempt to pull it out failed. Early the next morning, we returned with shovels and friends, determined to rescue the borrowed beach buggy, but when we arrived, the only part visible was about three inches of the top of the windshield. The tide had risen during the night, and the wave action caused the marvelous home-made jalopy to slowly disappear under the sand. I suppose it's still there where we left it almost sixty years ago; perhaps several feet under the Miracle Strip's wondrous white sand, waiting patiently to be rescued. Fortunately, Brother, Bob acted like he understood, took his loss well, and didn't bruise my body.

Today, the homemade beach buggies are a thing of the past, but the memories linger on. Driving on the beaches is prohibited. Manufacturers have developed many different types of vehicles that traverse the soft beach sand much better than the man-made ones, but I doubt they're having as much fun.

[1,2] Davis, Charlie, Growing Up In Pensacola, Self-Published, ISBN. 978-0-615-32657-3, 2009
[3]Ralph graduated from University of Florida Law School and practiced law in Pensacola.

Charlie with his brother Bill's Beach Buggy

Tom Brown Jr. and his Beach Buggy, ca. 1955

4

Brother Ben's Eulogy
Ben L. Davis, Jr.
1921 - 2013
Harper-Morris Memorial Chapel
September 13, 2013

Hello, everybody! I'm, Charlie, one of Ben's six siblings.

Ben's family, His wife, Jean; Children, Greg, Vickie, Moni, Larry, Marie and Margaret . . . and their families, want you to know they appreciate very much your joining us today to help celebrate Ben's life. We, of course, like many of you, mourn his death, but we have much to celebrate about his ninety-two years of life.

Colonel Butch Redding, USAR Ret., Ben's nephew, led us in prayer after a few comments and a testimony to his high regard for his uncle Ben.

In 1921, the year Ben was born, the life expectancy of a male child was far less than ninety-two years . . . in fact, his life expectancy was age 60. He outsmarted all those prognosticators and actuaries and did things his way, which was his style. It wasn't that he was hard-headed . . . well, let me take that back. Let's just say, he was determined to do things his way, which more often than not, turned out to be the best way. That's what I mean about his style. We thought about playing Frank Sinatra's record of "I Did It My Way," but changed our minds.

When he was diagnosed with terminal cancer, he was pretty cool about it. He said, "I've had a wonderful life, and a wonderful family," and then added, "Not too many people get to live 92 years." After a few moments of silence, he laughed and said, "That might be too long."

Our society often judges a man by how well he provides for his family and how he conducts himself in his dealings with others. Somewhere in the Bible, it's written, ". . . he who provides not for his family, has denied the faith." Ben always provided well for his family and, regarding his faith, he conducted his life and business dealings in a Christian manner. He surrendered his life to Christ some time ago. In a discussion with a minister recently, he told him that he thought he would be going to heaven and was confident he'd meet up with a lot of his friends there. "All your friends?" asked the preacher. Ben hesitated and laughed before saying, "Well, I can think of a couple that might not have made it." It was only recently that Jean discovered that Ben, for a long time, kept a small cross in his coat pocket. It's going with him.

Ben and Brother Bob

He had a reputation among his fellow realtors, developers and builders as an honest man. He was a very successful businessman and followed the acceptable rules of the business world and the laws of society. That was his style.

Years ago, some smart professor wrote that each couple had the responsibility to have at least two children . . . the idea was they must replace themselves so the population wouldn't dwindle. I doubt his theory was correct, but Ben must have taken it to heart,

Jean and Ben

because he considered his most important accomplishment, other than marrying Miss Betty Jean Thompson of Cantonment, was being the father of six children . . . 4 girls and 2 boys. He didn't foresee the local population

explosion, resulting in 15 grandchildren, 28 great-grandchildren, and 4 great-great-grandchildren, a total of 54. He loved them all, and they loved him. Shortly after his death, Facebook messages started showing up. For example:

1. Tammy Brown wrote, "Our Grampa! One of the most generous, caring, and most amazing men ever put on this earth. God took him home last night. I can't even express in words what he meant to me and my family! I love you Grandpa, you will be missed dearly."

2. Gary Miller wrote, "Grandpa was the kind of man that never judged his grandchildren but saw the best in all of us. I know in my heart I'm a better man because of him."

3. Steve Ribollo wrote, "My Grandfather, one of the greatest men I've ever known, passed away this evening at age 92 after fighting cancer and having a stroke. A hero and mentor to every man in my family. He was a great man and an awesome example."

4. Scott Ribollo wrote, "Lost my guiding light tonight. My dear Grandfather, Ben Davis. You were the greatest example ever."

5. Emily Daughtery wrote, "What a wonderful man heaven gained yesterday. I only knew him for a short time but his awesomeness

was apparent the first time I met him." She wrote this along with Ben's grandsons Curtis, Aaron and Ben Daughtery, her husband.

6. I spoke with Marie Abbatiello, Ben's oldest child, just before the services began, and she reminded me that Ben taught all of them to do the right things. She thought for a moment, and said, "What he really taught us was to respect God, Family, and Country."

Ben had the misfortune of being the first born . . . the oldest brother. We five younger brothers looked up to him, not because he was bigger, actually he was the runt of the litter, but because he had more things than we did. We would borrow stuff from him, like his shoes, shirts and socks when we were all younger. Later, we borrowed his car, his boat, his money, his castnet . . . you name it. He often said, "If there's really such a thing as reincarnation, I want to come back as a little brother."

The Siblings: Tom, Charlie, Emma Jean, Ben, and Bob. Not pictured: Brothers, Bill (1923-2003 and Jack (1936-1983)

He did have one thing none of us wanted to borrow. Back about the time he owned the Swamp House Fish Camp at Highway 90 and the Escambia River, we all enjoyed going frogging. He had ordered from a catalog a thing called a "Michigan Frog Grabber," which fit on the end of a pole and was designed to snap shut on a frog when, or if, you touched a frog with it. It didn't work, but Ben was determined to prove to the world that it would work. We teased him unmercifully, and the last time I saw it, Vickie had framed it, and it was hanging on the wall in his personal "man-cave" where he entertained his friends with delicious gumbo and fried mullet. We had a lot of fun with Ben over that "Michigan Frog Grabber."

Since there were six of us boys and one girl in our family, our sister, Emma Jean, was obviously spoiled. She had one bedroom, and we six boys had the other one . . . all to ourselves. Seven kids around one table was a crowd, but six boys in one bedroom was a mob. People not too familiar with our family often asked, "How many kids are there in your family?" and Ben's answer was, "Well, there are six of us boys and we each have a sister, so how many does that make?"

It was hard to get the best of Ben . . . in any situation. A while back I was in the car with him, and he had the radio on. A song was being played that was loud and noisy, current for the young crowds today. Ben immediately turned it off and said, "How in the heck can anybody understand what that guy's singing? The words don't make sense." I agreed and reminded him that when he was young, one of his favorite singers was Hoagy Carmichael. Ben replied with, "Right, he was great." I said, "His No.1 song was "Boop Boop Diten Datem Whatem Choo." What did those words mean, Ben?" He said nothing, but looked straight ahead and

smiled. Finally, he said, "You know you're a smart aleck, don't you?" (He didn't say, "aleck.")

There were not many things Ben couldn't do, or wouldn't do, if he wanted to do them bad enough. He had several shrimp boats over the years and kept all of us supplied with shrimp. He and our cousin, Tom Brown, have probably shrimped, fished and oystered every square foot of the local bays and some of the bays over in Alabama.

Ben was always jokingly accused of things that were not true, or only partially true, by his fishing and hunting buddies. One thing that was the absolute truth . . . something we all agreed on, was that it didn't matter whose boat he was in, his or somebody else's, he was the captain; like Butch said earlier, he was in charge. Now, he might not have actually taken control of the wheel, but he was in charge of giving directions and instructions . . . especially instructions. Tom Brown,Jr. had fixed up his own boat, and as a favor to Ben, he installed an expensive, comfortable Captain's Chair just for Ben. It shocked Tom when Ben enjoyed the chair so much that he didn't bother to give instructions. He just enjoyed the boat.

In his retirement he continued to have his hand in some real estate deals, especially properties he owned. He continued to be active in hunting, especially with his friend, Reynolds Atkins, in Mississippi. He also spent a lot of time fishing, shrimping and crabbing with his son, Greg, son-in-law Larry Barnard and Tom Brown Jr. His interests in growing stuff to eat increased, and each year his garden got a little larger. Soon, he was providing fresh vegetables to all his family and friends.

In recent years, he held court in his enclosed porch at their home in Holly-Navarre on East Bay situated in a subdivision he helped develop. His close friends and kin gathered for their daily "tea-party" to enjoy adult beverages and attempts at solving some of the world's more immediate problems. There were occasional disagreements that were patched up the following day.

Ben enjoyed a good, long, and full life. He gave more than he got and left a rich legacy for those whom he loved and enjoyed being with. His death leaves a void that can never be filled, and as Tammy wrote, "He will be missed dearly."

Butch provided a closing prayer. Later, at Bayview Park Cemetery, friends and relatives gathered while Butch Redding read verses from the Bible and offered a final prayer.

COL. Butch Redding, USAR Ret.

The Davis Family celebrated Ben's 90th Birthday at Ben and Jean's home on East Bay.
Rose Marie Kennedy Kaiser, Sandra Lockney Davis, Charlie Davis, Marilyn Korb Davis, Fannie
Stowe Davis, Bob Davis, Jean Thompson Davis, Ben L. Davis, Jr., Emma Jean Redding, Tom Davis,
and Sue L. Davis,

5

The Brown Family & Boats
(See "Brown Family Tree" at the end of the chapter)

It's amazing how so many members of a local well-known Brown family have "gone down to the sea in ships" and boats of all types for many generations, dating back to the 1700's. In some respects it's clearly traditional, as though being driven by a genetic predisposition to own and operate a boat or ship of some kind by many descendants of William and Nancy Brown. In another respect, the desire to be around boats by some of the relatives of the Brown descendants is like the spread of a contagious disease; scientists might even consider it an inheritance of acquired characteristics.

Nancy Brown was the daughter of a Creek Indian chief, so, maybe the passion for boats and anything that floats began with a canoe. Family and public records indicate the Brown family's local entry into the maritime industry really began five generations ago with their grandson, Jacob Brown (1849-1888), one of eleven children.

Books could and should have been written about the Brown family's influence in the towing, marine and related maritime industries in Northwest Florida and South Alabama, however, numerous and interesting articles

42

have appeared in magazines and newspapers over the years. It would be sufficient to write only about Jacob Brown (1849–1888), his son, Capt. William Ed Brown (1877-1957), and grandson, Capt. Shirley Brown, to have a great story. However, I believe it's important to show the reader how many of their descendants followed in their footsteps. Also, I think it is interesting to show how many folks related to the Browns, not of direct descent, who became involved with boats at so many different levels.

As the reader will discover, it is impossible to write much of anything about the Browns and boats without mentioning family names like Creighton, Johnson, Abercrombie, Davis, Rocheblave, Walker, LePoidevant and many others. At the risk of getting too far ahead of the story, I want to share a few lines from an article by James H. Chadwick, titled, "An Interview with Captain Shirley Brown" (grandson of Jacob Brown), published in 2010 by *Pensacola and Northwest Florida History Illustrated.* Captain Brown was asked if his

Capt. Shirley Brown ,
Owner of Brown Marine Service
(Courtesy of Ted Brown)

was a "large family," to which he replied:

Edmund Gaillard Creighton
(Courtesy of Charlene Johnson)

Son, my family was and remains so big that I believe I'm related to the whole world. My father, William Edward Brown, was born at my grandfather's home on Santa Rosa peninsula about a mile and a half from the Pensacola Bay Bridge. Grandfather {Jacob} called his home 'Faust.' Today the area is known as {Naval Live Oaks Plantation}. My mother was Emma Louise Creighton {Johnson}, and her parents were Edmund and Belle Deens Creighton. I had a full brother named Hugh Ambus Brown, we affectionately nicknamed 'Ham,' and a sister, Gladys Louise Brown {Workman}.

On my father's side, I had half-brothers William Edward Brown, Jr., and Thomas F. Brown,

Sr., and a half-sister, Doris Maude Brown. On my mother's side, I had half-brothers Charles H. Johnson and Ernest W. Johnson, and a half-sister, Flossie Aliene Johnson {Davis}. Like many families back then, we may not have had much money, but we never lacked for love.

Jacob Brown (1849 – 1888):

Jacob Brown, who died at age 39, was active in the maritime business. John Baroco, in a 1999 paper on "Descendants of Nancy Catharine Brown," wrote about him:

He is buried in St. John's Cemetery. He was a merchant trader; owned several schooners; carried freight mainly from Freeport, on Choctawhatchee Bay. He ran a ship repair facility on Deadman's Island off of what is now Gulf Breeze in Pensacola Bay.

Jacob Brown
(Courtesy of
Jimmy Mashburn)

In a talk given to the Gulf Breeze Historical Society in 1997, Shirley J. Brown, Chairman and CEO of Brown Marine Service, Inc., said:

My grandfather started a shipyard at a location known as Deadman's Island. In maritime language the term 'Deadman' isn't reference to a departed soul, but rather to a device used to restore life to wooden sailing ships at the turn of the century. Long before dry docks were in use, hauling large vessels out of the water in order to make repairs to the keel involved a bit of ingenuity and muscle.

Mother Nature provided a natural dry dock of sorts at Deadman's Island. Deep water just off shore made it possible for the large ships of that day to move in close where a thick cable was anchored to the Deadman. This was usually a large tree or a huge block of concrete with the bulk of it buried deep in the sand. The free end of the cable was looped around a stout mast on the ship then brought back to the Deadman where a winch was attached. This enabled the workers to slowly pull the ship over to one side exposing the underside so necessary repairs could be made.

Jacob Brown must have been a smart business man with lots of energy, because he accomplished much to have died at the young age of thirty-nine. It was convenient for him to have a shipyard at Deadman's Island since he and wife, Julia Annie Faust, homesteaded nearby on the bluffs about a mile-and-a-half east of where the Pensacola Bay Bridge was later built. Their eight children, three boys and five girls, were born there. The property, which Shirley Brown referred to above, is now in the Naval Live Oaks Nature Preserve, part of the National Parks Service. The high-bluff location is easily recognized today from the Pensacola Bay Bridge, and is popularly known by locals as "Butcher-pen Cove." Jacob and family also owned a waterfront home across the bay in Pensacola, situated about where Gulf Power Company's office building is located today, an area known as "Hawkshaw." All eight of Jacob and Julia Annie's children were born in the Gulf Breeze home on the bluff. The family traveled by boat back and forth across the bay, since the bridge had not yet been constructed.

Left: Jacob and Julia Anna's wedding picture.
Above: Portrait of Julia Anna Faust
(Courtesy of Jimmy Mashburn)

The only information I have regarding the death of Jacob Brown is from copies of news articles in the *Pensacola Daily Commercial*, dated April 28, 1888 and May 3, 1888:

April 28, 1888:

Bullets at a wedding—a long way from Childe Harold. There was a very warm entertainment in the eastern portion of the town Tuesday night. It appears there was a wedding n hand in which all of the interested parties were of the Great Brown family. Bad blood having existed for a considerable time between "Jake" {Jacob} and "Joe," a collision followed and in the melee "Joe" got so badly shook up that he was compelled to call into play a pistol from which he sent a ball into the head of "Jake." Fortunately the wound proved merely of a scalp nature. The wedding bells ceased ringing of course, when this rude interruption of the programme took place, and as soon as the combattants became composed and their respective scars in a measure healed, they will register their names at the municipal hotel {city jail}and tell all about it.

May 3, 1888:

Joe Brown, the slayer of Jake Brown whose funeral takes place this afternoon, will probably be given a hearing before a justice tomorrow. He is now in the county jail and regrets the circumstances which forced him to deprive a fellow man of his life. Notwithstanding the general belief and expectation that Jake Brown would recover from the wound he lately received in the head from a pistol ball, which was fired into him by a relative, policeman Joe Brown. He died at midday Tuesday.

Savine Brown—(1864 – 1942):

Jacob's sister, Savine Brown LePoidevant married Michael Guadian LePoidevant around 1876. He was a Customs Sea Captain, born in France. Michael LePoidevant first married Jacob's sister, Sena, who died shortly after their marriage; he later married Savine. They had six children; one of whom was Ellen Nora LePoidevant (1884 – 1969) who married Wilmer Walker, Sr. Our family lived near the Walker family in East Pensacola Heights and knew all of them well. My siblings and I often wondered how the Browns were related to the Walkers, and I never figured it out until now. I understand why Uncle Shirley said, "I believe I'm related to the whole world."

The Walker family was much involved in the commercial fishing industry, operating small bay boats to large ocean going vessels. The Walkers had what amounted to a family compound in East Pensacola Heights on Bayou Boulevard at the edge of Bayou Texar. On the bayou, in sight of the bayou bridge, the Walker family business included two large boathouses and docks that provided boat storage, rentals, repairs, charters, fresh shrimp and fish. Today, the Marina Oyster Barn Restaurant, owned by the Rooks family, occupies the location of the smaller boathouse.

Many of the young boys in East Pensacola Heights, myself included, worked for Mr. Walker, Sr., renting his boats, keeping the boats bailed out and clean and selling fresh shrimp and fish to walk-in customers. Mr. and Mrs. Walker had three daughters, Lois, Cathleen and Ethel; four sons, Wilmer, Jr., Douglas, Oliver and Maurice. All four of the sons were involved in the fishing industry.

Above from left to right: William Wilmer Walker, Sr. (Courtesy of Ted Brown), Doug Walker's Boathouse, and the Marina Restaurant

Hiram Brown—(1872 – 1894):
Hiram Brown, Jacob's oldest son, was sixteen when his father was killed. On February 4, 1894, six years after Jacob's death, Hiram drowned at age 22, along with four others when his sailboat overturned in a storm off Santa Rosa Island near Big Sabine. On February 5, 1894, *The Pensacolian* ran a story under the heading, "Five Men Drowned—Sad Ending of a Sunday Pleasure Excursion:"

At an early hour Sunday morning seven men left the city in a small sailboat to go to Big Sabine on Santa Rosa sound, about twelve miles from Pensacola, in search of shells. A heavy storm raged Saturday night and Sunday morning a strong norther was blowing. Friends tried to dissuade the party from venturing in a small sailboat but they would not heed.

They ran before the wind and quickly reached their destination. About 4 o'clock in the afternoon they started to return and were capsized shortly after leaving Big Sabine. The seven men clung to the boat in the icy cold water until five of them; Rollin, Mashburn, Mobley, Messick and Brown became exhausted and sank to their deaths. Rollin attempted to swim to the shore but sank before he reached it. The two other men continued to cling to the boat through the long hours of the night until noon yesterday when they were rescued by the lumber freighter, *Mamie,* in route to the city from Choctawhatchee bay.

Hiram Brown had been connected with boats plying between the city and Choctawhatchee bay for years, and was well-known here.

In the February 8, 1894 issue of *The Pensacolian,* an article about the tragedy included the following paragraph:

Hiram Brown, the boatman who was drowned near Big Sabine Sunday, was a brother-in-law of Officer M. J. Herrin of the city police force. Officer Herrin has obtained leave of absence and is making a vigorous search for the body of Mr. Brown.

L to R: Hiram Brown,

Walter, Ed and Hiram Brown

Courtesy of Jimmy Mashburn

Anna Eliza Brown--(1874 – 1952):

I include Anna Eliza Brown Herrin Abercrombie, although she was not directly involved with boats as were her brothers, Wm. Edward and Walter, and her father, Jacob. Anna married Marius Herrin, and they had eight children; four girls and four boys. Marius died in 1905, and in 1910, she married James Abercrombie, a widower with three children. He was involved with boats of all sizes and ships in his capacity as the elected Harbormaster for many terms. Anna Eliza and James Abercrombie had three children, a family structure, more familiarly known as "yours, mine, and our kids" situation. Her brother, Capt. Ed. Brown, Sr., my grandfather, as explained below, was the assistant Harbormaster under James Abercrombie.

Anna Eliza Brown
(Courtesy of Jimmy Mashburn)

The Abercrombie and Herrin families, like the Walker family, were among the early pioneering families of East Pensacola Heights. Many descendants of all three families continue to reside in the "Heights." Anna Eliza's two sisters, Jacob's two oldest daughters, Nancy Catherine Brown Burgoyne and Mary Elizabeth Brown Smith, lived together in East Pensacola Heights after being widowed. As a "paperboy" in East Pensacola Heights, I threw papers to numerous customers who were "kinfolks," a fact I was unaware of until long after I was grown.

Anna Eliza Brown, Marius Jefferson Herrin and James Edwin Abercrombie
(Courtesy of Jimmy Mashburn)

49

The Brown Sisters: Nancy Catherine, Mary Elizabeth, Anna Eliza, and Rosa Lena
(Courtesy of Jimmy Mashburn)

Capt. Walter N. Brown—(1880 - 1936):

Walter N. Brown
Yachtsman
(Courtesy of Jimmy
Mashburn)

Walter Nathaniel Brown was the youngest of Jacob and Julie Annie's three sons, and like his father and brothers, he became a licensed boat captain. He was born December 21, 1880 at the family homestead in Gulf Breeze, Santa Rosa County, Florida, and was eight years old when his father died. It has been difficult to obtain much history about Walter from relatives since he never married locally. As a young man he was active in the maritime business as a licensed boat captain, and ran unsuccessfully for political office before moving to South Florida where he married and established a family. Unfortunately his relationship with his Northwest Florida relatives deteriorated.

In recent years, sometime prior to 1991, Walter's granddaughter, who lived in Dania, Florida, mailed a manuscript to Jacob's youngest daughter (Walter's youngest sister), Rose Lena Brown Hendricks (1884 – 1991). The fifty-six page manuscript was titled, *Pirate Plunder in Florida Waters*. The sub-title was, A True Narrative as Told by Capt. Walter N. Brown to the Writer, Irma S. Pyle. I obtained a copy of the manuscript, which is an interesting read, but knowing what I know about Walter and the Brown family, it is difficult to

50

separate fact from fiction, even though the subtitle states, "A True Narrative."

His story begins with Walter as a small child, described as a "red-haired, freckled, little boy, in the month of July 1893," who loved to visit with his maternal grandfather who emigrated from Germany and owns a cabin on Santa Rosa Island near the Big Sabine. The grandfather obtains treasure maps from the dying captain of a Spanish schooner which had anchored in a cove near the cabin during a storm. He described the arrival of the schooner:

Walter N. Brown
(Courtesy of Jimmy Mashburn)

> The waters that had been so disturbed in the storm were now still and smooth. We could see the schooner which had anchored in the cove the first day of the storm. She was a trim little vessel, painted white, with red decks and cabin. She was sixty-six feet long, sixteen foot beam and drew five feet of water. Her name was the *Reflectar*, and her home port was Tampico, Mexico.

The story is action-packed but unstructured, and includes a search for and location of the treasure, but no recovery as a result of treachery and murder. Included in the mix are tragedies at sea and a legal battle to save the homestead located in Gulf Breeze. It is better written than expected, but disappointing in that I learned very little about Walter in his later life away from his Pensacola family. He died in 1936 and is buried in Dania, Florida.

William Edward Brown, Sr.
(Courtesy of Emma Jean Redding)

Capt. Wm. Edward Brown, Sr.—(1877 – 1957):

William Edward Brown, Sr., one of Jacob and Julia Annie's sons, was eleven years old when his father was killed. He was my step-grandfather, the only grandfather I ever knew, as both my natural grandfathers died before I was born. Captain Ed Brown, as he became known, was a widower with three children. He and his late wife, Maude Powell, had a fourth son who died in infancy. He married my grandmother, Emma Creighton Johnson, a widow with three children, then they became the parents of three children, so it became a "your three kids, my three kids, and our three kids" situation.

Papa Brown, Freddy and Mama Brown
(Courtesy of Charlene Johnson)

Later, after all the nine kids were out of the nest, they rounded it out to ten by adopting a son, Fred George Brown. All ten kids and their spouses addressed them as "Mama" and "Papa," we grandkids addressed and referred to them as "Mama Brown" and "Papa Brown," but on the waterfront and at the ports, he was Captain Ed Brown, a dominant figure among tugboat and barge operations. In addition to being a Harbor Pilot in Pensacola, he was also a Pilot Commissioner with the State of Florida. He eventually owned several tugboats, and was elected Harbormaster for several terms.

CAPT. W. E. (ED) BROWN
FOR HARBORMASTER
FRIENDS OF THE WATERFRONT

During World War I, Captain Ed Brown was employed by the Aiken Towing Company of Pensacola. In 1917, at age forty, he was ordered to relocate three tug boats and several barges to Panama City, Florida. It was a major operation; plans were to keep the tug boats and barges in Panama City for at least two years. The average number of crewmen on a tug boat back then was nine to twelve. The families of the crew members were also transported to new temporary locations in Panama City, as were the Brown family members. Back in those times, each family had at least one cow, some chickens and maybe a horse. My siblings and I grew up hearing about this armada of boats, barges, animals and kids, since my mother, at age fifteen, was one of the older kids on the trip.

Ed Brown, Harbormaster and friend,
Charlie Gonzalez
(Courtesy of Charlene Johnson

In his talk to the Gulf Breeze Historical Society, Shirley Brown said, "The operation took on the appearance of Noah's Ark, with the livestock taking up two barges while the crew and their families bunked down on the three tugs, the *Nellie,* the *Simpson* and the *Dixie.*" There has been much written and many talks given about this unusual voyage of people and animals, but my siblings and I always laughed when mom would tell about the cows getting seasick.

There are many other interesting sea stories involving Captain Ed Brown, but I've only heard bits and pieces over the years, and I'm concerned now that they'll never be told, especially since all but one of his children and step-children are deceased and only half of his grandchildren are alive today. One such story I heard portions of while growing up was about when he and his son, Tom Brown, my uncle, were stranded on an island after their tug boat, the *Bronx,* sank in the Gulf of Mexico. I knew it had to have been a perilous situation, because Uncle Tom once described to me, while crabbing with him and my cousins, how they ate raw crabs and snails and thought they were going to die. A few years ago, my cousin, Tom Brown, Jr., gave me a copy of the story of their 1926 rescue published in the *Mobile Register,* along with pictures under the heading, "Wives Greet Shipwrecks on Arrival in Mobile:"

> . . . . Captain Ed Brown, skipper; George Erain, deckhand; Captain A. B. Butterworth, owner; and Thomas Brown, 19-year-old son of captain Brown, of the storm-wrecked Pensacola tug, *Bronx,* as they arrived in Mobile midnight Friday after nearly a week of living death on a stormy sea and deserted Chendeleur Island in the Gulf. At the right is Mr. Butterworth and his wife; at the left, Mrs. Brown and her husband.
>
> The crew was brought to waiting wives and a mother in Mobile by the tug *Harry G. Lytle,* commanded by Captain C. M. Daughdrill and sent to the rescue of the marooned seamen by F. W. Crenshaw of the Gulf Towing and Wrecking Company.
>
> The men floated on a frail life-raft in a seething tempest for 52 hours after the *Bronx* went down 12 miles out of Pensacola Sunday, with little food, no water, and with their lives menaced by both the raging storm and man-eating sharks. At one time four sharks attacked the raft but were beaten off.

Capt. Ed Brown shown at the Wheelhouse of the *Nellie* in the Pensacola Port. (Courtesy of Ted Brown)

Their life-raft was completely wrecked off the Chandeleur Island, and there they spent 32 more harrowing hours with nothing to eat save raw crabs, until Brown, his son, and Butterworth succeeded in walking, wading and swimming to the lighthouse fifteen miles away on Thursday. Erin, who could not swim, was rescued Friday evening.

Captain Brown is well known in Mobile and Captain Butterworth, now port engineer of the Texas Oil Company at Port Arthur, once resided here.

Wm. Edward Brown, Jr.:

Captain Ed Brown's oldest son, Edward Brown, Jr., like his father and grandfather, followed in the maritime trade, as an engineer. Ed, as he was known was married only a year, when he lost his life shortly after WWI. He was aboard one of the many merchant ships, idled after the war and moored in Pensacola Bay. While preparing one of the ships for removal to Mobile, the ship's boiler exploded, scalding Ed severely. It was a horrible and excruciatingly painful way to die.

Shirley Brown with wife, Flora Guttman Brown

Captain Shirley J. Brown—(1913 - 2005):

It was only natural that Shirley Brown followed in the footsteps of his father and grandfather. His trip aboard his father's tug on that memorable "1917 Noah's Ark-like" journey to Panama City at age four cinched the deal; he was smitten. He liked to tell the story about going aboard his first boat at age one: "I fell off the family dock and landed in a small boat tied up there. I've been aboard boats ever since." He became Chairman and CEO of Brown Marine Services, Inc.

of Pensacola, a multi-million-dollar business he founded.

The October, 1977 issue of the *Via Pensacola* Magazine, published by the Port of Pensacola, included an article titled, "Pensacola's Brown Towing Company—40 Years of Moving Bulk Cargo." The unknown author was complementary of Capt. Shirley Brown's accomplishments in the maritime business, and explained how he began in 1936 with one tiny tug, doing work for the U. S. Coast Guard during the depression years. World War II's Southern boom opened up new opportunities, about which, Shirley recalled:

> The government needed asphalt to pave runways for airports that were springing up for military training all over the South. I got myself a used tug, bought an old freighter with the tug, hauling asphalt all thru the Gulf. That was the beginning, something we achieved with a lot of help from many good friends, including Capt. A. P. Ward who then headed a large towboat business here.
>
> Note: For an interesting story about Shirley Brown's wartime adventures, hauling asphalt out of Tampa to Pensacola, read, *Growing Up In Pensacola,* Chapter 51, "U-Boats in the Gulf of Mexico and Disaster on the Mississippi River."

Shirley's profitable venture in wartime hauling was the major reason for his company's rapid growth. When the war ended, he acquired property on Bayou Chico, and eventually acquired a large fleet of tugs, hauling gasoline and other bulk petroleum products to terminals throughout the Gulf Coast. In the late 1940's, Brown Marine Services, Inc. added a marina to their operations. The business included Shirley's son, Ted Brown, a licensed tugboat captain and President of the company, and his son-in-law, Bill Bryan, Brown Marine's Port Engineer and Caterpillar Engine Specialist. Eventually, Shirley's grandsons, Gary and Steve Bryan, both licensed tugboat captains, became involved with the company. Later, a nephew, Jack Brown, Tom Brown, Sr.'s son, a retired U. S. Army First Sergeant, also became a licensed tugboat captain and worked for the company.

Ted Brown with Toby Ward, Vice President of
Brown Towing Co.
(Source: *Via Pensacola*, 1977

In a 1996 article by James H. Chadwick in the *Pensacola Magazine,* titled, "A Man Named Shirley and a Boat Called Zeus," he wrote:

> Shirley Brown at 82 remains the guiding force behind the maritime business he founded years ago, equally at home in the wheelhouse or his office. 'I believe I have discovered the Fountain of Youth,' he likes to brag while pointing out of his marina window in the direction of Pensacola Bay. 'It's salt water!'
>
> To enter Captain Brown's office on Bayou Chico is akin to visiting a miniature maritime museum. Paintings on the wall vary from professional artists to the crayon renderings of children. All have the same theme—ships, boats and the sea. Model ships sit proudly on his desk top, and if you're as lucky as I was you'll hear a sea tale from this 'master mariner.'

Thomas F. Brown, Sr.—(1903 - 1989):

Thomas F. Brown, Sr.
(Courtesy of Dottie
McCluskey

Tom Brown, Sr. is the same 19-year-old deckhand that was stranded along with his father, Capt. Wm. Ed Brown, Sr., on Chendeleur Island following the sinking of the tugboat *Bronx* in 1926. Prior to that, he was one of the youngsters aboard the armada of tugboats and barges to Panama City in 1917, along with his brother, Wm. Edward Brown, Jr., half-brother Shirley Brown and step-brother, Charlie Johnson, Sr. He, like others in the Capt. Wm. Edward Brown family, grew up with a knowledge of tugboats, barges and the maritime business. Additionally, he married Marie Rocheblave, granddaughter of Ben Rocheblave, well-known Pensacola owner of tugboats and passenger boats in the late 1800's and early 1900's. (Tugboats: *Monarch, Mary Lee* and the *Flanders)*. Tom Brown, Sr. was a well-respected engineer aboard several tugboats during WWII, and afterwards before leaving the maritime world to own and operate a successful Pensacola automobile repair business until his retirement.

Capt. Charles Johnson, Sr.—(1899 - 1986):

Capt. Charles Johnson, Sr.
(Courtesy of
Charlene Johnson)

Charlie Johnson, Sr. was Capt. Wm. Edward Brown, Sr.'s step-son, my mother's brother and my namesake. He was an engineer and the "go-to" guy when a problem persisted. As a young man, he spent time in the U.S. Merchant Marines, having been raised around boats of all types, especially tugboats. Charlie Johnson's unique abilities were demonstrated in an article in the February, 1996 issue of the *Pensacola Magazine,* by James H. Chadwick, titled, "A Man Named Shirley and a Boat Named Zeus." Shirley Brown, Charlie's half-brother and founder

of Brown Towing, Inc. and Brown Marine Services, Inc., fell in love with a tugboat named, *Zeus.* She was tagged "The Bad Luck Boat" by all previous owners. Her owner was glad to sell, as were all previous owners.

Shirley said:

The *Zeus's* outward appearance belied any trouble that might be inside. She was one of the most beautiful boats on the Gulf Coast; 105 ft. in length and 22 ft. at the beam, the *Zeus* boasted 810 horsepower which was delivered from her Cooper-Bessemer diesel engine, one of the best at the time. After going along for about ten days, the timing chain broke. We fixed it and only a short time later she suffered a burned piston. When the boat burned the second piston, not long after we replaced the other one, I called the Cooper-Bessemer Company. After much discussion, Mr. Garries, an official with the company said, 'It's the only engine that has caused us so much grief.'

I called my half-brother, Charlie Johnson, praying he might have a solution. Charlie had worked his way up to president of the Aiken Towing Company; he owned a few of the same type engines I was faced with on the *Zeus*. Charlie loved a challenge, so he decided to take a few days off from being an executive in shirt and tie and change into a tugboat engineer in coveralls—trading an air conditioned office for an oily, hot engine room. He stayed aboard for about ten days, carefully observing every gauge, meter or just listening. Listening to the sounds all good engineers know, like a doctor with his stethoscope examining a patient.

Charlie called me at the end of his ride from Columbus, Georgia. 'I know what's wrong with your engine, but you are not going to believe me.' I told my brother that at this point in the game, I was so desperate; I would believe anything including magic spells. 'The engine is running backwards,' said Charlie. I replied that it's supposed to run backward. But Charlie persisted, 'That's not true. It's supposed to run for five to ten minutes backwards to stop the forward motion of the boat.'

Charlie suggested I buy a propeller with an opposite rotation from the one presently on the *Zeus*. What a turnabout! Almost like a new engine had been installed. No one had to lay a wrench on her after that except for an occasional adjustment. The "Never Sail" boat had been

58

transformed into "The Zeus—Super Tug." She gained a reputation for being a most reliable craft.

The *Zeus*
(Courtesy of Boat Photo Museum)

Charlie Johnson, Sr. owned and co-owned several tugboats. I remember as a kid, my dad and I going snapper fishing in the Gulf of Mexico with him and another uncle, Tom Brown, Sr., aboard a tugboat. Charlie Gonzalez, a local businessman and friend of theirs, was also on board the tugboat, which I believe was the *Nellie*, a tug, well-known around the local waterfront, and co-owned at that time by Charlie Johnson, Charlie Gonzalez, Shirley Brown and Bill Rosasco, Jr., President of Aiken Towing Co. and other enterprises.

As a kid, it didn't strike me as unusual to be deep-sea fishing from a tugboat, but I suspect other fishermen in the area probably considered it as a rare sight. As I recall, I was the only one doing any fishing, because the adults were enjoying their toddies and talking politics and business. I do look back all those years and wonder why the hell my dad brought me along. Frankly, I don't know, but I'm glad he did; it was a treat, and the men enjoyed themselves as much as I did.

As Shirley Brown would have agreed, Charlie Johnson was a man of many talents and knowledge about tugboats, diesel engines and the maritime industry. He designed and oversaw the construction of the *Bessie Lee,* a beautiful pushboat named after his wife. She was operated out of the port of Pensacola for years, and upon his death, his son, Capt. Jimmy Johnson, operated the *Bessie Lee* in and out of the Houston/Galveston ports.

The *Bessie Lee*
(Courtesy of Charlene Johnson)

Capt. Ted Brown, Realtor

Capt. Ted Brown-(April 16, 1951)
Like his father, Capt. Shirley Brown, his grandfather, Capt. Wm. Edward Brown, Sr. and his great-grandfather Capt. Jacob Brown, Ted Brown's destiny, as an only son, was the maritime industry, and specifically, to be part of the successful maritime

businesses his father founded. After graduating from Auburn University in 1972, he served two years active duty in the U. S. Army, and was the only U. S. Army officer with a U. S. Coast Guard Tugboat License. Ted was stationed at Ft. Eustis, Virginia as a Tugboat Platoon Leader, Operations Officer and then Supply Officer. Later, in the Army Reserve, he attained the rank of Captain with an MOS of Port Operations Officer.

Following his discharge from active duty, Ted joined Brown Marine Services, Inc., which at that time was mostly engaged in the transportation of petroleum products in barges on the Gulf Coast. Ted worked for his father's company as a licensed Florida Yacht Broker, and a Coast Guard licensed Tugboat Master before becoming president of Brown Marine services, Inc. As Capt. Ted Brown, he served as a Florida State Harbor Pilot Commissioner from 1992 through 2001.

After the death of his father in 2005, the family decided to reorganize the business and sell off all but the Marina & Boatyard, but to retain some of the investment real estate. Brown Marine Services, Inc. was dissolved but the Marine and Industrial Supply division was rolled into the Marina & Boatyard division and reincorporated into the present Audusson Marina, LLC, using the name of Pelican Perch Marina & Boatyard and Brown Marine Supply.

After the businesses were reorganized, Ted formed TBH Holdings, LLC, and is a licensed Florida and Alabama Realtor, active in all forms of real estate. His company developed and opened the Becks Lake Fish Camp in Pensacola. Ted is active in many worthwhile organizations, and is married to Kathy Horton Brown, who retired after practicing law as a board certified will and probate attorney. Ted and Kathy enjoy boating and other activities, which again proves, even after selling off all the company tugboats, "You (still) can't keep a Brown out of a boat."

Ted Brown and wife Kathy Horton Brown

Shirley Faye Brown Bryan—(March 10, 1936):

Shirley Faye Brown Bryan

Shirley Faye is Shirley Brown's only daughter and Ted's only sister. After the family's reorganization of the business, she became the owner of the Pelican Perch Marina and Boatyard and is actively working to improve it in many ways. She told me recently, "I've always loved that marina and enjoy being around it." She explained that the men thought tugboats, barges and boatyards was no place for a lady. The "men" were Shirley, her father; Ted, her brother; Bill, her husband; and Steve and Gary, her sons, all active in the business. They must have assumed she had enough to do as a well-respected, professional artist, but she could always persuade one of them to take her out on one of the boats to get good photos of boats and the water for her painting projects.

Shirley Faye has been a member of local artist groups for years, and was always on hand at local arts and crafts exhibits, such as the Gulf Coast Arts and Craft Festival and many other shows throughout the Southeast. She is a signature member of the Florida Watercolor Society, the Southern Watercolor Society and was asked to write an article for *Watercolor Magic Magazine,* featuring six of her paintings. Her art has been displayed for years in Pensacola's Quayside Gallery. Sandra and I are proud to have one of her works properly displayed in our home.

Shirley Faye Brown Bryan and her prize winning painting of a shrimp boat

Capt. Shirley Brown with the painting of his favorite tugboat, The *Janet* by his daughter, Shirley Faye Bryan

Bill Bryan—(June 20, 1931):

    Bill Bryan served as Vice President of Brown Marine Services, Inc. with a wide range of responsibilities ashore with the multi-division company. I was told that Bill's responsibilities were "to keep things running," which included the repair shops, the truck dealership, the Caterpillar and Detroit Diesel engine dealership, maintenance and much more. Bill is Shirley Faye's husband and was Shirley Brown's son-in-law. Their sons, Steve and Gary, were active with the company, as both became licensed tugboat operators at early ages.

Bill Bryan

Capt. Steve Bryan—(July 8, 1951):

    Steve Bryan and his brother, Gary, grew up around tugboats, barges, boatyards, boat engine repair shops and just about anything that had to do with the maritime industry. So, it should be no surprise to anyone that both of them became tugboat captains. They've operated tugboats all along the Gulf Coast, and were probably among the youngest to receive their Master's License. When Brown Towing Company was sold in 1993, Steve was the

Capt. Steve Bryan

Special Projects Manager, and went with the new company, Florida Marine Transporters, LLC. He is currently the Information Systems & Communications Manager with the company at its Mandeville, Louisiana headquarters. The company recently named its newest, modern tugboat the *Steven M. Bryan* in his honor.

Capt. Steve Bryan standing next to his namesake tugboat, the *Steven M. Bryan.*

Capt. Gary Bryan—(Oct. 24, 1953):

At the time Brown Towing Company was sold, Gary Bryan was a Tugboat Captain for the company, and chose to enter the marine salvage business. After several years he sold his company to Offshore Tugs Corporation of Stuart, Florida, and currently works for the company locally as a local Tugboat Captain. As the youngest grandson of

Capt. Gary Bryan

Capt. Shirley Brown, he is the last of the long line of Brown family members descended from William and Nancy Brown to enter the maritime industry

Capt. Jack D. Brown—(1931 - 2012):

Jack Brown, the youngest son of Tom Brown, Sr. was a retired, decorated First Sergeant in the U.S. Army. Jack served in the Korean War and two tours of duty during the Vietnam War. He was awarded the Army Commendation Medal for Meritorious Service in Korea, and three Bronze Stars during his Vietnam tours. Following his retirement from the U. S. Army, Jack became a licensed tugboat captain at Brown Towing Company, Inc. He retired after twenty years

Capt. Jack D. Brown

with the company. Jack loved to fish, but the only boat he operated after retirement was his fishing boat. Jack died on March 23, 2012.

First Sergeant Jack D. Brown
USA

Jack enjoying his favorite pastime, fishing.

Capt. Jimmy Johnson—(1925 - 1987):

Jimmy Johnson was the oldest son of Charlie Johnson, Sr. and as a young boy, spent time around Pensacola's waterfront aboard his dad's tugboats and those owned by Aiken Towing Company, where his dad was associated. It was only natural that Jimmy chose the U. S. Navy during WWII, where he served aboard U. S. Navy ships. While his ship was stationed at Guam, he was scalded by steam and returned to a Naval Convalescent Hospital at Glenwood Springs, Colorado. After the war, he attended the University of Florida for a period. In 1949, he graduated from Greer College in Chicago where he studied diesel engines and later followed the family tradition of being involved with tugboats and the maritime industry. Jimmy operated tugboats along the Gulf Coast and settled in Houston, Texas, where he

Jimmy Johnson
(Courtesy of Charlene Johnson)

was the main mechanic for Houston and Galveston pilot boats that guided the ships in the Houston Channel and Intracoastal Waterway through

Galveston. His son, Jimmy Jr., followed in his footsteps, or should I say "boat wake," as he too became involved with tugboats and diesel engines.

Jimmy Johnson at the
Wheelhouse of a tugboat
(Courtesy of Charlene Johnson)

Jimmy Johnson, Jr.
(Courtesy of Charlene
Johnson)

Charles Johnson, Jr.—(1944 - 2008):

Charles Johnson, Jr. was the youngest son of Capt. Charlie Johnson, Sr. As a young boy he worked with his dad on tugboats and the pushboat *Bessie Lee* where he learned about diesel engines. Charles didn't follow the sea as his father and older brother did, except for his time in the U.S. Navy aboard an aircraft carrier that provided him the opportunity to visit various ports in Europe. Like his father and brother, he worked in the engine room, albeit a lot different from the engine room in a tugboat. Charles worked for St. Regis Paper Co. (Champion), and upon retirement, devoted much of his time to building boats. He was recognized as an expert shipwright, a builder of boats, and during his retirement years, he built several boats for Brown Marine Services, Inc., one of which was named *Miss Lil* after his wife.

Charles Johnson, Jr
(Courtesy of Charlene
Johnson)

Tom Brown, Jr.—(3-25-28):

Tom Brown, Jr.

Tom Brown, Jr. is the oldest son of Tom Brown, Sr. As a young boy, he spent time around Pensacola's waterfront visiting aboard tugboats with his father, Tom, Sr. and his grandfather, Wm. Edward, Sr., an elected Harbormaster at the time. Tom joined the U. S. Navy and followed the family tradition when he became a coxswain—pronounced "cox's'n," an enlisted man who has actual, physical control of an open U. S. Navy boat. After his discharge from the Navy, Tom worked for Gulf Power Company until his retirement. During his years at Gulf Power Co. and in retirement, he always owned a boat of some kind. There is an old familiar adage or truism that's been around our close families for years, and that is, "You can't keep a Brown out of a boat," and Tom is a perfect example. Before and after retirement, Tom owned a small shrimp boat, and kept his family and others supplied with fresh shrimp, plus tons of fresh mullet. For several years after retirement, he operated a small tugboat, owned by his cousins, Alex and Tom Davis, Jr. in their marine construction business. At age eighty-eight, Tom Brown, Jr. hasn't slowed down much, although he has his grandsons throw the castnet when the mullet are running anywhere near his home on East Bay.

Tom Brown, Jr. enjoying life aboard the *Ben D.*

Wm. Edward Brown, III—(7-19-27):

The middle son of Tom Brown, Sr., he is known as Ed to some, and "Bubba" to those of us who grew up with him in East Pensacola Heights. He's been like all the other "Browns," you couldn't keep him out of boats either, however, the situation was different; his boats were submarines. The submarines he served aboard were the USS *Zugara,* a nuclear sub; and the USS *Lionfish.* After being discharged from the U. S. Navy, "Bubba," as I knew him, worked in a civil service position until retirement. In retirement, he was hired to teach the technology he mastered in the Navy and his civil service position.

William Edward "Bubba"
Brown III
(Courtesy of Tom Brown)

USS *Lionfish,* submarine

Ben L. Davis, Jr.—(1921 – 2013):

Ben L Davis, Jr.

I wrote about my older brothers, Ben and Bill, in several chapters of my first book, *Growing Up In Pensacola.* One in particular was about their ownership of a boat, the *Flossie A,* which, they modified from a badly damaged pleasure yacht into a commercial fishing boat shortly after WWII. With Shirley Brown's help, they contracted to transport crewmen to and from ships moored in Mobile Bay, a more profitable venture than commercial fishing. The business of operating a "water-taxi" went well until an employee mistakenly pumped gas through an abandoned gas cap, resulting in the fuel going directly into the bilge while tied up to the dock on the Mobile river. A spark ignited the fuel and the *Flossie A* was destroyed. For the full story about the *Flossie A,* see Chapter 23, *Growing Up In Pensacola.*

The loss of the *Flossie A* and the end of what was proving to be a profitable venture did not dissuade either of following their passion for boats. Although Ben was a successful Realtor, he continued to own one boat after another, especially small shrimp boats. He totally rebuilt a large commercial fishing boat, which when completed, he sold to one of Capt. Joe Patti's sons. For more information about Ben and his love for boats and fishing, I refer you to the Chapter in this volume, titled, "Brother Ben's Eulogy," and *Growing Up In Pensacola,* Chapter 37, "The Oldest Brother."

Ben Davis at the helm of his shrimp boat.

W. A. Bill Davis—(1923 – 2003):

Commissioner W. A. Davis
Chairman

Like, my brother Ben, Bill continued to own boats of various sizes, even though he was a Sanitarian with the Escambia County Health Department, and served as an elected Escambia County Commissioner. During that time he owned the *Native Dancer,* a commercial snapper boat, he docked at Williams Seafood Company. After retirement, Bill and his wife Carol lived in Gautier, Mississippi, where he owned the *Rampage,* a commercial boat he moored at their family home on Sioux Bayou. He made frequent trips to the Gulf of Mexico through the Mississippi Sound. On one such trip, while anchored in the Gulf, he was run down by a large shrimper out of Mobile, Alabama, sinking the *Rampage;* a collision that nearly cost Bill his life. An interesting footnote is that the captain of the large shrimper, who jumped overboard to help Bill, was a cousin he had never met, on our father's side of the family. For additional information about Bill and his boats, see *Growing Up In Pensacola:* Chapter 13, "Brother Bill's Eulogy," and Chapter 46, "The sinking of the Rampage."

Bill Davis aboard his
boat, the *Rampage*

As I suspected, it wasn't practical to think I could, in one chapter, adequately cover the interesting subject of the Brown family and their involvement in the commercial maritime industry over several generations.

I wrote above that somebody should write a book about the Brown family members and others involved with Brown Towing Company and Brown Marine Services, Inc. I hope someone will, because the companies

Shirley Brown founded employed over two hundred employees and operated dozens of tugboats and barges throughout the southeastern United States from their Pensacola location on Bayou Chico. The Browns have indeed made their mark in the maritime field and are a credit to the communities on the Gulf Coasts of Northwest Florida and South Alabama

Above: DPC-31, enroute to Cuba after WWII, with Tom Brown, Sr., and
Francis Rocheblave as Engineers
(Courtesy of Tom Brown, Jr.)

Below: Painting of two shrimp boats by Shirley Faye Brown Bryan

Top to bottom(1) The *Atlas,* The *Wind,* and The USS *Oriskany* (2) The *Cap'n Ace.* (3) The *Cap'n Ed.*
(Courtesy of the Boat Photo Museum)

Top to bottom: (1) The *Emma Brown*, (2) The *Nellie*, (3) The *Old Mack*. (Courtesy of the Boat Photo Museum

73

The *Quarterhorse*
Courtesy of the Boat Photo Museum

The *Janet*
Courtesy of the Boat Photo Museum

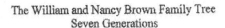

The William and Nancy Brown Family Tree
Seven Generations

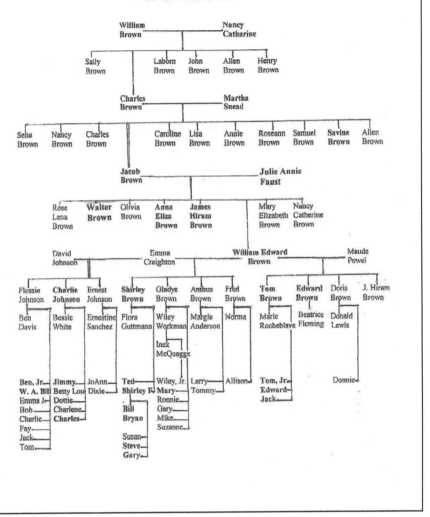

6

Em Hyer's Letters & the 1926 Hurricane

In the first volume of *Growing Up In Pensacola,* I wrote about Em Hyer (Mrs. J. Whiting Hyer) and her family, our neighbors in East Pensacola Heights, because of her love for animals and her obvious respect for nature. My siblings and I grew up on Bayou Boulevard, across the street from the Hyer family's property that consisted of several wooded acres, known to the community as "Hyer's Point," which included several hundred feet of waterfront on Bayou Texar. The family's beautiful, two-story home overlooks the bayou

Hyers Home in East Pensacola Heights

with clear views of Bayview Park and sections of East Hill, a community across the bayou.

The Hyers Family,
L to R, back row, John Hyer, Jr., John Hyer, Sr. J. L. Hall (Mike) and Edwin Wallace, Sr.
Middle row: Mrs. J. W. (Em) Hyer, Margaret Hyer Hall, Em Tucker Wallace.
Front row: Frances Hall Summit and Edwin (Ned) Wallace
Courtesy of Ned and Jean Wallace

While researching for the first story in 2009, I learned from Ned and Jean Wallace that Mrs. Hyer, Ned's grandmother, wrote several letters during the 1926 hurricane and its aftermath to her daughter, Margaret, a student at Florida State College for Women in Tallahassee, Florida (Florida State University).

My family moved to East Pensacola Heights in 1938, twelve years after the hurricane. I grew up hearing my parents and other adults talking about the ravages of the 1926 hurricane. It was before my time. The storm damaged the entire, panhandle of Florida, including the Gulf Coast of Alabama and Mississippi. Days earlier, the no-name hurricane had devastated Miami as it crossed over the state into the Gulf of Mexico, where it increased in intensity.

As I read excerpts from Em's letters, I recognized the names of many of our neighbors she referred to who had suffered damages. I was fascinated with her writing; it was a loving mother's well-written, honest report to a worried child about a disaster that damaged homes, families, friends, and all kinds of animals. She mixed descriptions of a disaster with that of a "dandy supper of roe-mullet (the mullet jumped into the neighbor's boat), broiled squab, and hoe-cake." I knew I would be writing a sequel to my book, so I asked Jean and Ned if I could use the letters for this story. It was disappointing to learn someone had "beaten me to it," but I was delighted to learn that "that someone" was Cynthia Dean.

Cynthia Green Dean

Cynthia Dean, a longtime friend, is the niece of Em Hyer's daughter-in-law, John Hyer, Jr's wife. Cynthia is an excellent writer, and very much involved in the West Florida Genealogy Society. She was chairman of the book committee that published *The Heritage of Escambia County, Florida.*

My wife, Sandra and I served on that committee with her, and have high respect for her professionalism. Cynthia is not only familiar with the letters, she is familiar with the individuals and families referred to in the letters written ninety years ago. Cynthia did a magnificent job of reducing the sixteen pages of Em's hand-written letters to only four, more readable pages, by typing the contents exactly as written, and inserting the relationship of those referenced. In addition, the typed version of the letters was published in *West Florida Footprints,* a publication of the West Florida Genealogy Society. I am pleased that Cynthia Green Dean has given me permission to use what she has accomplished with Em Hyer's letters, making these loving, informative, and in some cases amusing, messages from a busy mother about a major disaster back home.

I am grateful to Ned and Jean Wallace, current owners and residents of the Hyer's Point estate, for providing and sharing much information about the Hyers and their extended families. I also want to thank Ms. Frances Summit of Caro, Georgia, granddaughter of Em Hyer, who kindly allowed me to use the original letters. I've included a copy of the first page only of the original letters, suggesting it might be easier for the readers to imagine Mrs. Hyer writing while the storm in in full fury, with waves lapping at the front porch, the majestic trees bending to the wind, the trolley trestle destroyed and the bayou's high tide up to the level of the new bridge. It is interesting that she decided to write such a long letter to her daughter while, as she wrote, "we are in the midst of a most terrific storm." Following is a copy of the first page of Em's letters written on September 20, 1926, the day the hurricane struck Pensacola:

Monday Morn.

My dearest Margaret,
Well sugar we are in the midst of a most terrific hurricane. It has been predicted for several days so every one had ample time to prepare for it if there was any such thing but there is no such thing as preparing for a hurricane such as this. We took in most of our plants. tied up awnings nailed windows and doors. moved most every thing off the back porch & laid in a good supply of groceries. but no extra bread. We brought home every thing from St. Johns. and visited the Leonards - Bunnahams - invited them to come down & stay with us. if it got bad. Put the

In Cynthia's typed rendering of Mrs. Em Hyer's letters, there are no deletions or additions other than the information in parentheses and the dates the letters were written:

Monday Morning
September 19, 1926

My dearest Margaret,

Well, Sugar, we are in the midst of a most terrific hurricane. It has been predicted for several days so everyone had ample time to prepare for it if there was any such thing but there is no such thing as preparing for a hurricane such as this. We took in most of our plants, tied up awnings, nailed windows and doors, moved most everything off the back porch and laid in a good supply of groceries—but no extra bread. We brought home everything from St. Johns **(Cemetery)** and visited the Leonards—Brosnahams—invited them to come down and stay with us if it got real bad. Put the *Louise* in the cove and brought our skiff and Jack's up on the hill and tied them to the oaks. **(Jack Merritt, son of John A. and Mary Turner Merritt, Em's sister).** Well, it was a wise precaution for now Jack's is afloat, and ours is bobbing up & down. They are up on the hill 10 feet, I guess, from high tide. The water is up to the round flower bed, and good sized waves are splashing the big old century plant way up to the house nearby. Well, we are all going out to investigate things a little, and I will stop and go too.

Now we are back. You cannot possibly believe what we ran into. The water is past all belief. It is up to Bayview **(Bayview Park)** windows—no sign of a wharf or anything showing up but the roof and upper part of the building. You can step from the top of our bank right into the water. The lower magnolia limbs touch the water. John **(Em's son)** and Mike **(Em's daughter, Em T. Hyer)** rode me around among the trees in Jack's **(Merritt)** boat—up on top of the hill. We had to wade through water waist-deep to get around our lower garden fence—a large tree down across lower garden gate. Couldn't get in Mrs. Hall's front at all, **(Mrs. Hall, future mother-in-law of Em's daughter, Margaret who married Jay Hall)** her entire yard is water lapping up to her top step on her porch. She put on old togs and went with us. My, how she did wish for Jay. It lulled a little when we went on our tour, but it is awful now. Pigeon house most gone. John **(Em's son)** braced it, and now the braces are down.

Limbs of trees have torn a portion of the ridge board right over the dining room, and all the folks are up there getting it cut off. All our poles are down—no electricity, nor will there be for days, and no telephone poles, so—I bet we saw a hundred trees down, and you will never see your home again like it was when you left. That big old tree by the tank where the owls nest is down. Great big ones all around—top of both magnolias and mercy only knows what else, about 12 or 13 of ours and all the moss and leaves whipped off. Oh, there is someone in a boat, and they are being thrown out against our fence.

Later—Mike **(Em's daughter)** and I rushed to put on coats and went to see. It was Oliver **(son of Wilmer Walker, Sr.)** trying to bring their skiff up. Mr. Walker **(Wilmer Walker, Sr.)** brought his fish boat up, and Oliver misunderstood him and attempted to bring the skiff. Wilmer **(son of Wilmer Walker, Sr.)** went back and helped him—tied it up in the lane between us and Mrs. Hall's. It's all water you know, and a regular surf rolling just like the Gulf Beach. All kinds of animal life are panic stricken. We have a beautiful blue jay, pigeons, chickens, etc., in the house, and lizards & spiders & yellow jackets all over in a wild search for shelter. A huge porpoise was playing back in the cove when Mr. walker was putting up his launch, and a dandy big mullet got so frightened it jumped right into his boat. He tossed it over to me, and we had fresh roe-mullet, broiled squab & hot hoe cake for supper.

The Johnsons **(neighbors—Arthur Johnson)** had to go up to the store to get something to eat—had no way to cook and not a thing to eat. Mrs. Hall has no kind of stove either. Betty **(Betty Soule Merritt, wife of Jack)** was cooking on a 2-burner canned heat apparatus. John and Whiting **(Whiting Hyer, Em's Husband)** have gone to see the Brosnahams. They have returned now and report a wrecked mess for true. All of them are in Maybell's **(Maybel Brosnaham)** little house, and her living room was flooded, so John says. Their tents **(the Brosnahams were renovating their house and had put contents in tents)** until about 9 this AM, and then they went up in a jiffy. John says

Annie **(Annie Brosnaham, wife of George Brosnaham, Jr.)** looks like someone was dead. Every piece of their clothes, beds, furniture, ice box, electric stove, etc., all up side down in all this rain and blowing everywhere.

Well, I never can tell you all this mess, but I guess I had better stop. Abe **(Doris's beau, Abie Rule)(Doris Merritt, daughter of John A. and Mary Turner Merritt)** went to stay with aunt Addie **(Adelaide Turner Garfield, Em's sister).** Wasn't that nice? Wilmer Walker braved the hurricane and went to town, but we haven't heard any news. We really would like to hear from all our folks. Am mighty glad Tallahassee isn't in line to get this storm, but I dare say you felt it a little.

Mr. Walker **(Wilmer Walker, Sr.)** said the old street car trestle was going late this afternoon. It had broken loose from the pilings and was afloat. I hope it won't knock into our new bridge. All the railroad tracks from here to Escambia I think are afloat. So, I will have to send this letter by Montgomery. We are all lit up by candle light tonight. It's so dismal, and this howling wind and roaring waves makes one feel queer. Well, good night, honey, we are all going to turn in now. Hope we will all get through the night alright.

Lots of love,

Mother

Thursday Night
September 24, 1926

My dear Margaret,

The mails have all been so upset—we haven't heard from you in a coon's age. I wrote you a book on the hurricane day. There is just millions of the same kind of news, such as sheds and porches off—chimneys on nearly every house lying flat against the roof or on the ground, fences and arbors zigzagging, telegraph poles by the hundreds down and their wires dangling and draped in festoons from trees. Alcaniz **(street),** you know is brick paved over. Well, the wood blocks from Romana (street) floated "clear up" to Wright (street). They shoveled them off by the thousands. You could scarcely drive. Now they are on the grass plots, and it's OK.

You can't imagine anything to equal the wreckage that is the "mess" on the wharfs in the slip, but there is little actual loss, just such a mess.

Our city papers are the cutest things—light pink, and this one tonight is pale green, one sheet about 18 x 24. They have to use a little hand press. No lights yet, no phone and no water in town. Newport gives water, so does the ice plant. It looks like old timey to see people—everybody carrying jugs of water.

Jack (Merritt) Betty (Jack's wife, Betty Soule Merritt) took supper with us last night. After supper we all went in one car. Took Em (Em Turner Merritt Nickinson, daughter of John A. Merritt) a plate of "scamp" & then went over in the hill. (North Hill) A regular reunion at Dick's (Richard Turner, brother of Em Hyer) house block. Dick & his family, Filo (Filo H. Turner, Em's brother) & his spouse. (Marguerite). Bud (James S. Leonard) came up too, and Fan (Fan Turner Leonard, Em's sister) and Bud Jim (Bud Jim Leonard, son of James S. & Fan) came strolling by and stopped , so we had a nice time.

Mary (Dau. of Fan & James S. Leonard) has had fever for several days & Margery (dau. of Fan & James S. Leonard) is miserable. I haven't heard from them today. There are no schools in the city this week. They had to dry out and be cleaned up, so John (John Hyer, Em's son) and I went to the Cemetery (St. John's) early and had the crazy old car go punch, so we killed the whole day. Mr. Guethe had to come out to "Reimich" store, nearby, and towed us in. Then it took him hours to repair it at the shop. Miss Carrie had Whiting's (J. Whiting Hyer, Em's husband) car, so we were going to get a taxi when he got it fixed. We were so tired out from such a day; we just went fishing instead of picking up tree limbs and trash, so we had trout for supper.

An old sea captain gave Jack (Merritt) that scamp yesterday, and as they are cooking on a little sterno, they brought it for me to cook and asked themselves up to supper.

83

They were lonely and made the biggest kind of to-do over the supper—quite festive with 2 big silver candelabra. We all enjoyed it. We got a pitiful little leter from Catherine **(Turner, niece of Em & dau. of George Turner)** tonight. I must write to her a little, so good night sweet.

Loads of Love,

Mother

Monday Night
September 27, 1926

My dear Margaret

We received your letter today, and I have thought many times about the different things you told us. Charles Gonzalez told John that their house came very near going like the Howe's did. They all had to work like Trojans to save it. Huge timbers came over the breakwater, then over the railroad, then into their yard and rammed the pillars. I think their roof, that is to the porch, went off too. Mrs. Chap **(Mrs. Chapman Gonzalez)** said Bohemia **(area on Scenic Highway)** was ruined. We haven't been out their yet but we want to, and Mike **(Em's daughter)** is not working now.

Louverne has come back, so maybe she will take us out. Mary Patton **(sister of Annie Patton Brosnaham, Geo. Jr's wife)** is here, I think I told you, and she had to swim thru (8) rivers or creeks to get here after leaving Flomaton. One man was coming with them to look after his sweetheart. He had only his Sunday go to meeting clothes, so he ran over into the bushes on the edge of the river they had to ford, and put on his pajama pants and held his good clothes up out of the water. Then, after they got across, he disappeared for a few minutes into the bushes and lol he was spink & span and everyone else drowned. Mary had on her very best dress.

You know I really can't remember what I have told you about the storm, so if I tell you something I have already described, why please just excuse me. The Yacht Club is jammed up on the electric car trestle **(at Bayou Chico),** and Albert Quina, Bella said, lost everything he had.**(Bella Quina m. Richard Hill Turner, Jr., Em's brother. Albert is**

84

Bella's brother). It was all invested in a small mill (**Little Bayou Mill Co.**) right ther by the Yacht Club on that point, and the last stick of it washed away. There is a large Government boat sitting high and dry up on that island (**Brent's Island**) just in the mouth of Little Bayou, and I know without any exaggeration there must be all of 25 or 30 boats of various sizes setting up among the trees and on top of wharfs and half a block from water in Little Bayou.

The Draw on the Little Bayou bridge is a real sight. It is standing straight up only bent backwards till it touches the bridge and is twisted just as if it had been cloth. I told you Sanders Beach was washed as clean as my hand. I really don't know where the debris accumulated from those sheds.

Mike (**Em's daughter**) and Charlie were on the Palafox Wharf Sunday before the storm, and the *Tarpon* went out. Well, old Capt. Barrow (**Willis Green Barrow**) said he couldn't save her in that storm, so he beached her on Santa Rosa Island. He staid with her though, and Tuesday morning he came sailing into the wharf with a funny little piece of canvas stuck up on a row boat and reported that the old *Tarpon* was high and dry in the center of Santa Rosa. They have let him have a dredge, and they say in three days she will be afloat. There has been very little actual suffering though. Whiting (**Hyer**) said the Red Cross couldn't find any families who really needed aid.

Mr.Sherrill (**J. H. Sherrill—Sherrill Oil Co.**) had $500 sent him to spend upon the needy storm sufferers, and he wired back to his Oil people who had sent the money that there were no needy storm sufferers. That everyone was cared for.

Mr. Saltmarsh (**E.O. Saltmarsh, L & N R.R. official**) had open house at the depot, and anyone could go, day & night & get coffee and sandwiches, and he also had three Pullman cars lit up and running so as to care for any who may need it.

The San Carlos wouldn't give even a cup of coffee. Lots of their people went to Carrie's for food. Ferris-Lee lumber (**205 E. Main St.**) is a sight—it surely looks a wreck. It's just washed on the beach. I should think they could save much of it. Well, honey, Pa says I ought to be ashamed to write so much to you as you have to study some. Elizabeth

Monroe & Parilla were with Mary at C.E. last night, and Mike said she was just wild to know how you were "going." That means sorority, of course. In town this aft. Mike saw Mrs. Weis (**Mrs. Carl A. Weis**)—said she was buying yards & yards of sheeting for the families down on Main Street—that it was just simply washed away. I haven't been down there but I must go and see it to.

I haven't seen Fan (**Em's sister**) nor heard from any of my family today. Have been sewing—made 3 sheets & nearly finished one spread. Had a big okra gumbo for supper and it was A No 1. Had beautiful trout. "Daddy caught it with a hoop. Johnnie cleaned it like a man & Ma she fried it in the pan." Also a lovely soft shell crab. A monster for our breakfast this AM.

Tell me how you like the eats and so forth. Are your clothes alright, too, and have you plenty!
Well, honey, good night.

Loads of love,

Mother

They buried poor old Teddie Muldon this noon. I don't think there has been a soul at Gus Eitzen's grave since he was placed there.

Mother

Em Hyer's letters are unique because they are well written with wonderful descriptions of the broad array of damages caused by the hurricane and the matter of fact way she brings family and friends into the picture. With three letters, written over a one week period, she was able to cover a major catastrophe in a gentle way that should have assured her daughter that her family and friends back home were okay. The tone of the letters shows she was not afraid, and simply accepted what she was dealt and made the best of it. Some would think she was more concerned about the stress suffered by the animals around the property than about her own safety, which might have been the case, as it was her nature to harbor many different kinds of animals. As children, my siblings and I were always aware that Mrs. Hyer had a menagerie across the street that included everything from rabbits, squirrels, chickens and pigeons to flocks of geese and Guinea hens that roamed the neighborhood at times.

Anyone who reads Em's letters, and is only minimally familiar with the history of Pensacola, cannot help but be impressed with the family names she referenced, as it is an unintended list of, "Who's Who in Pensacola?" The fact is she is related directly or indirectly to most of them. They are all prominent Pensacola families, well respected, and much has been written about each of them.

Since reading Em Hyer's letters to her daughter, Margaret, I find it impossible to drive across the bayou bridge to East Pensacola Heights without looking over at Hyer's Point and thinking how great it would be to have a plate of Em's "dandy roe mullet, broiled squab, and hot hoe cake."

The *Tarpon* beached by the 1926 Hurricane
Source: *West Florida Footprints*, No. 32, 2011
Courtesy of Cynthia Green Dean

1926 Hurricane damage of Sanders Beach
Source: *West Florida Footprints*, No. 32, 2011
Courtesy of Cynthia Green Dean

1926 Hurricane damage of Bayview
Source: *West Florida Footprints*, No. 32, 2011
Courtesy of Cynthia Green Dean

The Yacht Club on the electric car trestle of the Dummy Line after the 1926 Hurricane
Source: *West Florida Footprints,* No. 32, 2011
Courtesy of Cynthia Green Dean

Streetcar trestle over Bayou Chico damaged by the 1926 Hurricane
Source: *West Florida Footprints*
Courtesy of Cynthia Green Dean

7

Eugene "Razzi" Rasponi

Every kid who attended A. V. Clubbs Junior High School in the 1940s and beyond, while Mr. Eugene Rasponi was teaching and coaching there, would have to agree he was greatly admired and respected. He was fondly referred to, and addressed by many students, as "Razzi;" he had a rapport with students that most teachers and coaches pray for. The school's 1947-48 annual, <u>The Aerial</u>, was dedicated to him.

DEDICATED
TO
MR. EUGENE RASPONI

Because we appreciate so much the work he has done in encouraging and directing our sports activities, and because we are so proud of our wonderful basketball team

My three older brothers, Ben, Bill and Bob preceded me at Clubbs School, and on my first day there, I met "Razzi" as he walked toward me in the hall. He looked at me and said, in mocked surprise, "Oh my God, not another Davis." Then, he laughed, shook my hand and welcomed me to Clubbs Junior High. He was like that with all the students. Of course, I knew most of the scary stories that didn't exactly endear Miss Nobles, the Principal, or the faculty to my older siblings. "Razzi" later reminded me of the time he caught my brother, Bill, smoking a cigarette up a tree on the school grounds. I was afraid to tell him two more brothers, Jack and Tom, would be attending Clubbs in the future.

Home Room 21

Abbott, Frank
Adams, David
Adkinson, Robert
Ard, Willie Ray
Askegren, Mauritz
Barrow, Gilbert
Bennett, Bobby
Bercau, Donald
Blackburn, Donald
Blackford, Bob
Blasky, Bill
Bonifay, Stanley

Bose, Bobby
Browder, John
Brunson, Perry
Bush, Charles Ray
Butts, Spencer
Carr, Ronald
Chavers, Foy
Chestnut, Vinson
Clarke, Clifton
Coleman, Dale
Coleman, Drew

Comer, Billy
Croft, Kyle
Crooke, Tommy
Cunningham, Carol
Cunningham, Donald
Daniels, Paul
Davis, Charles
Davis, Jimmie
Davis, Stanley
Diamond, Ronald
Dieckman, Robert
Douglas, Richard

Eugene James Rasponi, Sr. was born August 5, 1910 In Riolunato, Italy. He had one brother and six sisters; at some point in his young life, the family immigrated to America. He graduated from the University of Alabama, where he was a senior at the time Bear Bryant was a freshman.

After graduation, he taught and coached in Illinois for three years. In 1936, he accepted the position of Director of Physical Education at St. Florian Junior High School in Florence, Alabama. In addition to physical education, Coach Rasponi taught geography, history and civics.

"Razzi" married Ruth Christina Menne on August 3, 1940 in Peru, Illinois; they had two sons, Eugene, Jr. and Gary. He accepted a coaching and teaching position with A. V. Clubbs Jr. High and became the school's Assistant Principal. Later in his teaching career with the Escambia County School System, he became the Assistant Principal at Clubbs Jr. High School. "Razzi" died on November 6, 1995 at age 85, in enterprise, Alabama, where he is buried.

The following testimonies are from students who attended Clubbs Junior High School while "Razzi" was teaching and coaching there:

What we remember!! It's hard to believe that Razzi provided us a good physical education program and an intramural program. He taught us to have fun and enjoy sports. He did this on the small area at Clubbs. Razzi was a good teacher and basketball coach, and the basketball team won the county championship quite often. Many of us on the team went on and played varsity basketball at Pensacola High School.

"Razzi was my supervising teacher when I did my teaching internship from F.S.U. He was very helpful and taught me a lot. (Also gave me a good grade). Razzi ended his career in Escambia County as an Assistant Principal. (Jr. High School).

Eugene Rasponi was a good man. He touched the lives of many who attended Clubbs Jr. High School.

Gene Bridges
Pensacola, Florida

Razzi was a wonderful man & the first "coach" I ever had. I couldn't even spell "basketball" before I got to Clubbs and he got me interested. We beat Blount at PHS gym for title & Janie Cornwell (Cheerleader) dislocated her knee during the game, so we "Won one for Janie." I played second string center and I couldn't even push the ball off the backboard into the hoop, but I did in that game in 1st half. Mrs. Nobles (School's Principal) talked to the team at half-time and said, 'We need to make more plays like Scotty made, which was a laughing point for many years since it was about the only one I made all year. Wilmer (Wilmer Mitchell, his brother-in-law) laughs about it till this day. Razzi was a real gentleman and we were lucky to have him as our coach.

Laurence "Larry" Scott
Pensacola, Florida

I remember Coach Rasponi as being patient and showing compassion most of the time. He taught by demonstrating and showing, and if he ever lost his temper I didn't know it. With these traits, he was a good coach and motivator. I remember him as a fine person as well.

Note: He was especially good on defense, proven by the fact that our 8th grade

93

basketball team held Molino scoreless. The score was something like 20 to 0. I can't recall our exact score, but they didn't score. That was about 1949 in Molino on a dirt court. I might add, it was considered a road trip in those days, as was Brent and Ferry Pass. We got out of school half a day. Hooray

Bennie Early
Pensacola, Florida

I do remember playing basketball at A. V. Clubbs, and I remember Coach Rasponi as a very nice man, but I have no specific memories about specific events. I'm sure some of the guys will remember things, but I must apologize for my fragile memory that far back. The joke in our family is that Francis, my brother, has a memory like an elephant. Mine, not so much.

Noel Lindsey
Stuart, Florida

I didn't play on the A. V. Clubbs basketball team, but I remember Coach Rasponi as a good man. The thing I remember most is the time he wanted us to run to see who had the best time. We were lined up against each other on a hot day, and I didn't have my tennis shoes on, so I was barefooted. I made it about 20 yards before my feet were burning, so, I dropped out of the race.

George VanPelt
Century, Florida

Razzi created in me a desire to continue to play at a higher level. He taught me the skills that led me to be able to play varsity high school basketball and that resulted in my ability to receive a basketball scholarship to play at Georgia Tech. Good coaches never get the credit that they deserve and Razzi was a prime example of this. They can have such a positive influence on young students' lives.

Howard Snead
Signal Mountain, Tennessee

I contacted many other former students who were at A.V. Clubbs at the time Coach Rasponi was there, and every one had favorable comments about him. He was an asset to the school system, the community, and most of all, to his students. There's no way to know how many students were influenced in some positive way by "Razzi," but it would seem certain that most were.

UNDEFEATED—A. V. Clubbs Junior High basketball team was unbeaten during the past season, winning 11 games, including the county junior high title. The team scored 408 points to 174 for opponents, with Gene Bridges counting 163. Left to right above: First row, John Tringas, Jimmy Potts, Gene Bridges, Gene Middlebrooks, and Captain Howard Snead. Back row, Coach Eugene Rasponi, Billy Comer, Hobart Worley, C. C. King, and Robert Wheeler.

JUNIOR HIGH SCHOOL CAGE CHAMPS—Above are the members of the A. V. Clubbs Junior High school basketball team which won the county cage meet sponsored by Catholic High school last week and held in the Ellyson field gymnasium. Front row left to right are Johnnie Tringas, Billy Worley, Billy Comer and Bob Wheeler. Back row left to right, Eugene Rasponi, director of athletics, Jimmy Potts, Howard Snead, Gene Middlebrooks, Gene Bridges and Cecil King. (News-Journal Photo by Harting).

School Championship Basketball Team

They did it again! Our basketball team won the Escambia County Basketball Championship for the second consecutive time. Coach Rasponi really has a right to be proud of the team.

Billy Comer—Captain
Edward Restucher—Co-Captain

Wilmer Mitchell	Laurence Scott
Tommy Bridges	Donald Bercaw
Noel Lindsay	Don Allen Reynolds
Albert Reinschmidt	Thomas Mayne
Austin Wolfe	

*Top Row, 2ⁿᵈ from Left: Paul Daniels

Home Room Champions

98

A. V. Clubbs Cheerleaders :L -R , 1st Row: Thelma Holifield, Janie Mitchell, Ernest Mason, Jo Ann Owens, Gail Jackson
2nd Row: Perry Brunson, Gwen Miller, Janie Cornwell, Anita Faye Fowler, and Jimmy Davis

Traffic Boys: Tom Odom (Captain), Carlton Taylor, Tommy Bridges, Sonny Blackwell, Tim Barkley, Jack Eichelberger, Lynn Wilder, Lawrence Carrick, Willie Ray Ard, Charles Cannon and J. D. Tucker

Pictures for this chapter are courtesy of Aaron Grimsley

8

Five Flags Speedway

(Courtesy
of Dickie
Davis)

In the late 1940's and early 1950's my dad would often load up the family car with his youngest sons and oldest grandsons on Friday or Saturday nights, and they would be off to the "stock car races" at Pensacola Motor Speedway. The track was located near the intersection of Mobile Highway and Pottery Plant Road (Fairfield Drive), about where the Walmart Store is today. It was an appropriate spot because a popular racehorse track was previously in the general area. Dad was the County Tax Collector, and was given a family pass by J.J. Martin, who owned the Pensacola Speedway race track and the adjoining Martin Motel.

I was in high school during the time and remember the popular local drivers were J.C. "Jake" Hatcher, Sonny Black and Lamar Crabtree. One of Dad's grandsons was a young Dickie Davis, who caught a bad case of the "racing bug" about that time. While growing up Dickie raced in soapbox derbies, speedboats, motorcycles and no telling what else even before junior and senior high school.

Dickie Davis in the Soapbox Derby, Palafox Hill 1953
(Courtesy of Dickie Davis)

Much has been written about how stock car racing got started, and most agree its origin is rooted in the distribution of moonshine throughout Southern Appalachia, especially during the years of prohibition and the "Great Depression." Times were hard in the Appalachians and many families resorted to making and selling illegal liquor in order to survive. The demand was high for tax-free whiskey; production was simple and local, but distribution was a problem. The solution was delivery by fast, souped-up cars that could outrun the local sheriff deputies and U.S. Revenue Agents.

The 1958 movie, "Thunder Road," starring Robert Mitchum was about running moonshine in the mountains of Kentucky and Tennessee. It became a cult classic in the southeastern states. The drivers got better, and the cars got faster, inviting competition and bragging rights among the drivers, which in the 1930's eventually evolved into local organized racing events on improvised oval tracks set up in such places as cornfields and cow pastures. Thus, stock car racing was born. However, it was without any regulations; the accepted rule was, you "Run Whacha Brung." It's come a long way.

In the late 1940's, Bill France, Sr. recognized the problem racing faced was a lack of a unified set of rules among the different tracks. He spearheaded a meeting in order to form an organization that would unify the rules. The result was the formation of NASCAR in 1948 to regulate stock

Dickie Davis in Car 717
(Courtesy of Dickie Davis)

car racing in the United States. "Today, stock car racing is the largest spectator sport in America, drawing ten-million fans annually," according to Susanne Wise, Stock Car Collection Curator at Appalachian State University in Boone, North Carolina. Presently, NASCAR is a multi-million dollar industry and is still controlled by the France family, even though Bill France, Sr. died in 1992.

I don't know when J. J. Martin's Pensacola Speedway closed; I was away in the military like most of my friends. About the time the Korean War came to a close, a new race track was under construction on Pine Forest Road. Developed by L.H. Williamson, The Five Flags Speedway, a one-half mile oval track, opened on May 31, 1953. In an article by Alanis King in *SB Nation*, dated December 3, 2013, and titled, "Six-Decade Saga: The Tale of Five flags Speedway," he recalls:

> . . . during the inaugural race, the green flag was soon replaced with a red one as a result of a 14-car pileup on the dusty racetrack, and opening day was cut short due to unsuitable racing conditions on the makeshift track surface.

On June 14, 1953, Five Flags only NASCAR sanctioned Grand National Series (known as Sprint Cup Series today) was held at the speedway. Rain interfered, and only 140 of the scheduled 200 laps were completed. According to *Track History:*

> The legendary Lee Petty, Richard's father and Kyle's grandfather, appeared ready to charge to the front before the race was red-flagged. Herb Thomas, driving his Hudson Hornet, became the first and only person to win a Sprint Cup victory at Five Flags.

Drivers like Jake Hatcher, Sonny Black, Lamar Crabtree, Ivol Cooper, Onionhead McSwain, Rufus Johnson and others who thrilled fans at Pensacola Speedway continued the same at Five Flags, enjoying the new track lay-out and its highly-banked turns. Until the late 1960's, the Supermodifieds were the race car of choice at Five Flags. Unfortunately Sonny Black was killed at Five Flags in 1964, when he struck a wooden flag stand driving a Supermodified. Jake Hatcher also lost his life at Five Flags in 1965, driving his Supermodified No. 7 over one of the track's high banks.

Five Flags Speedway has changed ownership twice. In 1968, L. H. Williamson sold the track to Ohio Businessman, Tom Dawson, who initiated major changes. Alanis King wrote:

> With the arrival of Dawson, Five Flags' foremost racing class underwent a major shift: open-wheeled Supermodifieds were replaced with cheaper stock cars, and Late Models became the trademark of the speedway from that point on.

That same year, with the Late Models in place, Dawson introduced a long-distance event at the track; thus, the Snowball Derby, the track's signature event, was born, and has taken place every first weekend of December since its inception. The Snowball Derby is an independent event, meaning it is not officially sanctioned by any racing organization. In the past, it was sanctioned by Bob Harmon's All Pro organization and for one year by NASCAR when it acquired All Pro.

In a 1993 *Pensacola News Journal* article about Tom Dawson at the time of the 25th Snowball Derby, Jim Paulus writes:

Pensacola Stock Car Racing Poineers
(Courtesy of Dickie Davis)

Dawson moved from Ohio to Florida to get away from the cold and snow. So, what does he do? He puts on a race in December at Five Flags Speedway and gives it a wintry name. Dawson got the name of the race from a friend in Ohio who ran a hunting dog competition called Snowball Derby.

Paulus quotes Jim Grimes, a former sales manager at WEAR-TV who works in Rockford, Ill., who helped Dawson get the Snowball Derby started: "He took an old rickety race track and made something of it and brought credibility to racing in Pensacola."

The forty-seventh run of the Snowball Derby in December, 2014, was won by John Hunter Nemechek, 17 year old son of NASCAR veteran, Joe Nemechek. Chase Elliott won in 2011 at age 16 and again in 2015 at age 20. Jay Pennell of FOX Sports wrote:

> First run in 1968, the Snowball Derby is a premier short track late model race at the half-mile paved Five Flags Speedway. The list of winners is like a who's-who of racing names, including Donnie Allison, Darrell Waltrip, Pete Hamilton, Ted Musgrave, Rich Bickle, Jr., Kyle Busch, and Chase Elliott just to name a few. Other nationally-known drivers who have tried but failed to win the Snowball Derby are: Mark Martin, Matt Kenseth, Dale Earnhardt Sr., Bobby Allison, Rusty Wallace, Dick Trickle, Charles "Red" Farmer, and Mike Garvy.

Pensacola drivers have fared well in the Snowball Derby over its forty-seven year tenure. Wayne Niedecken won in 1968 and again in 1970. Dickie Davis, drew on his early experience in a Soap Box Derby, and then moved up through the race car divisions before winning the Snowball Derby in 1971 and 1973. Eddie Mercer, well-known local entrepreneur, won in 2005. Being a Snowball Derby winner is no longer an exclusive Man's Club. The first female driver to win was Tammy Jo Kirk in 1994, and eighteen-year-old Johanna Long from Pensacola who began racing at age fourteen, won in 2010. She's the daughter of well-known local driver, Donald Long.

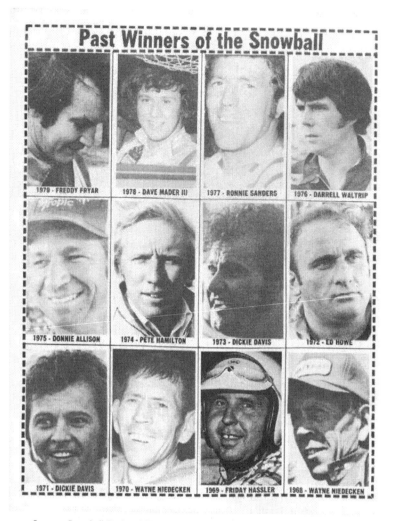

Past Winners of the Snowball

1979 - FREDDY FRYAR   1978 - DAVE MADER III   1977 - RONNIE SANDERS   1976 - DARRELL WALTRIP

1975 - DONNIE ALLISON   1974 - PETE HAMILTON   1973 - DICKIE DAVIS   1972 - ED HOWE

1971 - DICKIE DAVIS   1970 - WAYNE NIEDECKEN   1969 - FRIDAY HASSLER   1968 - WAYNE NIEDECKEN

Source: Snowball Derby, Official Souvenir Program. (Courtesy of Dickie Davis and the Bryant Family)

In Five Flag's Archived News, Dated November 18, 2011, under the heading "Snoball Derby: Once a Winner Always a Winner, " Elgin Trayler wrote:

They all went on to big accomplishments in their racing careers after winning the Snowball Derby, but the Derby memories come back to them like a cool Pensacola morning breeze. Dickie Davis, Butch Miller and Rick Crawford remember so well the day they won the Snowball Derby.

For Davis, Miller and Crawford, winning the Snowball Derby was a dream that came true. Seeing as more than 500 drivers have tested the biggest and most prestigious Super Late Model Race in the country, only 32 have accomplished the feat{35 as of 2015}. That stat alone shows how tough it is to get the title of Snowball Derby winner. These three drivers earned it—Davis on two occasions—as a feather in the cap of great racing careers.

'It's probably one of the best wins we've ever had,' said Miller, who won in 1987. 'It's one I will always remember and always cherish. We're on the back of that t-shirt—that's pretty cool.'

The t-shirt is a symbol of excellence like the Green Jacket at Augusta or the Borg-Warner Trophy at Indy. A checkered flag at the Snowball Derby lands a driver in racing immortality. The winner gets his or her name etched on the trophy, the t-shirts, the commemorative posters and much more.

'It's remarkable what the Bryant's have done,' said Davis. 'It just keeps getting bigger and bigger and I'm impressed.'

Davis was a pioneer in making the Snowball Derby what it is today. Back in the 1970s, the race was only a 200-lapper. Davis found a way to win the race twice, years before anyone else ever came close.

Wastle Spears
Source:
www.fiveflagsspeed

Tom Dawson continued ownership of Five Flags until 2007. In the interim several individuals contracted to operate the speedway, including Wastle Spears, along with his son and daughter-in-law, Terry and Helen Spears, who operated Five Flags from 1990 to 1997.

The Bryant's Dickie Davis referred to above are Tim Bryant and his family, current owners of Five Flags, having first operated under a lease for three years, before purchasing Five Flags in 2007. Bryant serves as general manager of both Five Flags Speedway and Mobile International Speedway. He is credited for the success Five Flags enjoys today. He is also one of the founding members of the Southern Super Series, where a common rules package for Super Late Models was established between Pensacola, Mobile, Gresham Motorsports Park, Fairgrounds Speedway in Nashville, Montgomery Motor Speedway and South Alabama Speedway.

The race classes that take place at Five Flags are: Super Late Models, Pro Late Models, Super Stock, Sportsmen, Bombers and Modifieds. I'm sure there are other events which I am not aware of.

We should be proud of the progress and success Five Flags Speedway has enjoyed over the years, especially since Tim Bryant has been in charge. The Snowball Derby is the signature race at Five Flags, but race fans are aware of the several championship races ongoing during the regular racing season that draw drivers and fans from all over the country. There are several charity events throughout the year that benefit local organizations. I encourage everyone who enjoys competitive sports to visit Five Flags Speedway, if you haven't done so. You'll be glad you did.

Kay, Randy, Bill, Ginny, Tim and Pat Bryant, current owners of the Five Flags Speedway
(Courtesy of the Bryant Family)

108

SNOWBALL DERBY WINNERS ROSTER

1968 Wayne Niedecken

1969 Friday Hassler

1970 Wayne Niedecken*

1971 Dickie Davis*

1972 Ed Howe

1973 Dickie Davis*

1974 Pete Hamilton

1975 Donnie Allison

1976 Darrell Waltrip

1977 Ronnie Sanders

1978 Dave Mader III

1979 Freddy Fryer

1980 Gary Balough

1981 Freddy Fryer

1982 Gene Morgan

1983 Mickey Gibbs

1984 Butch Lindley

1985 Jody Ridley

1986 Gary Balough

1987 Butch Miller

1988 Ted Musgrave

1989 Rick Crawford

1990 Rich Bickle, Jr.

1991 Rich Bickle, Jr.

1992 Gary St Amani

1993 Bobby Gill

1994 Tammy Jo Kirk

1995 Jeff Purvis

1996 Rich Bickle, Jr.

1997 Bobby Gill

1998 Rich Bickle, Jr.

1999 Rich Bickle, Jr.

2000 Gary St. Amant

2001 Wayne Anderson

2002 Ricky Turner

2003 Charlie Bradberry

2004 Steven Wallace

2005 Eddie Mercer*

2006 Clay Rogers

2007 Augie Grill

2008 Augie Grill

2009 Kyle Busch

2010 Johanna Long*

2011 Chase Elliott

2012 Erik Jones

2013 Erik Jones

2014 John Nemechek

2015 Chase Elliott

* Pensacola Drivers

9

Gordon Towne

In 1953, Gordon Towne came to town. That was sixty-three years ago, and the town "ain't" been the same since, and neither has Gordon Towne. He didn't come alone; three other Townes, his wife, Helen, and their children, Terry and Linn Dee, also made the journey from Orlando. The Townes probably entered Pensacola by crossing over the old two-lane Pensacola Bay Bridge, and then passed by other historical landmarks like the L&N Railroad Depot, "The Milk Bottle," and the San Carlos Hotel. There have been many changes in the town since their arrival, and

Gordon Towne,
Mr. WCOA

Gordon was in the mix, not only as Pensacola's leading radio voice, but through his involvement in local and statewide organizations. Gordon earned the respect and admiration from the citizens of Pensacola who recognized it was a good thing when the Townes came to our town.

Although Gordon was born in Minnesota in 1927, he became a Floridian at age five when his family moved to Winter Haven, where he graduated from Winter Haven High School in 1944. Like other young men his age, future plans were put on hold. As a member of "The Greatest Generation," he was soon serving his country as a Gunnersmate aboard a Destroyer, the USS *Fechteler*, in the Pacific Theatre. He and his fellow shipmates have remained in touch through the "Fechteler News," a newsletter, to which he occasionally contributes articles.

U.S.S. *Fechteler* DD 870, Gordon's "Tin Can"

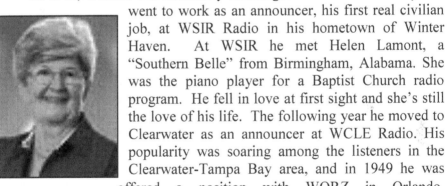

Helen Lamont Towne

In 1946, Gordon was honorably discharged from the U.S. Navy and went to work as an announcer, his first real civilian job, at WSIR Radio in his hometown of Winter Haven. At WSIR he met Helen Lamont, a "Southern Belle" from Birmingham, Alabama. She was the piano player for a Baptist Church radio program. He fell in love at first sight and she's still the love of his life. The following year he moved to Clearwater as an announcer at WCLE Radio. His popularity was soaring among the listeners in the Clearwater-Tampa Bay area, and in 1949 he was offered a position with WORZ in Orlando. Gordon is known for his great sense of humor, which was evident in the following news release from the Associated Press in 1949, a short time after he and Helen were married.

Orlando, Florida– Disk Jockey Gordon Towne (of W-O-R-Z) has learned a few sobering facts about the radio audience.

Mr. Towne recently married a young lady from Alabama. And he made this the subject of radio chatter-kidding the state of Alabama. For one thing he said of course folks in Alabama don't wear shoes. He said maybe the folks in Florida ought to send shoes to the folks in Alabama. Mr. Towne, as you may have guessed, has been swamped with over 100 pairs of old shoes from charity-minded Floridians. Towne plans to go through with it. He is shipping the shoes to the Mayor of Birmingham, his wife's hometown. So far, no comment from the Mayor.

Gordon with shoes donated for the folks in Alabama

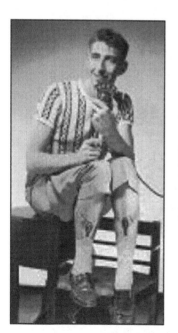

Gordon at WORZ

In 1951, Station WHOO in Orlando wooed him away from WORZ, and in 1953, Gordon accepted a position with WBSR in Pensacola. With his years' experience in radio, he started out as the morning announcer and by 1961 he had worked up to Program Director-Salesman. Under his guidance, WBSR became the major competition for arch-rival WCOA. In a Pensacola News-Journal article, the late Don Priest, WCOA News Director, recalled the first time he met Gordon: "It was at a local car dealer's showroom," Priest said. "He was trying to sell advertising to them. My first impression is that this guy is a real wheeler-dealer. I was impressed by his flamboyance and a little snake oil."

That same article went on to explain, "Towne was hired at WCOA shortly thereafter."

Gordon spent the next twenty-eight-plus years at WCOA, starting out in 1961 as Morning Announcer and Salesman. In 1973 he was appointed Sales Manager. Two years later, the station was sold to Summit Communications of North Carolina, and Gordon was promoted to General Manager of WCOA. That same year he was elected

Gordon Towne
Pensacola radio
personality and
WCOA manager

Courtesy of the J. Earle Bowden Family

113

Vice President of Summit Communications of Florida. During the ensuing years, Gordon, WCOA, and Summit prospered under his leadership.

In the mid-1980s, Gordon put together an offer to become the owner of the station he worked for and loved for twenty-eight years. Unfortunately, his bid was unsuccessful and the station was sold to another group. As a result, Gordon resigned. In a <u>News Journal</u> article, Don Priest said, "Towne's resignation came as a shock." In the same article, Al McLeod, Gordon's longtime friend and golf partner, said, "Towne had a subtle sense of humor, did some kidding and ragging of different well-known people. He had a real quick wit and was sharp on the comeback."

Gordon's reaction to leaving WCOA was: "It's hard to turn your back on this. It's a chapter that you're closing in your life," adding, "I'm going to just sit back and watch the paint peel." Those who know Gordon are aware he couldn't sit still long enough to watch the paint applied much less peel. It was and continues to be his nature to be involved.

Master of Ceremony Gordon Towne at a PSA Meeting with guests Jack Nicholas and Son

For starters, he's been active in the Pensacola Sports Association (PSA), Hospice, Northwest Florida Blood Center, Inc., Pensacola Country Club and Florida Association of Broadcasters Board. Gordon has always been a fisherman, a tennis player, a golfer, a biker, and a runner. He once finished a 10K run in 55 minutes. A few years back, he took on archery hunting and began participating in the Fiesta of Five Flags.

Gordon and Buz
Windham are
both active
members of the
American
Cancer Society

Fiesta of Five Flags Marathon

Even today, at age eighty-nine, Gordon's activities are far too many to include in this essay, but one that is a must is his involvement with the

Gordon and Helen

American Cancer Society. As noted in the PNJ article, "The death of fellow WCOA worker Sally Henderson of cancer led Towne to the local chapter of the American Cancer Society." Don Priest said, "It had a profound effect on a lot of us, but in Gordon's case it started him in getting very active in cancer work." In 1966, he chaired the Harry Ordon Fishing Rodeo and raised five-thousand dollars for the American Cancer Society. Gordon served on the Society's board of directors and for several years chaired its annual fundraiser, the Cadillac Ball. He was chosen to head the state society's public information division, and was awarded the American Cancer Society's prestigious National St. George Medal. He was Chairman of the Board, American Cancer Society, Florida Division—1992-93.

As you might have surmised, Gordon Towne is a man of many passions, number one, his love for Helen, his bride of sixty-seven years, his children, grandchildren, and two great granddaughters. Another passion is, of course, his love and respect for his church, the First Baptist Church of Pensacola, where his family are long-time members. Gordon isn't shy about sharing his Christian beliefs, or discussing others' thoughts on religion.

We both attend the Joe Harrell Men's Bible Breakfast, a non-denominational group that meets each Wednesday morning in the Wright Place at First United Methodist Church. It's a mixed-bag of guys from different churches in the area who meet to share the Bible and enjoy a great meal. A unique part of the get together each week is when Gordon is

116

invited to the podium to lead us in prayer before the guest speaker is introduced. All of us look forward to his part, because his skill as a Master of Ceremonies comes through loud and clear. A newcomer to the group would naturally expect him to immediately lead us in prayer, but Gordon will first challenge us on some current event or share something interesting or amusing. He usually follows by reading a short, interesting faith-based story that has a Christian message. Then, he says, "Pray with me, please."

Gordon leading the Joe Harrell Bible Breakfast at the First United Methodist Church

In 1993, at age twelve, Gordon's grandson, Gordon Ross Jones, wrote the following tribute to his grandfather, titled, "My Hero."

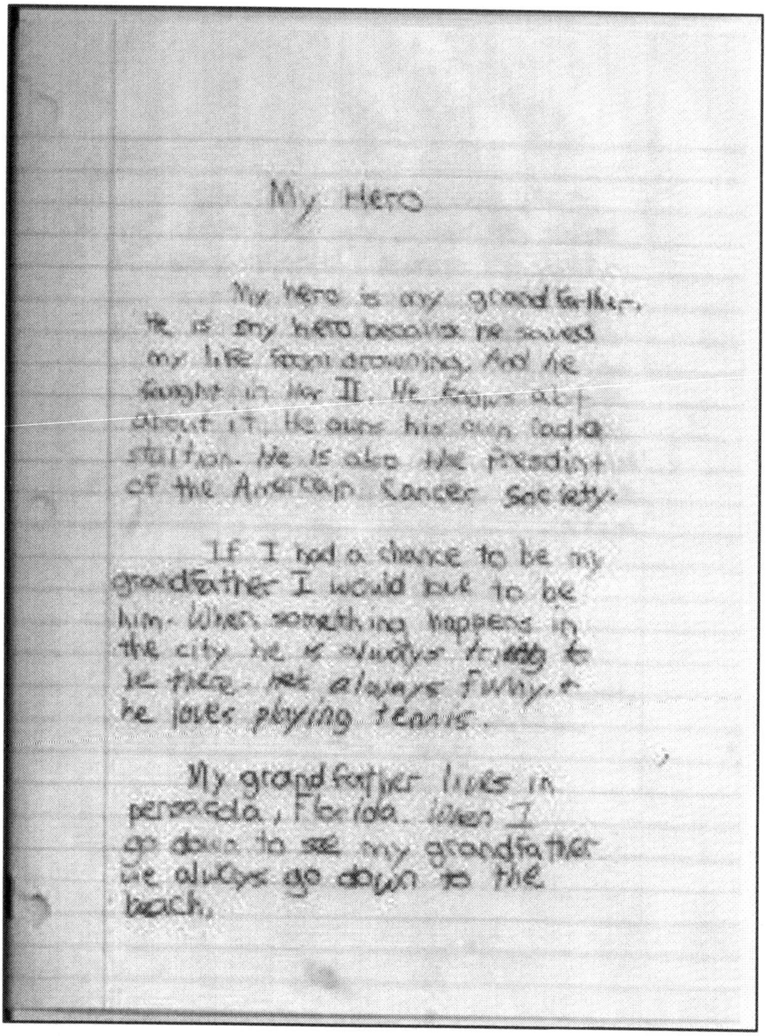

My Hero

My hero is my grandfather.
He is my hero because he saved
my life from drowning. And he
fought in War II. He knows alot
about it. He owns his own radio
station. He is also the president
of the American Cancer Society.

If I had a chance to be my
grandfather I would but to be
him. When something happens in
the city he is always trying to
be there. He's always funny, +
he loves playing tennis.

My grandfather lives in
pensacola, Florida. When I
go down to see my grandfather
we always go down to the
beach.

My grandfather favorite
thing to do is go ~~sha~~ snow
skiing. He also enjoys playing
alot. He plays the drums
and the organ. And hes
actually good at them.
And last but not leas he
collect stamps. And he
alway carries a $2 bill
around + we have the same
name.

Compliments by
Landon Ryan Jones
1998

119

Another of Gordon's passions might surprise some of you—he's a "hoofer." That's right, he's a tap dancer! Neither Jimmy Cagney, Sammy Davis, Jr, Shirley Temple, nor Bojangles, could do it better. Of course, they're all dead, leaving Gordon in a class of his own, which "ain't nothing new" folks. Gordon Towne has always been in a class of his own.

Gordon dancing at Bayview Park

Gordon is the center of a performance at PHS in 2010.

10

Hopkins Boarding House, Hoppy's, and the Hopkins'

I don't know who coined the phrase, "Movers and Shakers," but whoever it was, they must have been thinking of the Hopkins family. Pensacola and Escambia County are fortunate to have more than one generation of this hardworking, dynamic family, made up of outstanding individuals who succeeded in most everything they did. In return, they contributed to the community in numerous ways. Their giving back helped make Northwest Florida the attractive destination it is for individuals, businesses and organizations.

Although it was the twentieth century, Elbert W. Hopkins, Sr., his wife, Idell, and sons, Junell (J.B.) and-six-weeks old Elbert W. Hopkins, Jr. (E. W.) were true pioneers. In 1928, during the "Roaring Twenties," while

The Hopkins Family: E.W.., Jr., E.W., Sr.., Vernon, Mrs. Hopkins and J. B.
(Courtesy of E. W. Hopkins)

Prohibition was in full swing, they moved to Pensacola from Wallace, which was a small community between Pace and Chumuckla, Florida. It was the year Herbert Hoover defeated Al Smith for President. Hoover would later promise Americans that, "Prosperity is just around the corner," which, in retrospect, could have been the Hopkins families prophesy. However, neither the Hopkins nor the world knew the "Great Depression" was "just around the corner."

"The Blue Light," North Davis Highway
(Courtesy of E. W. Hopkins)

122

As the crow flies, it was less than twenty-five miles from Wallace to where Elbert, Sr. opened his first of several businesses in Pensacola. He leased a service station and garage from J. H. Sherrill with the Pure Oil Company. It was located on North Palafox Street in an area north of town known as Golden, and just south of Fairfield Drive (previously Pottery Plant Road). Idell's half-brother, Harvey Dixon, and the Crabtree brothers, Lloyd and Kenner, worked in the small auto-repair garage in the rear of the station. The family lived in part of the service station, which was their first home in Pensacola. That was eighty-seven years ago, and in the middle of the "Great Depression," but the family survived due to hard work and determination, a character trait of the Hopkins family members.

E. W., Sr., (2nd from right) with
E. W., Jr., J. B. and employees.
(Courtesy of E. W. Hopkins)

According to E. W., Jr., "Our next move was about 1931 or 1932 to North Davis Highway where Dad ran another service station and roadside place with a dance hall, known as 'The Blue Light.' That move was a step in the right direction, but there were problems, as E. W. explained: "Mom suffered a near fatal accident when some drunk drove through the front door and hit her, and later, in about 1935, The Blue Light burned. It was a total loss. Mr. Sherrill helped by financing a new English Tavern station with a new dance hall."

THE SPEARMAN BREWING COMPANY
PENSACOLA, FLORIDA

My own family lived in the Brent area, near the English Tavern, and my brother Bob recently reminded me that Elbert, Sr.

123

took him along with J. B. and E. W. to the grand opening of Spearman Brewery, which was located on Barrancas Avenue and Government Street. Bob said he remembers the brewery's motto was "The Pure Water Does It," but he didn't understand what it meant, since he and E. W. were only seven years old at the time.

E. W., Sr. (center) with the Crabtree Brothers
(Courtesy of E. W. Hopkins)

In 1937, Elbert, Sr. sold the English Tavern to the Merritt's, a local family. He then built and opened the new Parkway Café about a mile south on Davis Highway at the "Golden cut-off" to Old Palafox Street. "The Parkway Café was a success," said E. W., adding, "but my dad was restless, so he started another business, an auto parts and wrecker service on Davis Highway, about where Quigley Electric is today." (Davis and Texar Drive).

During World War II, Elbert, Sr. worked at Pensacola Naval Station as a mechanic while also running another new venture he called Hopkin's Boarding House at 615 North Spring. (It's not to be confused with the popular Hopkin's Boarding House later established at 900 North Spring street). E. W. worked as a "tack-welder" at the shipyard and helped out at the boarding house. J.B. was in the Air Force during WWII.

Following the end of WWII, Elbert, Sr. closed down the boarding house and opened Hoppy's, a sundry and gift shop, next door to the Y.M.C.A. on Palafox Street. It was a big hit with us students at Pensacola High School, guys at the Y.M.C.A., members of First Baptist Church and the telephone operators at the nearby Southern Bell building. Years later, when the sitcom, "Happy Days," first appeared on television, it reminded many of us of pleasant times at Hoppy's, since it was the most popular gathering spot after school. There were other businesses downtown with similar soda shops, like Hannah's Pharmacy, Woolworth, Kresses, Newberry and Walgreens. As I recall, E. W. was in charge, and none of us called the future Marine Lieutenant a "soda-jerk."

After receiving many requests for small lunches, mainly from the

124

ladies at Southern Bell, Arkie Dell Hopkins, Elbert, Sr's sister-in-law, was asked if she would like to try doing the lunches. She agreed and prepared the lunches at Hoppy's for several months in 1947-1948. The price for lunch, which included a meat, two sides and a roll, was fifty-nine-cents. Arkie Dell realized there was a definite need for an economical place for people to have lunch, and in 1949 she opened a restaurant and rooming business across the street from Hoppy's at 415 North Palafox. She also called her new business, Hopkins Boarding House. Business was good. In 1951 she purchased the McGaughy house at 900 North Spring Street and moved her business there. She became affectionally known as "Ma" Hopkins, and over the next sixty plus years, lunch or dinner at Hopkin's Boarding House was a must for all of the locals and most of the visitors to Pensacola. I could fill a book with favorable comments by locals and visitors who enjoyed lunch there, but one particular description on Facebook by a former resident of Pensacola pretty well sums up the reaction of most diners who enjoyed the friendly atmosphere where "the boarding-house-reach" was required. On June 5, 2008, cajunhippiegirl wrote:

> "It was a great place, in an old Victorian House. It operated as a boarding house for many years as well as a restaurant. My parents went there on dates in 1949, and we ate many a meal there after church on Sunday through the 60s & 70s until we moved to the East Coast of Florida. You could still get a 'pully bone'/"wish-bone" as one of the pieces of fried chicken, which was to die for. If you asked your server, they would bring you a plate of just "pully-bones." This was the practice right up until they served their last meal. On Fried Chicken day you had to get there early, and sit out on the big front porch which was full of rockers, fans and benches. What a treat. You could find people from all walks of life on that porch waiting for the same fried chicken as you. There were always at least two entrée's and numerous side dishes and salads. There was always desserts & pitchers of sweet tea on the table. Everything was served 'Family Style' and it was nice to chat with people you didn't know at your table. If you were lucky you got to sit at the big round table with the lazy susan in the middle, it made the passing of the bowls a lot easier. They also did a great breakfast. Everything was always so fresh and just like 'Grandma' made. I was so

Hopkin's Boarding House
(Courtesy of Frank Hardy, Jr)

sorry to see it close. It was an institution in Pensacola, everyone from there knew about it and many people from out of town stopped in anytime they were in Pensacola."

In Pensapedia ,the Pensacola encyclopedia, it's written, "A variety of other dishes were served, many of which have been included in regional cookbooks, including the Junior League of Pensacola's *Some Like It South.* Hopkins Boarding House was so well known, two years after it closed, a Facebook posting in United States Forum, www.fodors.com, dated May 11, 2006, someone asked, not knowing Hopkins Boarding House was closed, "Would you recommend it? It was named one of the top 10 'all you can eat' restaurants by Epicurious Magazine." In a reply to the query, someone wrote, "I used to eat there quite frequently in the mid-1980s, as I lived in Pensacola . . . I do recall it had wonderful fried chicken and I seem to remember something about biscuits or cornbread being exceptional. It used to be served family style. You would have judges and bankers sitting next to construction workers."

Unfortunately, in 1954 Arkie Dell became ill, and her sister, Blanche Wolf Stubbs, ran the business for the next seventeen years. Sadly, in 1986, Arkie "Ma" Hopkins died. Her son, Ed Hopkins, took over the business. Hopkins Boarding House thrived over the next ten years under the management of Vicki Hopkins, his wife. Ed and Vicki were divorced, and faced with the requirements of managing the business and the duties of his law practice, he decided to close the restaurant in 2004 and seek a new owner. Before that could be arranged, Ed Hopkins died on a hunting trip with his son on September 11, 2004. Hopkins Boarding House never reopened, and the house was purchased by Elise and Don Gordon, who turned it into a private residence.

Years earlier, on October 27, 1934, a third son, Vernon Hopkins, was born into the Elbert W. Hopkins, Sr's. clan. At an early age, Vernon went to work at Merrill-Lynch and remained with the firm for twenty-five years, while living in Mobile, Atlanta, New York, Little Rock, and Memphis. Upon retirement in 1984 he returned home to Pensacola to join First Mutual Savings & Loan, where E. W. was President. He became manager of First Mutual's brokerage company, retired from the bank in 2006 and moved to Ocala. Currently, Vernon and wife, Carolyn, have plans to move to Orange Beach, Alabama, to be closer to family.

In 1947, both J. B. and E. W. enrolled at the University of Florida; but after the first quarter, E. W. transferred to FSU for a semester before returning home to resume working at Hoppy's. In September, 1948, he was one of the 128 students who enrolled in Pensacola Junior College's first class, held in the old Aiken home on Palafox Street. He attended Auburn University from 1949 to 1951 and was awarded a commission in the U. S. Marine Corps. Eighteen years later, he became president of the PJC Foundation, and in 2005, he was named a Fellow. According to PJC's Compendium Magazine: "Recently, the Foundation paid homage to six Founding Fellows who laid the ground work that has led to 40 years of success: Crawford Rainwater Sr., E. W. Hopkins Jr., M. J. Menge, Warren Briggs Sr., Howard Rein and Gaspare (Tam) Tamburello." E. W. was also named a Fellow at the University of West Florida, where he was awarded an honorary doctorate. He was, in a quiet way, dedicated to education, evidenced by having served eight years on Florida's State Board of Regents.

E. W. was active in community organizations early on, such as Pensacola Jaycees, Pensacola Sports Association, Kiwanis, member of the Santa Rosa Island Authority, and a founding member of St. Christopher's Episcopal Church on 12th. Avenue. After years with Mutual Federal Savings and Loan, and retiring as President, E. W. worked another twenty-five-plus years with John Carr and Company as a Real Estate Broker. He enjoyed belonging to various other organizations, such as the United Way, Fiesta of Five Flags, State of Florida Ethics Committee, Mayor's Task Force, Diabetes Foundation, Junior achievement, and of course, the Chamber of commerce, from which he received the Hall of Fame Award in 1978.

E. W. and his wife, Jan Richardson Hopkins, a Pensacola native, were blessed with three daughters: Dinah Ricketts, Sarah Perkins, and Kate

E.W. Hopkins

When E.W. Hopkins became the second president of the PJC Foundation, he brought a unique perspective to the fledgling organization. Hopkins was one of the history-making 128 students who comprised the college's first class in September 1948.

"Those first five or six years, working with President Ashmore and President Harrison, were devoted to building up the organization. Sometimes it was hard to identify our PJC graduates because the college was still so young," Hopkins said.

An early Foundation event that Hopkins especially enjoyed was the Honors Program Banquet where PJC scholarships were presented to the valedictorians, salutatorians, and students with the top test scores at each high school. The banquet was sponsored by the company he worked for, Mutual Federal Savings and Loan, along with Crawford Rainwater's Hygeia Coca-Cola Company, and the Pensacola News Journal.

E.W. and his wife, Jan Richardson Hopkins, are both Pensacola natives. They have three daughters: Dinah Ricketts, Sarah Perkins and Kate Stradtman; and three grandchildren.

Stradtman. E. W. and Jan celebrated their sixty-fourth wedding anniversary on October 20, 2015.

J. B. Hopkins
(Courtesy of Stella Hopkins)

J.B. graduated from the University of Florida's Law School in 1951, and became the Assistant County Solicitor that same year. He was highly respected by others in the legal community, and enjoyed a long, successful and productive career. While practicing law, he served two terms in the Florida House of Representatives, 1954-1956 and 1956-1958. In 1958 he sought the office of State Senator, and ran against the incumbent, Philip D. Beall, but lost. He ran again for State Senator in 1966, and garnered more votes than Bernard Penn, and John C. Boles, but not a majority. Although he led John Broxson by 526 votes in the primary, J. B. lost to John in the run-off by 5,243 votes.

J. B.s two terms as State Representative were very productive for Escambia County and West Florida. As a member of the "Pork Chop Gang," a voting bloc of Panhandle legislators, he quickly earned the reputation of being a "tiger," as well as other less flattering terms from his

Governor Leroy Collins signing a bill creating University of West Florida. The Escambia delegation from R to L, Rep. Webb Jernigan, Senator Philip D. Beall, Jr. and Rep. J. B. Hopkins.
(Source: Pensapedia, 7/17/2016

more liberal fellow legislators from down state. In his first term, he failed to get a bill passed that would make Pensacola Junior College a four-year institution; however, he had drafted a bill calling for the creation of a four-year university in Escambia County. As will happen, a fellow lawmaker copied his bill, substituting "Palm Beach" in lieu of "Escambia County," and immediately submitted it ahead of J. B.s bill. J. B. is quoted in Pensapedia as follows: "His bill was ahead of mine, but it said, 'Palm Beach.' I went over and said, 'You so and so, you know my bill was ahead of yours—you copied mine . . . I want to put 'and Escambia County' on that bill, and he said OK." The bill was passed, and along with passage of additional related bills, which J. B. drafted, the University of West Florida became a reality. During his time in office, the St. Petersburg Times twice recognized J. B. as one of the State's top ten lawmakers.

Without any chance of exaggeration, one could say that J. B. Hopkins was actively involved in more organizations during his life than anyone else in the history of Pensacola, and what makes that so unusual is the fact that he was usually in charge at some point in his association. There are too many organizations to list, but those who knew J. B. well, were aware of his passion for the legal profession, and consequently his involvement in all professional groups. He was the legal counsel for the West Florida Homebuilders Association for forty-five years. In his younger years he was active in the Jaycees, local and national, and was involved for many years with the Chamber of Commerce. He was a founder of Scenic Hills Country Club, and a charter member and board member of the U.W.F. Foundation. It should be noted that he was a member of Masonic Lodge 15, involved in Scottish Rite, and was a founding member of the Hadji Shrine

(L-R) Vic Damone, J.B. Hopkins, Doug Sanders, Mayor Roy Philpot, and Bob Hope at Pro-Am Party for Pensacola Open

Source: Stephens, Jerry.
Loud Pants…Smooth Lies.
PSA Foundation.
March, 2002

Temple in Pensacola. J.B. left his mark in many ways. In 1993, the Student Enrollment services building at U.W.F. was named, "The J. B. Hopkins Hall."

J.B., his wife, Stella, and their four daughters were charter members of Holy Cross Episcopal Church in Pensacola, where J.B. taught a Sunday school class for men, and was a youth training teacher. Later, they transferred their membership to St. Christopher's Episcopal Church. As reported in Pensapedia, "In July, 2002, Hopkins had an operation to remove a brain tumor, but was told by his doctors that he had less than a year to live. He passed along cards to his fellow parishioners at St Christopher's Episcopal Church that read, 'What I have is bad. It is malignant, inoperable and terminal . . . I am OK with all this and I do not want you to be sad, either. I want to die as I have lived—with all the dignity, independence, faith and laughter I can muster.' He passed away on November 9, of that year."

J. B. and Stella Hopkins with daughters: Belrene, Holly, Julie, & Terrie
(Courtesy of Stella Hopkins)

I trust that by now the reader understands it would require a book-length publication to adequately cover the exploits and contributions the Hopkins family has made to Pensacola, Northwest Florida, and beyond. Perhaps there is a genetic predisposition for hard work and dedication to family, church, and community within each member of the Hopkin's family that predates their settlement in the little town of Wallace, Florida.

E. W. Junior's Birthday, 1930

J. B., E. W. Sr. and E. W. Jr

J. B., Vernon, and E. W., Jr.

132

E. W., J. B. and friend, 1930s

E. W. and J. B. Christmas, 1933

Below: J. B. and E. W. in Miami, 1937

11

Hunting

Bo Spot, Frank Davis, and Cricket

In the South, a strange phenomenon takes place every year during the fall and winter months. Many, supposedly normal, men will forsake the comfort of a warm, comfortable bed and the companionship of a loving wife, or whoever, to go sleep in the woods on the cold ground, usually in a tent or under some alternative makeshift shelter. These same people complain if the room temperature at home isn't just right, if the coffee is too weak or too strong, if someone has used up all the hot water, or if the food tastes a little different. Yet their tolerance for lack of creature comforts, badly prepared food and no toilet facilities is unlimited while in the woods. Why the hell is it like that for some men? Well, it's hunting season, that's why. It's that sacred time of the year when the male ego is overcome by some ancient genetic predisposition to sally forth into yon woods and slay the bag limit of the creatures of the forest and the birds of the air just because they're there. And it's okay to kill them with any size cannon we desire. Looking back at my own years of hunting, I suppose it was a man thing, but God it was fun.

When I was much younger, I was more excited about the opening day of hunting season than I ever was about Christmas and the arrival of Santa Claus. While a student at Annie K. Suter grammar school, I made the transition from sling-shots to a "Red Ryder" B-B-Gun and later to a "Benjamin Pump" air rifle. If members of the Audubon Society had taken a survey about that time, they would have recorded a sharp decline in blue jay, mockingbird, and sparrow populations in the area of 700 Bayou Boulevard in East Pensacola Heights. My brother Bob gave me a single barrel, sixteen gauge shotgun when I was thirteen years old. I shot my first duck, a Green-winged Teal, on Bayou Texar near the bayou bridge. Our family dog "Rosie," a mixed-breed bulldog, was with me and I tried desperately to get her to swim out and retrieve the little duck, but to no avail. So I stripped down to my "birthday" suit in full view of morning traffic flowing across the bridge and swam out to retrieve my prized kill. A couple of years later I killed my first Mallard at "Jenny's Hole," ** a favorite swimming hole on Carpenter's Creek.

I got my first taste of deer hunting when I was sixteen. Bob took me along with him on a weekend hunt with "Uncle Cousin" D. L. Johnson*, who had a hunting camp just off Wright Road in Okaloosa County, near Ft. Walton Beach. We hunted deer with dogs in the Eglin Air Force Reservation, where I shot my first deer on the first drive of the first day of hunting season. I was excited about killing my first deer but remained disappointed that Florida deer were so small. I expected a stag as large as "Bambi's" father. It was on my first deer hunt I became familiar with the long-standing rule of deer hunters, which is: "Hunt deer one day—hunt dogs three days." A year later I shot my second deer, a beautiful eight point, which fell right at my feet. As I watched him struggle to get up, he looked me in the eye and

I felt sorry for him, so I gave up deer hunting. I had him mounted though, and proudly showed him off as I moved throughout the Southeast. For several recent years he rested comfortably in our attic, keeping company with a mounted pheasant my wife, Sandra, shot years ago in Korea. Today he's been moved to Fairhope, Alabama, where he's mounted on the wall of my son-in-law, Eric Beall's "man-cave," along with a couple somewhat larger Alabama mounts.

Although I gave up deer hunting, I still enjoyed bird hunting, especially duck hunting with a trained retriever. My friend Pat Quinn, who today is the Director Emeritus of the Zoo in Gulf Breeze, convinced me back in the 1960s to purchase and train a golden retriever for duck and dove hunting. Pat did the same, and after several months of rigorous training, following the rules from a Field Trial Manual and the classic book, <u>Training Your Retriever</u>, our dogs developed into intelligent, obedient, well trained retrievers, and a delight to work with.

By having a well-trained retriever like my dog "Cricket," a whole new world of hunting opened up for me, and the thrill of the kill was no longer most important. The real thrill, the flush if you will, came from observing how well she responded to voice and hand signals when retrieving ducks from the water or marshes and downed birds from the field. It was good to have a hunting partner who loved to jump in the cold water to retrieve a duck, knowing I no longer would have to strip down to my "birthday suit" to fetch the kill.

Cricket of Carpenter's Creek

One memorable duck hunting trip took place in the mid-1960s on Lake Blackshear in Southwest Georgia. I was hunting with a friend from Americus, Georgia, and due to very cold, stormy weather we decided to cut our trip short and return to the cabin on the other side of the lake. The small boat was overloaded with the two of us, Cricket, several dozen decoys, shotguns and ammunition. About half way across the lake, the weather worsened, and it was too late to turn back. The wind and waves were too much for the small boat; after taking on too much water, the boat capsized, dumping us, Cricket, and all of our equipment into the freezing water. We didn't panic, but we were scared . . . and cold as hell. I sent cricket toward the shore, a good distance away, but she kept swimming back to us. A cardinal rule I had absorbed was: "Don't leave the boat." We didn't, and counted on the strong wind to push us to shore. After a couple of hours we realized that the outboard motor had broken off, but secured to the boat with a steel cable it was serving as an anchor. We were going nowhere.

Charlie and Frank Davis on the Escambia River

My hunting partner, a medical doctor, informed me that if we didn't get out of the cold water soon, it would be too late. I knew he was right, so we decided to swim to shore, even though we neglected to bring life preservers. I was exhausted from attempting to remove my hip waders, which I had worn while setting out the decoys. Fortunately, we had two seat cushions which we managed to hold onto when the boat overturned. I never had confidence in seat cushions, but they saved our lives that day. We left the boat and swam the long distance to shore, using the seat cushions to keep our heads above water. It was difficult, as we were exhausted, plus, I still had one leg stuck inside the waders. It wasn't amusing then, but we laughed later when telling how that faithful Cricket continued to swim back and forth to us as we slowly made our way to shore.

Other more enjoyable memories of hunting were trips to an area known as Upper Piney Reach on the Apalachicola River. For several years in a row, my brothers and I joined several friends as we made the trip to Wewahitchka, Florida, where we launched our boats on the Chipola River and made our way to the "Mighty Apalachicola." After traveling about ten miles downriver to our destination, we pitched camp for a week or more. Our trips were always planned around being home for Thanksgiving. Each year we were like new scouts on our first campout. As I reminisce about those trips, I marvel at how much discomfort we were willing to "enjoy." I'm too old to rough it now, even though modern technology and equipment have improved the creature comforts of sleeping in a tent on a freezing night. Still, I miss those wonderful hours around a campfire, listening to big lies and amusing, ridiculous jokes, mostly about each other. Though three of my brothers, a nephew, and several close friends who were "regulars" have since died, I cherish the memories. Hunting is a privilege we enjoy because we are blessed with so many freedoms in our country. As a former hunter, who grew up loving the water and the woods, I continue to appreciate Robert Louis Stevenson's famous poem, "Requiem," especially the last two lines:

Requiem
Under the wide and starry sky,
Dig the grave and let me lie.
Glad did I live and gladly die,
And I laid me down with a will.
This be the verse you grave for me:
Here he lies where he longed to be;
Home is the sailor home from the sea,
And the hunter home from the hill.

Robert Louis Stevenson

*See chapter titled, "Uncle Cousin D. L."
**See chapter titled, "Aunt Jenny's Swimming Hole"

12

Jerry Maygarden

To paraphrase the Scriptures, "What good can come out of Brownsville?" The answer is obvious; a lot of good folks have emerged from the West Pensacola community. Some of us remember Brownsville as it was in its good ole days before I-10 sucked away all the east-west traffic from Highway 90. Frankly, I never knew the established boundaries, but during my Cushman Scooter days, I considered everything west of Cagle's Restaurant or Peanut George's Liquor Store and East of

Jerry Maygarden

Myrtis and Louis Maygarden, Sr.

Martine's at the "Circle" as Brownsville. As for north and south, Cervantes Street was the dividing line. The lyrics in one of Phil Harris's songs, "It ain't no town and it ain't no city. . . " pretty well fit Brownsville, then and now.

Years before I-10 was in the planning stage, Maygarden's Grocery Store, located at the corner of P and Cervantes Streets, was a fixture in "downtown" Brownsville. The store's owner, Louis Ameal Maygarden, grew up on the Alabama peninsula near Ft. Morgan, but he and his brother Paul moved to Brownsville when the 1906 hurricane destroyed much of the Mobile-Ft. Morgan area. After a short stint as streetcar conductor, Louis spent the rest of his life in the grocery business in Brownsville, providing a service to many friends and neighbors in what was then a busy section of West Pensacola.

Lou & Jean Maygarden.

Courtesy of the
J. Earle Bowden
Family

Maygarden's Grocery Store was a popular gathering spot for friends and family, as well as politicians and sportsmen. In addition to groceries, gas, and occasional sage advice, many mullet fishermen valued Louis Maygarden's hand-made castnets. He had many friends. As for the question, "What good can come out of Brownsville," the Maygarden family members are at the top of the list.

In addition to running a grocery store, Louis Maygarden was an avid fisherman. He didn't just make castnets—he personally used them in local waters to provide fresh fish for his family. He and his wife had three children, Lora Walters, Ruth

McDonald, and Louis Ameal Maygarden, Jr., known locally as Lou Maygarden, a well-respected, prominent banker. Lou is currently retired and in his nineties, but he's still active in church and other activities. He served in the U. S. Navy during WWII, and flew in PBY's in the Panama Canal Zone in search of German U-Boats. Banking became a family affair, as Lou's wife Jean was also a career banker, and she too is now retired.

After the war, Lou and Jean's family grew. Their sons, Jerry Louis Maygarden and his brother Randy Ameal Maygarden ran the streets of Brownsville in their short britches in the summer time, and during those early years they always made an after-school bee-line from Allie Ynestria School to Maygarden's Grocery Store, their favorite place. There's no end to what Jerry and Randy absorbed about life and other mysterious things while doing their chores in their granddaddy's store. In his book, Inside The Bubble, Jerry wrote about their grandparent's mom-and-pop grocery store:

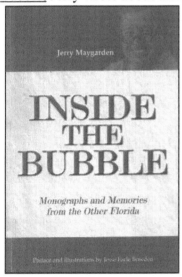

You can learn a lot hanging around an old grocery store, stacking cans and sneaking an occasional "Jacks" cookie. Nothing ever went bad in my granddad's store. If it started to look a little ripe, he would take it home for us to eat. I was probably 10 years old before I figured out that bananas were actually yellow. I thought they just came into the world bruised, brown and destined to become pudding.

They obviously received good advice and guidance from their granddad and parents, because both are very successful in many ways, especially their chosen fields. Randy's profession is public education and he's a dedicated teacher at West Florida High School. Jerry, a proven visionary with many successful careers behind him, is difficult to describe in a few words. Thus, in the balance of this chapter I'll attempt to cover only some of his many accomplishments.

Courtesy of the J. Earle Bowden Family

When You Reach September

An Editor's
West Florida Essays
and Other
Episodic Echoes

JESSE EARLE BOWDEN

Where to start—that is the question. It's like selecting the best cookie at J's Bakery; they're all good. Since I must start somewhere, I've solicited the help of the late Jesse Earle Bowden, Editor Emeritus, Pensacola News Journal, author, and historian. It's appropriate because not only were Earle and Jerry good friends with respect and admiration for each other, but both enjoyed an early exposure to a family grocery store. Earle's father owned J. W. Bowden's Grocery Store in Altha, Florida, so he too probably had an early reckoning about the color of bananas.

Earle wrote the preface and provided several illustrations in Jerry's fascinating book, Inside The Bubble, which was published in 2004. He alluded to a few of Jerry's successes in the early part of the preface, which he titled, "Homegrown Visionary":

> Reading these thoughtful essays and speeches of sandy-haired Jerry L. Maygarden, one sees the blossoming of a homegrown Pensacola and Florida Legislative leader, a respected visionary with the gift of oratory who cherishes the historic past and intrepidly confronts the futuristic challenges of the twenty-first century.
>
> Here is a voice flowing easily, one of vision easily heeded. Here are the ideas and thoughtful commentaries of a Vietnam War veteran, a popular former mayor of Pensacola and a Republican majority leader of the Florida House of Representatives.

Onetime student government president at the University of West Florida, Jerry became a UWF administrator at his alma mater before finding his career calling as a health care professional and hospital foundation administrator, first at Sacred Heart, now Baptist Health Care.

On completion of his political career—he began as a member of the Pensacola City Council; his fellow elected councilmen chose him to follow Mayor Emeritus Vince Whibbs as ceremonial mayor—the Pensacola News Journal wisely recruited the community leader as an editorial page columnist.

Jerry's resume includes many well deserved awards and recognitions, but, of course, he considers his family his most important achievement. His wife, Rhonda Fosha Maygarden is a registered nurse. Their son, Louis A. "Trip" Maygarden is an Attorney, and he and wife, Adrienne, live in Pensacola. Jerry and Rhonda's daughter, Morgan is married to LCDR Timothy Gleason, U. S. Navy. They currently live in Pensacola with their two daughters, Emma Grace (7) and Addie Mae (4) Gleason. In 1980, Jerry and Rhonda lost their infant son, Charles Morgan Maygarden. Much later, Jerry wrote in one of his columns: "There is no greater pain for a parent than losing a child."

The Maygarden clan was very active in the Richards Memorial Methodist Church in Brownsville. Jerry wrote about the family's longtime church membership in another of his columns:

> There was always something going on for young people—softball, basketball, and a thing we called 'Singspiration.' I couldn't carry a tune in a No. 2 wash tub, but regular Sunday school attendance, and participation in the youth choir was the price of admission to everything else. If it meant singing a few lines of "Amazing Grace" in order to play on the church basketball team, I would clear my throat and embarrass the entire family.

After years of negative changes in the Brownsville area and families and businesses dwindled, the Maygardens moved their membership. Jerry wrote:

We actually left Richards Memorial to start a new church on Nine Mile Road. For seven years we were missioners and charter members of St. Luke United Methodist church. We built a home downtown on Zarragosa Street in the Historic District. We lived just a few blocks from First Church and we both adored Rev. Henry Roberts. So, we found a new church and moved our letter in 1992.

Ardienne and Trip Maygarden

Jerry & Rhonda

Tim, and Morgan, with Emma Grace, and Addie Mae

The rest of the family also became members of the First United Methodist Church on Wright Street in downtown Pensacola. As expected, the Maygarden family continued their active participation at First Church.

Rhonda is past president of the United Methodist Women, she and Jerry attend the annual meetings of the Alabama-West Florida Conference of UMC, and Jerry is a former board member of both the UMC Children's Home and the Alabama-West Florida UMC Foundation. In addition, Jerry is a former Church Administrator, past chairman of the Joe Harrell Men's Bible Breakfast, and many other leadership positions. Lou and Jean are active members and Lou attends the Bible breakfast group. Randy is a long time usher at the Sunday morning services.

The Lou Maygarden Family

As an editorial page columnist for about two years, Jerry wrote numerous stories about many subjects, and most of those articles are in his book. Those of us who have read any number of his articles, his book, or any of his other publications, are aware he is an excellent writer. It's not just because he earned two degrees in communication arts from the University of West Florida and has a God-given natural talent for writing and speaking. Nor is it because he's crammed his life with major concerns and experiences, some of which Earle Bowden alluded to in the preface. It's all of the above, combined with a deep faith and love for family and country. Jerry has been involved and done more in his lifetime than perhaps a dozen other average men of average intelligence could accomplish. A few examples include:

(1) Served in U. S. Navy in Vietnam under combat conditions.

(2) Earned Bachelor's (1974) and Master's (1975) in Communication Arts at the University of West Florida and Associate of Arts: Liberal Arts (1972) at Pensacola State College.

(3) Phi Kappa Phi, Academic Honor society, UWF (1974); Distinguished Service Award, Sigma Alpha Epsilon/Florida Sigma Chapter (1993); The Highest Effort Award for Government Service, Sigma Alpha Epsilon (1994)

(4) Proprietor: J.L. Maygarden Company (2000—Current)

(5) Director: Coastal Bank & Trust of Florida (1991—Current)

(6) President & CEO: Greater Pensacola Chamber of Commerce (2013—2015)

(7) President & CDO: Baptist Health Care Foundation (1989—2013)

(8) Exec. Vice President: Sacred Heart Foundation (1983—1989)

(9) Vice President: University of West Florida (1978—1983)

(10) Served eight years on the Pensacola City Council, three of which he served as the Mayor of Pensacola. (1985—1994)

(11) Served eight years in the Florida House of Representatives from Escambia County, three of which he served as the House Majority Leader. (1994—2002)

(12) Founder and Chairman, Ronald McDonald House Charities of N W Florida (1981).

(13) Founder and President, Propeller Club, Historic Port of Pensacola, (2005).

(14) Charter Member, Leadership Escambia and Pensacola-LEAP (1983).

(15) Community Leader of the Year, Greater Pensacola Chamber (1988).

(16) Outstanding Young Man in America, United States Jaycees (1977).

(17) Fellow, Rotary Intl. (1989-Present), President, Rotary Club of Pensacola (2009).

The JERRY L. MAYGARDEN ROAD: The City of Pensacola named a new road in Jerry's honor. It's a beautiful drive that runs from

Summit Boulevard, along the southern perimeter of the Pensacola Airport to Spanish Trail. Jerry's brother, Randy, jokingly said: "It's appropriate to name it after a politician because it's a short street and doesn't go anywhere."

In September, 2002, Jerry was in his final term as State Representative and was invited to be a member of a trade delegation to Cuba from the City of Pensacola. At the time, there was a false sense of optimism that the United States was considering lifting trade sanctions against the communist regime. A year or so earlier, the U. S. did relax restrictions when a hurricane devastated the island nation. U. S. companies had begun exporting agricultural and medical products as a result. The objective of the Pensacola delegation was to secure an agreement with Cuba to use the Port of Pensacola as the point of embarkation for American goods to Cuba. It was a reminder of an old popular American slang expression, "to take a message to Garcia," derived from an essay titled, A Message To Garcia, by Elbert Hubbard regarding facts leading up to the Spanish-American War to free Cuba from Spain. The Pensacola trade delegation arrived in Cuba one-hundred-and-three years later "to take a message to Castro."

The delegation got a treat they weren't expecting—a six-hour lunch with dictator, Fidel Castro. Jerry sat across the table from Castro, giving him an opportunity to have a dialogue with the communist leader. Following are brief excerpts from one of his Pensacola News Journal columns about the visit:

> I sat across the table from one of history's most disliked revolutionaries, Fidel Castro. For more than six hours we sat and listened as he boasted of numerous great works provided the Cuban people. In the afternoon, our conversation settled on public education, so I seized the moment to remind Castro that one of our revolutionary fathers, Thomas Jefferson, insisted that a nation could not remain free and ignorant.
> 'Jefferson said that?' Castro scoffed. 'You are quoting Jose Marti,' he charged smugly. There was a moment of uneasy silence.
> Marti must have read Jefferson, I retorted. Laughter broke the silence before the interpreter could translate my words.

Jerry meets with Fidel Castro, the leader of Cuba

Before departing, I asked Castro if there was a message for my governor—the brother of President George W. Bush. He paused to think while chewing a mouthful of shredded pork and Asian rice.

The United States,' he said, carefully avoiding any reference to the president, 'must learn to take poverty seriously.' He looked up and down the table to assess the impact of his words. 'The people of this hemisphere are desperate for a standard of living comparable to yours.' He pointed a bony finger in our direction and went on at length about U. S. wealth and our ability to improve the quality of life for every person in the Americas. 'They (the Mexican people) will risk everything crossing the border into Texas,' he said. 'Even our people will paddle a rubber tube 90 miles to have just a little of what you have in Florida.' His final words on the subject reverberated throughout the room. 'If the U. S. doesn't find a way to share its wealth with the poor countries of the world, it will be overrun by immigrants.

According to Jerry, he's been called "a right-wing redneck" by some and "a liberal jerk" by others. I don't believe he's either, but being from Brownsville, he's probably closer to the former than the latter. Let's face it, when a person becomes involved in as many "things" as Jerry has, and accomplishes as much as he has, people might begin to wonder if he's normal and start calling him names. The fact is, he's not normal—he's supernormal. A normal person can't do what he does. We both attend the Joe Harrell Bible Breakfast on Wednesday mornings, and I've been tempted to follow him as he leaves the church because I'm convinced he jumps into a phone booth and changes into whatever attire it takes to leap over tall buildings and do all those other super things he does.

Courtesy of the J.. Earle Bowden
Family

Anyone who only partially followed Jerry's activities as a City Councilman, Mayor, State Representative, read his editorial page columns, or heard only a few of his many speeches, is aware he has fought tirelessly to keep our beautiful waterfront and beaches open for the use and enjoyment by the public. Remember, he and his granddaddy were mullet fishermen years ago and knew the value of having recreational access to our bays and bayous. Every voice counts and Jerry has never been shy about having his voice heard. Thus we look forward to the UWF Argos's football team's 2016 opening season.

Thirteen years ago, Castro heard Jerry's voice loud-and-clear. His was only one of many such voices "history's most disliked revolutionary" heard over the years which eventually prompted changes in the Cuban regime, allowing further lifting of trade restrictions recently by the United States.

In addition to all the above, Jerry is, by all definitions, a "True Gentleman."

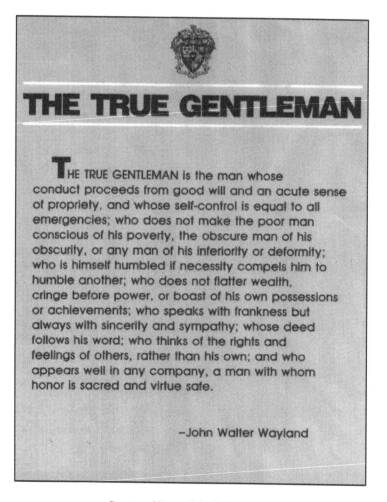

THE TRUE GENTLEMAN

THE TRUE GENTLEMAN is the man whose conduct proceeds from good will and an acute sense of propriety, and whose self-control is equal to all emergencies; who does not make the poor man conscious of his poverty, the obscure man of his obscurity, or any man of his inferiority or deformity; who is himself humbled if necessity compels him to humble another; who does not flatter wealth, cringe before power, or boast of his own possessions or achievements; who speaks with frankness but always with sincerity and sympathy; whose deed follows his word; who thinks of the rights and feelings of others, rather than his own; and who appears well in any company, a man with whom honor is sacred and virtue safe.

–John Walter Wayland

Courtesy of Sigma Alpha Epsilon Fraternity

13

John E. Frenkel, Sr.
"The Breezy Boy from the Gulf"

With the mention of Yazoo City, Mississippi, most folks would immediately think of comedian Jerry Clower. They would be right, of course, but there was another Yazoo City native, John Frenkel, whose migration east was a blessing for many, especially for Pensacola and Northwest Florida. In 1899, young Johnnie Frenkel, at age six, came to Pensacola and, in the ensuing years, became one of Pensacola's outstanding citizens. He is remembered for his thirty-six years as an effective leader in the city's financial affairs, and was instrumental in the founding of radio station WCOA (in 1926) and the Pensacola Interstate Fair (in 1935). Like his fellow "Yazoo City" native, he was an excellent entertainer who was known for having a fine voice. His theme song was *Down Pensacola Way.* He often referred to himself as "The Breezy Boy from the Gulf."

Johnnie was born in 1893, the "Gilded Age," which was better known as the "Gay

John E. Frenkel, Sr

151

Nineties." Grover Cleveland was the new president. It was also the time of an economic depression that historians call the "Panic of 1893." Unemployment was extremely high, which gave rise to a highly publicized "March on Washington" by unemployed laborers dubbed "Coxey's Army." Some time prior to Johnnie's sixth birthday, his father, Emile Frenkel, died, leaving his wife, Mollie Lowenstin Frenkel with nine children, Johnnie being the youngest. The Spanish-American War was underway and William McKinley was president when, in 1899, Mollie and her brood moved to Pensacola to join Sam, her eldest, who was working in what would become their beloved hometown.

The Breezy Boy from the Gulf

J. M. Hilliard was Mayor of Pensacola and William D. Bloxham was Florida's governor. Pensacola was a small town, known mostly for its deep harbor, navy yard, and timber industry. It turned out to be just the place for Mollie Frenkel and her nine energetic kids: Sam, Maurice, Charles, Edward, Benjamin, Clarence, Clara, Eva, and John.

According to family records, "Johnny started growing up. He began working at the early age of seven, selling newspapers and doing other odd jobs. In 1908, fifteen-year-old Johnny became a bank runner at the old American National Bank. This was the start of his post-school career."

152

Johnny had inherited a natural talent for singing and he was in demand at local events around town. His son, Don, recently recalled, "My Dad had fond memories of the years he and several of his friends acted in local Minstrels. He admired Al Jolson and the well-known 'Cotton Blossom Minstrels' that toured the country in the pre WWII years. These were popular entertainments of years past."

Johnny was one of the early originators of the "St. Aloysius Minstrels," which later became the "Holy Name Minstrels." Johnny wrote the skits and songs, taught others the lyrics and how to act the parts. His Minstrels became an annual benefit event for the Sisters

of Mercy of Pensacola. They were proud of Johnny. So was his Rabbi at Temple Beth-El.

During World War I, Johnny entered the U.S. Navy and served as Chief Yeoman in the Navy Pay Corps. He left the Navy in 1919 and became the assistant auditor of the Emergency Fleet Corporation. In 1922, Johnnie went on to become the City Clerk and Treasurer for the City of Pensacola, and while in that position, was elected Secretary of the Civil Service Board in 1931. The following year he was promoted to City Comptroller. In 1948 he became the city's Director of Finance, and retired in 1958 after thirty-six years of service.

In a Frenkel family album, it's written, "While playing in the Holy Name Minstrel he (Johnny) sang and danced the song, 'Peggy,' with Miss Lillian Blanche White, (a registered nurse from a long-standing local family). From here a romance began." They were married on September 25,

1928, and remained sweethearts and constant companions until her death in 1971.

Ms Lillian
Blanche White

John and Lillie's Wedding

In the interim, they were blessed with three children, Moljean, John, Jr. and Don.

John, Lillie, John, Jr., Moljean, and Don

In 1926, John, Sr. had a major hand in getting Radio Station WCOA started in Pensacola. The call letters stood for "Wonderful City of Advantages." He traveled with Harvey Bayless, Mayor of Pensacola, to Atlanta and then to Washington D. C. in an effort to give WCOA and Pensacola a voice on the airways.

WCOA from studios in the San Carlos Hotel

In 1927, Celia Myrover Robinson wrote in the magazine, *Florida on the Gulf*:

So Mayor J. Harvey Bayless and City Clerk John E. Frenkel made a trip to Atlanta, and there met W. Van Nostrand, Jr., supervisor for radio for the southeastern district, who accompanied them to Washington, where the Florida representatives, Senator Duncan U. Fletcher and Congressman J. H. Smithwick helped them to get in conference with the powers that be. Permission was granted to the City of Pensacola then to install WCOA.

WCOA took (to) the air during the last part of last February (1926), on a 222 meter wave length and 500 watts power. Mr. Frenkel volunteered as public servant to sponsor the station as a city institution. He not only assumed responsibility for its physical well being, but he took charge of the programs. Having a good voice himself, he has not neglected the musical phase of the broadcasting.

WCOA Staff – City Hall – 1930
Back row: Charles Hauteman (Receptionist), Beecher Hayford (Chief
Engineer), Johnny Frenkel (Station Director).
Front row: Byron Hayford (Engineer), Bob Reed (Announcer-pianist),
Jimmy Sanders (Salesman), Victor Land, (Announcer)

On October 18, 1984, Larry Wheeler, staff writer with Pensacola News-Journal wrote a fitting tribute to John Frenkel, titled, "Taking Us For a Ride: John Frenkel And His Fair." He wrote, "Frenkel recalled that during the 1920s, while organizing a Mardi Gras carnival, he met a young fellow who represented a traveling show. In 1935, that same fellow returned to town and asked Frenkel to throw a fair so the traveling midway would have a date to play between Alabama and their winter quarters in Tampa. 'That's how the modern Pensacola Interstate Fair began,' Frenkel said."

The first Fair was held in 1935 at Cervantes Street and Pace Boulevard. From there it moved to the corner of Garden Street and Pace Boulevard. In 1940 the Fair purchased its first permanent location on Pottery Plant Road, later known as Fairfield Drive, where it prospered over the next twenty years. The Fairfield location was centrally located, but urban sprawl had its effect, and the property was sold for a local development.

Ribbon cutting ceremony: Frenkel, TT Wentworth, .Ms Fairest of Fair. Mr. Blount,. Governor. & Mrs. Collins. Charlie Carter, and John Frenkel. Jr.

In 1968 , the Fair purchased the property at 6665 Mobile Highway on West Highway 90. The fairground and its structures were built from the ground up and the first fair was held at this location in 1969. The Fair currently owns over seventy acres at the site.

(Much more is written about the phenomenal successes of both the Pensacola Interstate Fair and Radio Station WCOA, and separate chapters on each are included elsewhere in this book. I believe it is important to include a brief summary of both institutions in this chapter in order to reveal the visionary magnitude of John Frenkel, Sr.).

Upon his retirement in 1958, after thirty-six years with the City of Pensacola, fellow employees and other friends had a surprise party for Johnnie at Bartels Restaurant. It was a well-planned affair, patterned after a popular television series. They called it, "This Is Your Life—John E. Frenkel."

John, Sr with his sons, their wives and his grandchildren

His family, many friends, local dignitaries, and government officials were in attendance. Tom Siler, City Personnel Director, as Master of Ceremonies said,

> Mr. Frenkel, this is a long-planned party put on as an honor to one who has not only given thirty-six years of faithful and dedicated service to the City of Pensacola, but one who has played one of the greatest parts in developing our city into the outstanding government it now is. But even greater, this is a tribute to you as a man—a man who has led an exemplary life—devoted to his family, true to his friends, completely sincere and honest in his convictions and just in his many official capacities with an ever-present sense of humor.

As is usual in such testimonial dinners, several prominent friends rose to tell amusing stories about Johnnie, to the crowd's delight; others spoke of his honesty and integrity, something everyone had known for years.

Recently, I was privileged to peruse an accumulation of cards, letters, and photographs Johnnie's family had saved over the years. Most were letters he wrote to his wife, whom he affectionately called "Lili." He obviously adored her, because he wrote her a long love letter every anniversary of their marriage. In the mix were letters congratulating him on his retirement from: Oliver J. Semmes, Jr., City Manager; Crosby Hall, Chief of Police; and Congressman Bob Sikes. As for photographs, there were many, but of note were autographed photos from Vice President Hubert Humphrey, Congressman Bob Sikes, and President Gerald R. Ford. Included was a thank you letter from Mary Call Collins, wife of Governor Leroy Collings, to Johnny and Lili following a visit to Pensacola.

One can only admire John E. Frenkel's extraordinary journey through a life that came to an end on February 17, 1988. He was ninety-four-years old. He lived an exemplary life of integrity, proving that something good can, and did, come out of Yazoo City.

14

The Judge

On July 14, 1950, precisely at noon, the Reverend Billy Graham was ushered into President Harry Truman's oval office. It was his first visit to the White House. In Korea, at approximately the same time, eighteen-year-old Private First Class Joe Tarbuck and his buddies in the 63rd Field Artillery Battalion of the 24th Infantry Division were suddenly surrounded by hundreds of North Korean communist troops and forced to surrender.

By the time the Reverend Graham had used up his allotted twenty minutes, PFC Tarbuck and about three dozen of his fellow captives had their hands tied behind their backs and faced an irate machine gunner who was preparing to shoot them. After only nine days in Korea, the war was over for PFC Tarbuck. As a POW, he would spend the next three years, one month and two weeks in pure hell. He and his fellow prisoners suffered unbelievable deprivation, torture, and other examples of man's inhumanity to man, from which most of them did not survive.

PFC Joseph Q. Tarbuck

Years later, the Corporal, who had morphed into retired Circuit Court Judge Joseph Q. Tarbuck, reluctantly explained the circumstances leading up to his capture and the incidents immediately following their surrender:

I was in Headquarters Company and Captain Green came to our building and asked for a volunteer to walk a distance of several miles from our building to the area where the artillery was situated and check the communication wires running from Headquarters Company to the artillery site for someone had been cutting them at night. I made the trip, repaired a break in the wires and arrived at the artillery site. I think that was the last time I volunteered for anything.

The next day, on July 14, about 12:00 noon, the North Koreans attacked our position and about 1:00 P.M. we surrendered. Some of the infantry had fallen back to our position and were bathing in a nearby stream and were killed there. Some of our soldiers tried to run through rice paddies surrounding us on three sides and were gunned down.

There must have been 35 to 40 of us at this position. Our hands were tied behind us with our own communication wire and we were lined up on the road in three rows; the first row sat, the second row knelt and the third row stood. I was in the second row. A North Korean soldier rolled a water-cooled machine gun with large, iron wheels out onto a dam dividing a rice paddy, flipped up a gunsight and was apparently going to kill us. I remember trying to decide what to do, kneel in a fully upright position so I would be killed immediately or fall down as soon as the shooting began, hoping I would be missed and might be able to escape after the enemy moved on.

At this time a North Korean officer came out on the road, stood to our right and began a colloquy with the machine gunner. When it seemed the machine gunner was intent on carrying out his mission of killing us, the officer drew a large pistol from his holster and aimed it at the machine gunner and uttered a few words. The machine gunner dropped the sight on the gun and rolled the machine gun off the dam. This was the first of two occasions that we were scheduled to be put to death.

162

The Korean War had begun less than three weeks earlier, when on June 25, 1950, the North Korean Communists launched an unprovoked attack on South Korea. PFC Tarbuck had joined the army in 1949, shortly after graduating from high school and was stationed in Japan as part of the occupation forces following WWII, which had ended less than five years earlier. His artillery battalion was loaded aboard U. S. Navy LST's and transported to Pusan, South Korea, arriving on July 5, 1950. They boarded trains and proceeded toward the front line, optimistic about the outcome. They had been assured the North Korean soldiers would withdraw ". . . as soon as they saw our uniforms." After all, it was termed a "Police Action."

Unfortunately, America's early entry into the Korean War did not go as planned; in fact, it was a disaster. We were ill-equipped against the Russian supplied North Koreans, especially the Russian T-34 Tanks. On June 29th, many American civilians were captured, and six days later, on July 5th the day PFC Tarbuck and his 63rd artillery battalion arrived in Korea, the first American soldiers (part of Task Force Smith, also from the 24th Division) were captured. Private First Class Tarbuck's group of captives in the Kum River area were grouped with POWs from other battlefields and marched north toward Seoul, during which time they were beaten, especially when they were marched through the front lines of the North Korean soldiers. The summer of 1950 was very hot in Korea and the food the North Koreans provided consisted of watered-down, tasteless soup of millet, rice, and sometimes a small amount of vegetables. Many in the group were barefooted, as the North Korean soldiers had confiscated their shoes, jackets, helmets, shirts, plus everything they had in their pockets, including watches and rings. Thirst was a major problem as they were given no drinking water. They scrounged what water they could from streams and rice paddies, giving rise to serious stomach problems.

When Corporal Tarbuck (American soldiers were promoted one grade upon being captured) and his fellow POWs crossed over the Han River into the captured city of Seoul they became part of a mixture of civilians and soldiers that had swelled to over eight hundred frightened souls that were housed in school buildings. The civilians were mostly missionaries, diplomats, priests, nuns, and other mixed families taken captive just after the war started. All were forced to attend lectures and communist indoctrination sessions, a technique that would later be referred to as "brainwashing." This large group of POWs would later become known to Korean War historians as the "Tiger Survivors."

The large group of POWs departed Seoul by train and traveled north to arrive in Pyongyang, the capitol of North Korea, after several days of hiding in tunnels and mountains by day to avoid detection by Allied Forces. At Pyongyang CPL Tarbuck, like all the others, continued losing weight as the food was in small amounts of rice and millet. Nor was there any medical attention, sanitation, bedding or any effort to combat the lice. Housed in school and farm buildings, many of the wounded died from lack of treatment. The weather turned cold since winter arrives early in North Korea.

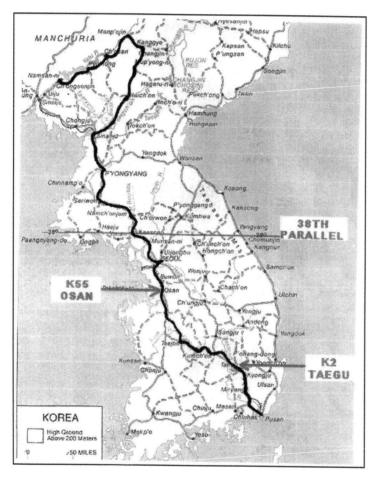

The route the POWs marched to the prison camps.

164

As winter set in, many of CPL Tarbuck's fellow POWs died from exposure. They had been force-marched to the frontier town of Manp'o, situated on the Yalu River, across from Manchuria. At that time Communist China entered the war; the Allied forces had driven north to the Yalu River in places. Thousands of Chinese troops entered North Korea, crossing over the Yalu River from Manchuria at Manp'o. Corporal Tarbuck and his fellow POWs—soldiers and civilians, including women and children—were out in the cold.

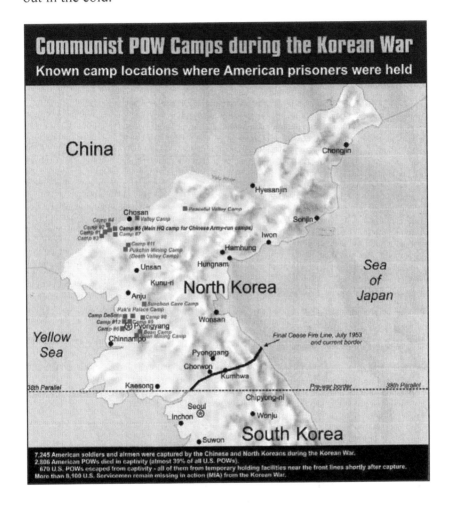

In mid-October, 1950, the long column of POWs departed Manp'o, and were marched from town to town and forced to sleep beside the roads or in fields. In October, the weather in North Korea was freezing and windy.

The POWs were marched out onto a large cornfield. Judge Tarbuck, in an interview a few years ago, explained:

> We dug holes in the ground and pulled cornstalks over the top of us to keep from freezing to death.

On October 31, 1950, appropriately on Halloween, CPL Tarbuck and most others who had survived up to that point thought that it couldn't get any worse, but unfortunately, it got worse, much worse, when a North Korean Major from the Security Forces took over the group. He was brutal and had no compunction about killing someone if they didn't keep up with the march. The POWs referred to him as the "Tiger," and the cruel treatment he imposed on the POWs on their march in freezing temperatures from town to town will forever be known as the "Tiger Death March." At that point in the war, the Allied Forces were rapidly advancing north, and the POWs were force-marched from the "corn field" to different towns to avoid being liberated. The POWs prayed they would be liberated, but in retrospect knew the "Tiger" would have killed every one of them before allowing that to happen. Several years ago, Judge Tarbuck responded to that concern in an interview:

> That was October, 1950, when the 82nd Airborne was supposed to drop and perhaps try to rescue us. This North Korean Commanding Officer that we called the "Tiger" heard about it and started to herd us all into a large tunnel. We had civilians with us, Catholic nuns, and I know we had a bishop from England, just different people from different countries that were there working in South Korea at the time they were taken prisoner. As we were being led into the tunnels, the nuns started to cry and make the sign of the cross, so we figured then that we were going to be killed in that tunnel.
>
> The "Tiger" evidently didn't want us recaptured by our own troops so he was going to kill us. And then, understand this is what we learned later, he got word that the, I think it was the 82nd Airborne, had a lot of men killed, for it was a very bad drop, and so they weren't going to be able to rescue us. That's when we started the 110 mile march farther north. So, that was the second occasion that we thought we were all going to be killed.

Korean War historians are well acquainted with the "Tiger," whose real name was Chong Myong Nil. I have no idea what happened to him after the infamous "Tiger Death March," but I'm sure there are many former POWs who would like to know. According to my research, he was responsible for the shooting death of eighty-nine POWs, many of whom he personally shot. He is recorded as being responsible for the first witnessed atrocity in the Korean War, when he personally shot Lieutenant Cordus Thornton in the back of the head in front of all the POWs. Judge Tarbuck explained:

> The Lieutenant had allowed us to drop a soldier, who had died, by the side of the road without the Tiger's permission. The Tiger asked the North Korean soldiers what he should do with the Lieutenant, and they all shouted: "Shoot him!"

In October, 1951, CPL Tarbuck and the remaining survivors, now referred to as the "Tiger Survivors," were turned over to the Chinese. Years later, Judge Tarbuck was asked in an interview, "What it was like being with the Chinese as opposed to the North Koreans? His reply:

> Well, it was much better. On occasions, we even got meat. Once in a while I think they would give us a pig or something like that, which we would clean and our cooks would cook. It was much better; we had rice instead of millet which is better for you. We had better food, better clothing.

On August 31, 1953, CPL Joseph Q. Tarbuck was released, as the hostilities had ceased, and he returned to his sister's home in Fort Walton where his father also resided. Many Korean War POWs had difficulties adjusting to their return to civilian life. They struggled with depression, flashbacks, nightmares, and many other issues; not CPL Tarbuck, he was strong emotionally and physically and was ready to get on with his life. When asked what the first thing he did when he returned home, his reply was:

> I don't know that I did anything special. I was just very glad to be back home. I know the gang, my friends that I left, had what they called a block party for me and another person from my neighborhood who was also captured. He was captured much later than I was, but that was it.

Joe Tarbuck, a civilian again, didn't waste much time taking charge of his future. He lived in Fort Walton Beach, Florida to be near his sister, Rose, a nurse at Eglin Air Force Base. Six months after his release he enrolled as a freshman at Florida State University. I met him that February, 1954, when he pledged the same fraternity I had pledged the previous semester. There were several of us returning military veterans in the fraternity, but all of us, veterans and non-veterans, admired Joe. Of course, there were many reasons to admire him because he was a nice guy, but what amazed us most about him was he didn't act like we expected someone to act who had been through what

Joe at FSU

he had been through. Simply put, he was normal, mature, and pleasant to be around. He enjoyed the university life; he played hard, studied hard and made good grades.

I recall stopping by his room at the fraternity house and was surprised to find him squatting in the middle of his room, holding a cup of something with both hands. I learned the cup contained hot water. The squatting position while sipping on hot water was an Asian habit he had picked up while a POW. I wish I had taken his picture.

Another incident worth writing about happened when a missionary, a former Korean War POW, was the guest speaker at one of the student Christian organizations on campus. Joe, along with "Mother Holton," the fraternity's House Mother, and several guys from the fraternity house attended the lecture. During the presentation, Joe whispered to Mother Holton that he knew the missionary. Following the presentation, she and Joe approached the Missionary, and pointing to Joe, she asked: "Doctor, do you recognize this young man?" The man's response was surprising and emotional. He said; "Do I know him? He saved my life more than once." I wasn't there, but those who listened in on the exchange were emotionally impressed. The missionary accepted an invitation to visit the fraternity house that same evening, and he and Joe exchanged stories that kept all of us mesmerized until the wee hours. So, how did Joe save the Missionary's life? Well, we learned that CPL Tarbuck, the future attorney at law and Judge, was a thief—not a real thief, but a real Robinhood type of thief. He stole food from their North Korean captors. The missionary explained that many fellow POWs were starving to death and how Joe managed to steal from the POW camp warehouse, large, round wheels of dried, pressed, soy beans to secretly feed them. Joe never mentioned that to any of us before that night.

It's only natural to wonder how a POW like Joe continued to believe in the existence of a loving God after facing a firing squad more than once; witnessing fellow POWs being shot and beaten to death by vengeful guards, and observing many others succumb to harsh treatment and starvation. It's interesting to know that Judge Tarbuck is a current member of St Francis of Assisi Episcopal Church in Gulf Breeze which he has attended faithfully for many years. For twenty-plus years he regularly attended the Wednesday morning Joe Harrell Bible Breakfast at First United Methodist Church. Yet, most telling of his uninterrupted inner strength and faith is the fact that while a POW, CPL Tarbuck constructed a small cross from scrap wood, which he used daily to pray the Rosary alongside the Catholics in captivity with him. He still has that cross.

After graduating from FSU in 1957 with a degree in geology, Joe enrolled in the College of Law at the University of Florida and received his law degree in 1959. Upon passing the Florida Bar exam, he joined the law firm of Richard P. Warfield for about one year before entering his own private practice. While establishing his very successful law practice, he married Pensacola native, Carolyn Williams. Joe and Carolyn had four children: Joey, Billy, Chris, and Beth, who grew up in the family's Gulf Breeze home overlooking Pensacola Bay. Active in professional and civic activities for years, Joe served as president of the Society of the Bar of the First Judicial Circuit and president of the Gulf Breeze Rotary Club. In addition, he was an avid outdoorsman for years. He and Carolyn enjoyed membership in hunting and fishing clubs such as the Hit N Miss Club and the Toeshemoe Club, both located in Alabama.

In 1978, after twenty-three years in private practice, Joe Tarbuck, Attorney at Law, became Judge Joseph Q.Tarbuck, when Governor Bob Graham appointed him to the bench as Circuit Court Judge, First

Judicial Circuit. He remained on the bench for the next twenty-three and one-half years, retiring in 2000 due to Florida's mandatory retirement age. Judge Tarbuck served his profession for forty-five years, plus was often called to try cases after retirement due to heavy caseloads. Sadly, Carolyn died in 2001, interrupting their plans to spend his retirement years together.

Judge Tarbuck is often asked if he suffered from flashbacks or post-traumatic-syndrome as a result of being a POW in the Korean War. People are amused with his usual answer:

I have a flashback that really interests me and I think it's funny. After I was practicing law, I used to have dreams that I was captured again and I had to go through all the Korean experience again. I also had dreams that I had to go through law school again, and I hated the dream that I had to go through law school again more than I did of being captured again. I had a hard time in law school. I was not prepared for it. I graduated with a degree in geology from FSU so I was not the typically prepared student going to law school. It was very strange and different to me.

Judge Tarbuck wrote the following when asked if he had ill feelings or harbored any animosity about the POW experience:

I have no regrets or remorse for having gone through thirty-seven-and-one-half months of captivity under the North Koreans and then the Chinese. I was repatriated on August 31, 1953 and returned from Korea with an experience and background that later in life enabled me to develop a deeper understanding of American Foreign Policy.

Some people say we lost the wars in Korea and Vietnam. I do not agree with that thinking. The United States and the United Nations showed the communists that they would not stand by while aggressor nations tried to impose a new political regime or a new way of life on neighboring nations. We showed that we will sacrifice our lives and property to preserve the freedom which we love and cherish.

The Korean Police Action will never be a 'Forgotten War.'

As of this writing, it has been sixty-three years since Corporal Tarbuck was released from the POW camp in Korea, and sixteen years since Judge Tarbuck retired from the bench. At age eighty-five, he is still going strong and has remarried. He and wife, Anita, are constant companions. They enjoy friends and family, but most important, they enjoy each other,

Judge Tarbuck and his lovely wife Anita

and have sampled every menu at every popular restaurant in Pensacola and Gulf Breeze. The Judge still lunches regularly with old friends, Bob Bell, Dr. Don McLeod,* Bill Pennewill, Jack Gardner, and others to discuss football, politics, kids, grandkids, and current ailments. Judge Tarbuck has done much to earn the respect of his nation, fellow legal professionals, his family and friends. His fellow military veterans paid tribute to him by selecting him as the Parade Marshall for a Pensacola Veterans Day Parade. The citizens of Pensacola and Gulf Breeze are fortunate to have him as part of our two communities and have benefited from his examples of strong leadership.

*Dr. Don McLeod died May 4, 2016

15

"Miss Faye"
56 Years at Jerry's Drive-In

Much has been written about Jerry's Drive-In, one of Pensacola's favorite restaurants, but in recent years, Faye Schneidewind, one of the restaurant's long-time waitresses, has been getting the headlines, and rightfully so.

Jerry's Drive-In circa. 1950

Jerry's owner, Ray Wessel and Faye in the
earlier years

Congressional Record

PROCEEDINGS AND DEBATES OF THE *111th* CONGRESS, FIRST SESSION

The Honorable Jeff Miller of the First District of Florida

Washington, Monday, November 2, 2009

RECOGNIZING FAYE SCHNEIDEWIND FOR 50 YEARS SERVICE TO JERRY'S DRIVE-IN

Madam Speaker, I rise today to recognize Ms. Faye Schneidewind upon the occasion of her 50th year of loyal service to Jerry's Drive-In, a Pensacola, Florida landmark. Miss Faye is an intimate part of the fabric of our Northwest Florida community, and I am proud to recognize her on this achievement.

Faye Schneidewind grew up in Pensacola and still lives only a few blocks from Jerry's. The 80-year old great-grandmother started working as a waitress at the diner when she was just 21. After a few years away, Miss Faye returned to Jerry's on November 5, 1959, her sister's birthday. She has been serving the customers at Jerry's ever since. Miss Faye knows just about everyone who walks through the doors at Jerry's, and always provides a warm smile, a hot meal, and good conversation. She is as much a part of the history of Jerry's as memorabilia stretching across its walls.

Jerry's Drive-In is a truly family restaurant. Originally named Jerry's Barbeque, Jerry's Drive-In was opened by Jerry Glass in 1939. Raymond "Grandpa" Wessel purchased the restaurant in the early 1950's with his son Bill. The Wessels lived in an apartment above the restaurant. Even after the restaurant was sold, Mr. Wessel continued to maintain his residence above Jerry's. Jimmy and Pam Halstead bought Jerry's in 1997 and have continued its tradition of great food and great service.

Madam Speaker, on behalf of the United States Congress, I am honored to recognize Faye Schneidewind on 50 years of dedicated service to Jerry's Drive-In. She is and always will be an invaluable part of our Pensacola heritage. My wife Vicki and I wish Miss Faye, her daughter, her three granddaughters, her nine great-grandchildren, and her entire extended family at Jerry's all the best for continued success.

Recent newspaper articles about Faye and her career at
Jerry's Drive

Everything that counts   Sunday, October 25, 2009   Hwy. 29 just south of Kingsfield Road   968-3083

A half-century of service

Jerry's Drive-In honors Pensacola's favorite waitress

Rebecca Ross • rross@pnj.com

They call her Miss Faye. If you've been to Jerry's Drive-In, you've probably seen her, holding court at the bar. The 80-year-old great-grandmother is as much a part of the landmark diner as its faded sports pennants and fried grouper sandwiches.

On Nov. 5, Faye Schneidewind will celebrate 50 years of loyal service at Pensacola's favorite greasy spoon.

"Everyone loves Miss Faye," said coworker and manager Sharon Johnson. "She's just a sweet lady. Jerry's wouldn't be the same without her."

The Pensacola native grew up and still resides just blocks from Jerry's.

She first started working as a waitress at the diner when she was just 21, waiting to join her then-husband who was stationed in Hawaii. When she divorced and returned home a few years later, she went back to Jerry's.

"I just needed a job," Schneidewind explained. "I remember the date I started, Nov. 5, because it was my sister's birthday. I've been there ever since."

She reckons she has served thousands of

4E   Pensacola News Journal • pnj.com   Sunday, October 25, 2009

SUNDAY ETC.

Jerry's

FROM 1E

"Oh, she knows everyone's story," Sommers said. "She can tell you about almost anybody in Pensacola."

Age doesn't seem to be slowing Schneidewind down. Though she works only Tuesdays and Thursdays, she keeps busy just about every day of the week.

"I don't like to stay home by myself," she said. "If I didn't have a reason to get out of the house, I'd just stay in my pajamas all day."

Cataract surgery has kept her vision sharp and Schneidewind behind the wheel. She listed off a schedule that would impress a social butterfly 50 years younger.

Gary McCracken gmccracken@pnj.com

Faye Schneidewind, a waitress at Jerry's Drive-In, checks on her customers at the counter. Schneidewind, 80, has worked at the restaurant for almost 50 years.

174

Right: Faye Schneidewind is shown with previous owner Ray Wessel at Jerry's Drive-In in 1960.
Special to the News Journal

Schneidewind working at Jerry's Drive-In. She has worked at the popular East Pensacola Heights restaurant for almost 50 years. She will celebrate her 50th anniversary on Nov. 5.
Gary McCracken/
gmccracken@pnj.com

BETH RAMIREZ DE ARELLANO/News Journal correspondent photo
Jerry's Drive-In employee Faye Schneidewind, left, has heard 40 years worth of stories and bad jokes from regulars like Ralph Bird and Leo Snyder.

175

Most of us who grew up in East Pensacola Heights during the pre-WWII years and after, knew her as Faye Johnson, the youngest of Ola and Viola Johnson's five daughters. The Johnson family home was only three blocks from Jerry's Drive-In. Faye was twenty-one when she first went to work at Jerry's, but she didn't work very long; she left to join her U. S. Navy husband in Hawaii. It was 1950, and the Korean War had just begun.

Left: Faye, her Mother, Viola, and all her sibling, Ruby, Dorothy, Doris, Lois, and Faye.

Below: Ruby, Dorothy, Doris and Faye

Faye returned to work at Jerry's on November 5, 1959 after her marriage ended in divorce. She said she remembers the date because it was her sister Ruby's birthday, who also worked at Jerry's.

On November 5, 2015, she celebrated her 56th year at Jerry's Drive-In, at which time she was a young 86 years of age with no plans to retire anytime soon.

In 1950, when Faye left for Hawaii, Jerry's Drive-In was a single concrete-block building, founded by Jerry Glass in 1939, with a "curb" or "car-hop" service in the rear. The only "car-hop" I remember at Jerry's was "Foster," a black guy many of us got to know well. He was there for years, and as teenagers, some of us knew we could go to Foster to purchase beer-to-go—always in a sack, looking just like hamburgers and French fries. While in high school, I had a Cushman Scooter, which had a small storage compartment under the "buddy-seat." Foster would bring me enough ice to keep the beer cold. It was like an ice-chest on wheels. I doubt Ray Wessel, the owner at the time, was aware of how Foster was conducting business in the back, but I know my dad sure as hell didn't know how I was conducting business on my scooter. He would have skinned my head—and more.

Jerry's was a gathering spot for me and my friends during high school, and while home on military leave, or between semesters while in college. We had other places in East Pensacola Heights we frequented, that is, those places that would tolerate us, like George Jordan's "Scenic Terrace," a popular night club, and John Oliver's "Nob Hill," one of our other favorite watering-holes. By the time we got older with more responsibilities, such as a family, work, or a business to run, the "Terrace" and "Nob Hill" had ceased to exist. Fortunately, Jerry's Drive-In was still going strong, with help from Faye, "Neenie" Buchanan, who also grew up in East Pensacola Heights, Ray, "Mom," (Ray's wife), Bill, (Ray's son, who also managed the restaurant), and all the others who made it a fun place to gather.

As for my high school buddies, many of them have "crossed over the bar," but the crowds at Jerry's today includes our kids and grandkids. The above long-time owners and employees, who made the place famous, are gone also—except Faye, the "Grande Dame of Waitresses,"—who's there on Tuesdays and Thursdays, happy to see her many friends and customers as they are to see her.

Jerry's Drive-In is working on its eighth decade in business, without interruption, except for a two month shutdown due to a kitchen fire in 1999. During those 76 years, there have been only three owners: Jerry Glass, the Ray Wessel family, who moved from Indiana to make the purchase in 1952,

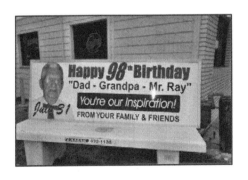

Birthday Bench for Ray Wessel

Faye, her grandson, Kevin and Ray Wessel

and the current owners, Jimmy and Pam Halstead. During the 47 years under Ray Wessel's ownership, many changes were made to accommodate larger crowds, and only God knows how many burgers, shakes, mullet and liver plates were sold. The stock value of major beer companies was maintained by the sheer volume of the suds consumed at Jerry's on the corner of Cervantes Street and Perry Avenue. The trend continues under the Halstead's, who purchased the restaurant from the Wessel family in 1997.

Above: Faye and Jerry's owner Jimmy Halstead.

Right: Faye with owners Jimmy & Pam Halstead

In an interview with Jimmy Halstead, published on December 14, 2000, Beth Remirez de Arellano of the Pensacola News Journal wrote:

> Owners Jimmy and Pam Halstead, who bought Jerry's from . . . Ray Wessel . . . say they decided no changes needed to be made in the successful establishment. "When we bought it, I think people thought the place was gonna change so much—but we haven't changed anything. We make our own soups—we make it all."
>
> Another place they didn't want to make changes was with their loyal workers. "Faye has been with us so long, said Jimmy, and so has Flossie (food preparation—kitchen.) I just think I need to thank them," he said.

That was almost 15 years ago, and "Miss Faye," as she is affectionately known, is still there—doing what she's always done, pleasing her customers.

: Above: Faye, happily serving her
                    customers.

  Right: Faye with her nephew
  Norbert Houston and family.

Below: Faye, with her sister Doris
  Wright, and niece, Lois Wright

In another Pensacola News Journal article about Faye and Jerry's, written by Rebecca Ross on October 25, 2009, in celebration of Faye's 50 years of service, Ms. Ross wrote:

> Strong management and close friendships are what keeps the energetic octogenarian at Jerry's Drive-In. "I've had good bosses," Faye said. "I just love all of them. They've all been so good to me. And the staff and customers are just like family. I've watched our regular customers grow up, and now they're bringing in their own babies. I just love talking to everybody."

Jerry's Drive-In is just as popular today, as it has ever been, and perhaps even more so. People come from all over the surrounding two counties to eat at Jerry's to enjoy the people and read and laugh at the hundreds of humorous and sarcastic bumper stickers, plaques, pictures, and sports pennants mounted on all the walls. New generations of young guys and gals consider Jerry's their favorite gathering spot, like my generation did. Many of us silver-haired or bald headed old-timers still frequent Jerry's, not only for the great food but to experience again the nostalgia of the good times with old friends in years past. As for the food, my favorite is still the mullet sandwich, with side orders of baked beans and hush-puppies with coffee or beer—God, it's good, especially when it's served by "Miss Faye.

Update:

In December, 2015, Faye decided to retire after fifty-six years at Jerry's. Jimmy and Pam Halstead went all out to honor her with an extraordinary retirement party that included various gambling tables and slot machines, complete with professional operators, dealers and play money. Old friends, customers, and employees enjoyed the special event that lasted into the wee hours. It was a fun time, as always, at Jerry's.

Above: The Retirement Party
Below: Faye and her Family at the Retirement Party

181

Above: Faye with daughter, Norma Jennings, granddaughter, Dianna Sorensen, and great grand-daughter, Maryn Sorensen .

Below: Faye with Norma, son-in-law, Bud Jennings, granddaughter, Becky Smith, and great granddaughter, Reagan Smith.

Above: Pam Halstead toasts Faye with champagne before cutting the cake.

Below: Erick Colado with Faye

182

Darius Brown

Kevin , Dianna Sorenson, their daughter,
Maryn, and sons, Jaren and Kevin

Tommy Ellingson

Above: Charlie and Faye's sister, Doris.

Left: Popular Pensacola Bartender Bill Johnson.

183

Antwon Brown

Malia Wright and Erick Colado

Gabe Prim

Willie Lewis

Rachel Bonifay

Willie Lewis and Michael Rosburg

Elle Bardsley

Kenny Leonard

16

The Mullet Toss

"Throwed Rolls," the successful gimmick used by a popular Gulf Coast restaurant is amusing to most people, but tossing a dead mullet, a delicious food fish, in a competitive sporting event "ain't" so damn funny to some of us who live here on the so called "Redneck Riviera." We enjoy catching and eating the elusive, popeyed, Black Mullet (Mugil cephalus) and the White or Silver Mullet (Mugil curema). We would never think of using either as a ball or discus in a "Mullet Toss," as they do at a very popular and often crowded bar and lounge situated on the Gulf of Mexico beach along the Florida-Alabama line. They are too tasty to waste, and sometimes too darn hard to catch.

I've never attended a "mullet toss" event, which must be an original idea of the owners of the establishment on Perdido Key. As I understand it, a customer becomes a participant by paying an entrance fee, and the winner is the one who tosses the mullet the greatest distance across the "State Line" into the sand dunes. It must be fairly profitable for the owners because the mullet toss has been a regular event for several years. I would agree that businesses and organizations have a right to have as many mullet tosses as they desire, and as the old saying goes, "I will defend their right to do so," but that still doesn't make it right. Why not use something other than food, such as "buffalo chips" or "horse biscuits?" There's an unlimited, renewable supply, and after a few beers, who cares, it's the challenge and the spirit of the competition that counts.

Besides being a culinary delight, the mullet is an interesting fish. It's a true vegetarian, which should please the health food folks, since it feeds on aquatic plants and algae. They are found all over the world, and are made up of about eighty to one-hundred species. The average adult size of our local striped (black) mullet is about eighteen to twenty inches long, and one to two pounds in weight. They travel in schools, but to see a single mullet is common. I've always considered that lone mullet as being on a recon mission, looking out for fishermen, and now, "discus collectors" for a mullet toss.

A real mystery about the mullet is the fact that it occasionally jumps in the air for no apparent reason, although much has been written about this behavior. Another thing that is unique to the mullet is the fact that it is the only fish in the world that has a gizzard. We know, of course, that birds have gizzards, and we know that birds fly, so perhaps it's possible that since the mullet also has a gizzard, it has a genetic predisposition to want to fly, which may be the answer to the above mystery. Several years ago someone wrote an article in the Pensacola News Journal, claiming that the mullet was indeed a bird, since it had a gizzard. Who knows, maybe someday the mullet will become the state bird. It would be a good thing because then the Audubon Society might get involved, and we could sic 'em on the "Mullet Tossers."

Mullet are caught in nets, not on hook and line. For years, the commercial fishermen on both coasts of Florida and the entire Gulf Coast used "gill nets," which could be hundreds of feet long. When schools of mullet were spotted, the boat would surround the school of fish by making a circle, doling out the net as it went. The fish, in an attempt to escape, frantically "gilled" or caught themselves in the net, and were brought into the boat as the net was retrieved. A "trammel net" was used in the same manner, but was different from the "gill net" in that it was made up of double layers of net, the outside mesh larger than the mesh of the inside net. When the circle was made, and as the fish panicked they pocketed themselves by forcing the small mesh net into the larger mesh net. Neither of these nets can be used in Florida today because of the Florida Net Ban that was enacted several years ago. The only legal way to catch mullet in Florida today is with a "castnet," which a hand held net, personally thrown by the fisherman. Since the net ban went into effect, the mullet population

Above: The author throwing his castnet from the dock.
Below: Bob Joseph making a great cast from author's dock.

has increased tremendously, and many commercial fishermen are earning a living by catching mullet with their castnets. Unfortunately, Alabama does not have a net ban, and allows the use of the large nets.

The primary reason for catching a mullet is to eat it, not to "toss it," and when preparing it for the table, the mullet is the most versatile of all fish caught along the Gulf Coast. Everyone has their own favorite recipe, but the mullet can be fried, baked, broiled, smoked, canned, used in chowder or soup, in salads and smoked mullet pate' plus there are other recipes we've never heard of. You haven't lived until you've had a mullet sandwich at Jerry's Drive In, or mullet plates at Chet's or The Marina Oyster Barn.

The mullet roe is sought after worldwide, especially in Japan where it is considered a delicacy. Most of the commercial fish houses ship both yellow and white roe to many foreign countries. Locally, when mullet roe is fried, baked or smoked it is delicious, but if not eaten sparingly, one should not stray too far from the loo.

Several years ago, the State of Florida decided to launch a worldwide marketing program for the Florida mullet, and in the process, it was suggested that the name of the mullet be changed to "Lisa." It was as though the state had decided to take the first born child from each family in Florida. There was a tremendous uproar from both commercial and sport fishermen. They would have nothing to do with the name "Lisa" for their beloved mullet. The program was eventually cancelled, but not because of the opposition to the name change; it was discovered that canned mullet had too short a shelf life due to its oily content. This was years before the world's sudden demand for Omega-3 Fish Oil.

I trust the reader will understand that the mullet is a favorite for many of us in the Florida Panhandle, and that we consider its place is on the table and not tossed in the sand.

"The Mullet Toss" was first published in Emerald Coast Review XVI., page 16.

(Courtesy of the West Florida Literary Federation

17

"My" 1926 Model T Roadster

During the late 1940s, when I was a student at Pensacola High School, my older brother Bill owned a service station in East Pensacola Heights, located just past Jerry's Drive-In on Scenic Highway (now Cervantes Street). My mode of transportation at the time was by bicycle and borrowed cars. I had obtained my driver's license, and was always borrowing cars. This was a time when most families had only one car, but I was lucky because I had three older, married brothers who owned cars. Fortunately, Bill was quite a "horse trader" and made a deal for a 1926 Model T Ford Roadster. He didn't give it to me, but he let me have it for a few months, and I used it like it was my own. I drove it everywhere, or as long as I could keep gas in it, and it helped to have a big brother who owned a gas station.

A 1926 Model T Ford
Source:
ConceptCarz.com

Henry Ford's Model T, or "Tin Lizzie," or "Flivver" as it was colloquially known, was a wonderful vehicle, a fun car to drive, but very different from the cars I had previously driven and learned to drive in. The Model T was advertised as "three speed," meaning it had two forward and one reverse drive. It had no clutch, and the transmission was controlled with three foot pedals and a lever mounted on the driver's left side. There was no gas pedal either, since the throttle was controlled by a lever mounted on the steering column just under the steering wheel. To move forward I would increase the throttle, push down on the left pedal, which engaged the bands wrapped around the transmission drum. The little roadster was then in low gear. When the right speed was reached, I would push the floor lever forward, lift my foot, and the car would literally jump into high gear. When it entered that wonderful "chug, chug" sound and feel, I would increase the throttle, and we were off and running. There's no other sound like a Model T as the little four cylinder engine struggled to please. The middle pedal engaged the reverse gear, and the right pedal engaged the transmission brake. The floor lever served as the parking brake when pulled all the way back.

During my early years of living in East Pensacola Heights, the old bridge across Bayou Texar joined Gadsden Street on the west side of the bayou, not Cervantes Street, as it does today. Gadsden was the main route to connect to Palafox Street and downtown. However, drivers had an option to switch over to Cervantes Street from Gadsden Street, and vice versa, at the park between 15th and 16th avenues because the streets cut diagonally through the park. The west end of the bayou bridge connected to a steep hill at the east end of Gadsden Street in front of the Mirador Apartments. That steep hill was a big problem for me and my "Tin Lizzie," but I learned through trial and error, while holding up a lot of traffic, that it climbed better in reverse. So, each morning, on my way to school, I would stop about half way across the bridge, turn the little "Flivver" around, and back up the hill. It worked every time. I don't know if there was a flaw in Mr. Ford's engineering or if the problem was on my end, but a compromise between the machine and the hill was reached.

My friends loved the Model T as much as I did, so the rumble seat, as well as the front seat was usually occupied beyond capacity. Once I was driving across the old wooden toll bridge to Pensacola Beach, overloaded with friends; guys were even standing on the running boards. Although I slowed down considerably at the toll booth, I ran into the back of the car in front of me. Several of my friends were thrown off, and rolled all over the bridge. None of them were seriously hurt, nor was either car damaged. The other driver was mad as hell, and my friends managed to show their butts. Mr. Bonifay, who managed the bridge and ran the toll booth, was ready to throw the pride of the Ford Motor Company and its loud-mouth occupants into the Intracoastal Canal. Frankly, it was the design of the Model T that saved the day because that particular model did not come with a front bumper, and fortunately, the front wheels extended beyond the front of the car, preventing damage to either vehicle.

Charlie "Driving Miss Marie," his niece Marie Abbatiello ,in Brother Bill's 1926 Model-T.

It was probably a good thing when Bill decided it was time for me to return the wonderful little Model T. I sure hated to give it up, but I appreciated Bill's generosity. Now, in my old age, I have labeled and filed away these good memories along with memories of old girl friends, my dog, Rosie, the Catalonia Park all-star team, my first speckled trout, my paper route, the old Scenic Terrace, John Oliver's Nob Hill, and of course, the first time I saw Sandra Lockney in that itsy bitsy, teeny weenie, rose-colored bikini at the Royal Arms Apartment's swimming pool.

18

My Beautician, Ann Barnes

Forty years ago, in April, 1975, a frightened, pretty, sixteen-year-old Tuyet Doan and her parents, Khim and Mau, boarded her uncle's small shrimp boat in Vung Tau, on the coast of South Vietnam. Saigon, the capital, was falling to Communist North Vietnam's Army (NVA) and the Viet Cong, marking the end of the Vietnam War. The Doan family was afraid of the Communist Regime. With her parents and other relatives on board, they cautiously entered the South China Sea. After being adrift for ten days, they were rescued by a U.S. Navy ship and taken to a refugee camp at the U. S. Navy Base on Guam. Later, they were flown to the U. S. Marine Corps base at Camp Pendleton, California.

Ann and her parents Khim and Mau
1975

193

Today, Tuyet Doan is the much admired Ann Barnes, a successful beautician at Pensacola's Continental Hair Design on Beverly Parkway. Her forty-year journey from being a young girl in a war-torn country to becoming an American citizen, a wife, mother, grandmother and business woman is remarkable and inspiring. For several years she's been my barber and my wife Sandra's beautician.

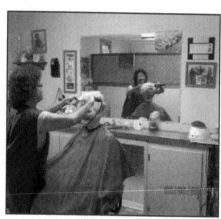

Ann always makes us handsome and beautiful. Well, at least, she always improves our looks!

Prior to fleeing Vung Tau, Ann's parents owned a floating restaurant. Unlike the world famous restaurants of Vung Tau Harbor, theirs did not have accommodations for guests. Instead, it was more like a floating kitchen; their customers were boaters and fishermen who purchased their meals to go. Ann recalls helping her mother prepare the meals. Everything had to be made fresh as very few people in Vietnam had refrigeration; they made frequent trips to the market.

It was obvious in early April, 1975 that Vietnam would soon fall to the advancing NVA since the North Vietnamese Government had violated the Paris Peace Accord. The citizens of Vietnam watched as the American civilian and military personnel in Saigon, along with tens of thousands of South Vietnamese civilians loyal to the Americans and the South Vietnam regime began evacuating the city. On April 18, 1975, President Gerald Ford created the Interagency Task Force (IATF) for Indochina. The IATF was given the responsibility to transport, process, receive and resettle Indochina refugees, mostly Vietnamese, to the United States.

All nearby countries in Southeast Asia declined to accept the Vietnamese evacuees and refugees, fearing they would have them permanently. However, Governor Ricardo Bordallo of Guam agreed to grant the Vietnamese temporary asylum. Guam was twenty-five-hundred miles from Vietnam. The U. S. Navy's Seventh Fleet was alerted to stand by to pick up refugees fleeing by boat. The commander of U. S. Naval forces on Guam was ordered to accept, shelter, process and care for refugees as they were removed from South Vietnam. Sometime prior to South Vietnam's capitulation on April 30th, Ann's family boarded their shrimp boat and slipped away from Vung Tau and their ancestral homeland, Vietnam. They were among the forerunners of the estimated two-million "Vietnamese Boat People" who left Vietnam between 1975 and 1995.

The boat trip from Vung Tau was considered dangerous because they could be stopped by the South Vietnam military that was on the look-out for deserters. The military and political situations created a mistrust of everyone. Even more dangerous was the possibility of harm from pirates and others fleeing Vietnam seeking a means of escape. They entered the South China Sea from Vung Tau with no definite destination in mind. It's unknown if the family knew U. S. Navy ships had been patrolling near the coast of South Vietnam to assist refugees. Fortunately, after ten days at sea in the small shrimp boat, they were spotted by a U. S. Navy ship and taken aboard. Many more were rescued, and since the ship had limited sleeping accommodations, the refugees huddled on the deck until they reached Guam and the refugee camp. A week later, after much processing and orientation, Ann and her parents were flown to the huge refugee camp at the U. S. Marine Corps Base at Camp Pendleton, California.

A counselor at Camp Pendleton advised Tuyet to change her name to Ann, because, she said, "You look like an Ann." When Ann was sharing this information with me, she laughed, and said, "The counselor tactfully explained that the Vietnamese pronunciation for Tuyet sounds much like the English word 'twit.'" That must have been a shock to Ann, or Tuyet, to give up a name she had for sixteen years. Frankly, I'm glad she agreed to change because Ann is a sweet name and it fits her. Also, I wouldn't be comfortable calling her "Twit," especially when she has a pair of scissors in her hand.

After several months at Camp Pendleton, Ann and her parents, Khim and Mau Doan, were sponsored by the Redeemer Lutheran Church of Nassau, New York. Their sponsor family was the Rev. Theodore Grant and his wife, Nancy, of Hicksville, New York, a community on Long Island. Ann and her parents lived with the Grants their first eight months in Hicksville before moving into a rented, converted farmhouse, which the neighbors painted and renovated for them. They lived there three years, during which time Ann completed high school. Reluctantly, they decided to move to Pensacola where they had relatives and friends who had settled here earlier. The Doan's adored the Grants and appreciated what they and the community did for them, but Long Island didn't have a large enough Vietnamese population and they found the winters unbearable. Their move to a warmer climate was typical of what most other Vietnamese refugees did after resettlement.

Home Is Where Her Heart Is

For refugee, it's still Hicksville

By Jennifer Sinco Kelleher

Tuyet Doan Barnes wasn't born in Hicksville and lived there for only three years when she was a teenager. Yet Hicksville long felt like home to her, so she came back this week after a 24-year absence.

"I've always felt that this was my home," Barnes, 42, of Florida, said. "This was the first place I was exposed to a new country, new customs."

It was where her family got its start in the United States after fleeing the fall of South Vietnam in April 1975, with the help of Redeemer Lutheran Church in central Nassau.

Afraid of the Communist regime, the Doan family left Vung Tau, Vietnam, on a small shrimp boat with no destination in mind.

The family lived with the Rev. Theodore Grant and his wife, Nancy, for eight months before moving into a rented, converted farmhouse on Meadow Lane, where they lived for three years. They later moved to Florida, because Long Island didn't have a large enough Vietnamese population and they found the winters unbearable.

Barnes, who was 15 when she arrived in Hicksville, kept in touch with the Grants, even after her parents passed away, her mother in 1993 and her father in 1996.

But when Barnes and her husband, Richard, arrived in Hicksville Monday after driving from Pensacola, Fla., nothing looked familiar to her.

"Everything was so different until we turned the corner of Old Country Road and Levittown Parkway," she said yesterday. Then the memories came flooding back — memories of Thanksgiving dinner in the Grant house on Bridle Lane, of her father, Khim Doan's, pet squirrel, of seeing snow for the first time.

Nancy Grant, who considered Barnes' mother, Mau Doan, her sister because they were close in age, said Barnes looked "a little more sophisticated."

Since Monday, Barnes and the Grants have been reminiscing about the Doan family's immigration experience and have visited Redeemer Lutheran Church. Barnes, who stayed with the Grants, returns to Florida today.

Barnes remembers her mother sobbing as they left their country. Afloat for about 10 days, they were rescued by a U.S. Navy ship and taken to Camp Pendleton in California.

Meanwhile, members of Redeemer Lutheran Church saw a need to help refugee families and decided to sponsor one.

Raising funds and educating the community about the Vietnamese, the Grants prepared to open their home to the Doan family.

Barnes said she never felt discriminated against in Hicksville. But because Barnes had to act as translator for her parents for tasks such as shopping and doctor visits, she didn't have much of a chance to socialize.

Her father, however, was determined to not let culture separate him from the community. Barnes remembers her father making friends with Puerto Rican families he worked with at a factory.

Barnes laughed heartily as she recounted watching her father attempt to salsa dance at Puerto Rican parties, while her shy mother stayed in a corner.

Grant said the Doan family's time in Hicksville helped bring the community together. A local real estate agent found a home for the Doans, and in one weekend neighbors painted and renovated it for them.

Even though the Doan family was Catholic, they never felt pressure to repay Redeemer Lutheran by compromising their faith, Barnes said. The church even enrolled Barnes in St. Ignatius Catholic School.

"In Vietnam, different denominations had so many conflicts," Barnes said. "It amazes me how the Lutheran church here didn't expect anything in return."

Because Barnes was the Doan couple's only child, she felt many of her childhood memories disappeared with their deaths. "I have a lot of memories here," she said. "When my parents were gone, I felt all my childhood was gone — until I came here."

'I've always felt that this was my home. This was the first place I was exposed to a new country, new customs.'

— Tuyet Doan Barnes

Tuyet Doan Barnes, left, who arrived in the United States as a refugee from Vietnam more than 25 years ago, reminisces yesterday with her sponsor family, the Rev. Theodore Grant, retired pastor of Redeemer Lutheran Church, and his wife, Nancy, at their Hicksville home. She stayed with them once again while she visited from Florida.

196

Originally, the U.S. Government strategically resettled the Vietnamese refugees evenly throughout the country to avoid so-called "Little Vietnams." Many families, like the Doans, relocated to warmer areas to be with other Vietnamese and avoid the unbearable northern winters. Today, the highest concentration of Vietnamese in the U.S. is in California and Texas. Many of us are glad the Doans chose Pensacola.

The family arrived in Pensacola in 1979, which was a better fit, with its year-round mild climate and fairly large Vietnamese community. With the work ethic for which most Vietnamese are known, Ann and her parents did whatever it took to make a better life for themselves. Recently, she recounted how it was necessary to take many low-paying jobs those first few years before she pursued an education in cosmetology. She passed the state exam thirty-one years ago, and has been a beautician and barber since. With her professionalism and great personality she has developed a large clientele among both men and women.

During those years, Ann married, and is the proud mother of two girls and two boys. As of now, she has eight grandchildren . . . and counting. Khim and Mau lived to enjoy their grandchildren. Mau Doan died in 1993 and Khim Doan died in 1995. Ann's marriage ended in divorce, but fifteen years ago, she married Richard "Rick" Barnes, the love

Ann, Rick and their beautiful family

of her life. Rick is a U.S. Army veteran, from Pensacola, and the son of a preacher. She now has a large extended family, and they own a nice vacation home on Lake Juniper near DeFuniak Springs, just eighty-five miles east of Pensacola. Ann is a dedicated fisherman, or fisherwoman, something she must have learned from her time with family in Vietnam.

Ann, the fisherman

Life is good for the Barnes family. Ann's son, Danny, a U.S. Marine, had several tours in Iraq and returned home safely. They are strong supporters of V.F.W. activities, and enjoy traveling.

Danny in Iraq

Above: Danny and some of his Military friends
Below: Danny and his proud Mother

199

A while back, Ann persuaded Rick to get rid of his motorcycle and they purchased a boat; now she can seriously stock up on fish. Recently, she and Rick purchased a motorhome; they enjoy the RV lifestyle, especially when they tow their boat to their favorite fishing spots.

Ann and husband Rick enjoy traveling and fishing whenever they have a chance.

They are both sports enthusiasts and she's a walking almanac on college and professional football. She'll eat your lunch on facts. She's like all other barbers and beauticians, they get too darn smart when it comes to sports and politics. Everybody admires Ann and appreciates her sense of humor. On occasions, I ran late for my appointment with her, but always called to let her know, "I'm on the way." Her usual response was, "No problem, if I don't have enough time, I'll cut as much as I can." That inspires me to be on time.

Sandra and I look forward to our time with Ann, but there is one thing I wish she would change: the "Florida Gator" pennant hanging on her wall. A "FSU Seminole" pennant would look much better.

19

"My Brother-In-Law In Raiford Prison"

During a weekly meeting of the Joe Harrell Bible Breakfast at First United Methodist Church, Gordon Towne, a member of First Baptist Church and a longtime member of the non-denominational group was in charge of the program. We looked forward to what Gordon had in store for us because he always made it interesting. That particular morning he decided to have each of us participate in the program by identifying a person who had a significant influence on our own personal Christian life.

Rev. Norman Redding

That wasn't a difficult question, and I was glad to have an opportunity to tell my fellow "breakfast clubbers" about my brother-in-law, Norman Redding, who spent twenty-five years at Florida's Raiford Prison.

Norman grew up in Mulberry, Florida, a small town east of Tampa, where he and his brother played high school football. The family later moved to Pensacola and he became a civil service employee at Pensacola Naval Air Station during World War II. In 1945 Norman and my sister Emma Jean were married, and he continued his job at the Navy base while attending the new Pensacola Junior College at night to study accounting. By the time their son Norman, Jr. (Butch) arrived, the accounting curriculum must have aroused an entrepreneurial spirit in Norman, and he chose to test the business world, while keeping his day job. I was about fourteen at the time, and when not in school or throwing my paper route, I helped Norman and his dad build the structure for his new venture, Reddings Curb Market, on Scenic Highway (now Cervantes Street) in East Pensacola Heights. Emma Jean and Norman's parents ran the business.

It was some time after Reddings Curb Market was introduced to the people of East Pensacola Heights that Norman agreed to teach me how to drive. He owned a Model-A Ford. I don't remember the year make, but it was in excellent shape. I remember the gear shift and dimmer-switch was on the floor, and the horn had that ooga-ooga sound. I really liked that old car, and would love to have one just like it today. As I recall, Norman graduated to Buicks sometime in the post-WWII 1940s when the American auto industry began making automobiles again. He was a Buick man for many years, but not before I dented the fender of his Model-A when I hit that telephone pole in front of our house on Bayou Boulevard. Was he upset? Heck no—he laughed. He pretended to be more upset about the broken eggs than the fender. That was Norman; to know him, was to love him. He had the patience of Job, and a heart of gold. The curb market venture didn't make it, and Norman continued with the old fashioned way of making a living—his job, plus he kept books for businesses on the side. He was making it, but what many of us didn't know was something of a personal and spiritual nature was gnawing away at Norman. That heart of gold was troubled.

Norman was, as we say in the South, "a church goer." He and Emma Jean met at and were married in East Hill Baptist Church. They became charter members of the Heights Baptist Chapel, which was sponsored by East Hill Baptist Church. It was at this point in their young marriage that Norman revealed what was gnawing at him. He believed God had called him to the ministry. In 1952, after much prayer and consultations they made the decision to go for it and were off to Birmingham, Alabama to attend Howard College (now Samford University). After graduating in 1955, he enrolled in the Baptist Seminary in New Orleans, and our brother Bill moved them to New Orleans in a "fish truck" he borrowed from

Norman and Emma Jean Redding

Williams Seafood Company, which Norman thought appropriate since the fish is a symbol for Christianity. How could anyone doubt it was a genuine call to the ministry from God, when the student rolls up to the school of divinity in a truck with a large symbol of Christianity emblazoned on each side? They did, however, arrive with one less piece of furniture than they started out with. While crossing over Lake Pontchartrain, their bedsprings, the forerunner of the innerspring mattress, fell from the truck, stopping vehicles both ways in the bridge's heavy traffic. They did what good Christian folks would do: they quickly threw the bedsprings into Lake Pontchartrain and continued on their way.

His first sermon after being ordained was to the congregation at the Heights Baptist Chapel. Some of us in the family humorously refer to that morning as probably the chapel's first miracle when my dad shocked us all by answering the call and dedicating his life to Jesus Christ. No one, not even Norman or my mother, knew of his plans to do so. This is not to infer that Dad was some sort of heathen as he wasn't. He was a good person and did attend church in the past when my older siblings were young. My grandparents were Anglicans and after settling in America became Episcopalians, but I have no idea if dad and his siblings attended church with them; that's another one of those many questions we neglected to ask. What I learned over the years was that Dad was entering the church one Sunday, in the early years of his thirty-two years as an elected county official, and someone jokingly said something like, "Hey Ben, it must be getting close to election time," suggesting his reason for being in church was to get votes. Unfortunately, Dad, a tall, red-headed, former railroad-man and local baseball team manager took it as a personal affront and stopped going to church. So, we considered it a miracle that Norman, his son-in-law, brought him back to the flock. He was a Christian. I know, because a few hours before he died, he assured me he was going to Heaven. Norman did a wonderful job conducting his funeral service.

Norman Redding

While attending the seminary, Norman pastored the New Hope Baptist Church in Franklinton, Louisiana. Fresh out of the seminary, he accepted an invitation to be the preacher at a small church at Brushy Creek, near Greenville, Alabama. Small also applied to the salary, however, what they lacked in salary was made up with good food and other tangible assets. Emma Jean said they always had a freezer full of meats and vegetables donated by the church members. His salary was determined by the congregation's offerings, so Norman naturally preached on the importance of tithing.

Their next church was at Hokes Bluff, in Gadsden, Alabama. While there, Norman learned of an opening for a chaplain's position at the Florida State Prison in Stark, Florida. He applied for the job, was interviewed, and hired. It was a position he was well qualified for and a life-changing event for the family. They moved to Starke in December; 1962 in a real moving van without the usual Christian symbol on its sides. Norman spent the next twenty-five years at the huge Raiford Prison, ten of those years as the Death Row Chaplain. I enjoyed conversations with him about the goings on at the prison; he was always willing to answer even the most ridiculous questions. I did learn most of all that it was a dangerous place, even for a chaplain. A person had to spend only a short time with Norman when he spoke about his relationship with prisoners, especially those on death row, to realize he was truly a man of God, and wasn't just putting in his time until retirement.

Norman had compassion for everyone there, even though most were there for heinous crimes. He told me about conversations and prayers with the condemned men, even as they walked to the electric chair (known in Florida as "Old Sparky"). He spoke to me about those prisoners who became true born-again Christians, not just temporary "jail-house" conversions. He also talked about his disappointments in not being able to reach some of those who were about to be executed. They rejected everything about Christianity and all other religions. Perhaps the most surprising thing Norman said during one of our conversations years ago was that he believed there were many prisoners who should never be released back into society. I wouldn't have been surprised if a guard had made that statement, but knowing deep down inside that Norman was to me the best example of a godly man and I assumed all men were salvageable in the eyes of God. Today, I'm a lot smarter, which I suppose comes with age, and I agree with him. I've had to remind myself that Norman didn't say God didn't love them all, he simply meant they were dangerous and should be locked away forever to protect society.

Norman sitting at the table where he counseled inmates at Raiford Prison

Norman was encouraged to write about his ten years experiences as a death row chaplain, but he refused. He obviously believed his dealings were confidential and private between himself, the prisoner, and God. Makes sense to me, but it would have been interesting reading. He did write a book, but it was more of an instructional manual on Scripture and its uses.

Being a chaplain in a prison like Raiford is potentially dangerous and Norman did have several bad experiences, a couple of which he wrote about in his book, since doing so would not violate anyone's confidentiality.

In a chapter about his belief in angels, his first sentence was, "February 20, 1966 will be a day I will never forget." He continued by explaining that it was a Sunday, and he had conducted four worship services and spent a number of hours in counseling. He walked through the metal detectors, out of the building, and headed down the steps to the double chain link fence that was twenty feet high, topped with three feet of looped barbed wire. Attack dogs were spaced at one-hundred yard intervals inside the fence. Two gates, operated by the guard tower, separated the dogs from the people. The tower waved him in and closed the gate behind him. Suddenly he realized he was closed in with one of the huge vicious guard dogs that are trained to kill. The tower guard made a mistake. The huge dog barked, growled and attacked, reaching Norman in two or three leaps, charging for his throat. Norman jerked his right arm forward causing the dog to miss his mark and slam hard against the fence with such force it startled the guard dog on the other side of the fence. The two dogs tried to attack each other through the fence, which gave him time to edge over to the exit gate and yell to the guard in the tower, who in his excitement opened the gate on the opposite side of the fence. After much yelling from Norman, the guard closed the gate and slowly opened the exit gate, allowing him to squeeze through while kicking at the dog which had turned back to him. He could have been killed, but escaped unhurt, which he attributed to intervening angels. He further explained his belief in angels with applicable scripture. The guard in the tower apologized to Norman, and subsequently quit before he was fired.

In another incident Norman wrote about, he was required to attend the execution of a prisoner named Charles who had murdered his wife. The condemned man requested that Norman conduct his funeral, which he agreed to do. After the execution, Norman learned from the prison administrators that there was a death threat to anyone who participated in Charles's funeral. The threat came from the family of the person Charles had murdered. The prison officials cautioned Norman not to conduct the funeral and if he did so he would be on his own. Norman vowed to do so, as he had promised the man he would. A lieutenant volunteered, without the institution's sanction, to accompany Norman, and he stayed with him during the services. Fortunately all went well.

Norman retired from the Florida Prison System in 1988, but remained active in their family church in Starke. Both their children, Butch and Christie, were married with families of their own, but they were always a close-knit, Christ-centered family, with much activity centered around Norman and Emma Jean's home. They were a happy family and did many things together.

PRISON SETS CHAPEL RITE

TALLAHASSEE, Nov. 29 (UPI)—State Prisons Director Louie Wainwright said today dedication ceremonies will be held Dec. 3 at the new chapel in the east unit of the state prison in Raiford.

Housing 1,200 prisoners, the east unit was opened in 1961 but because there was no chapel, religious activities were held in a dining room.

The new chapel, seating 210 persons at each service, will provide space for religious activities, directed by Chaplain Norman Redding.

Sadly, Norman died from Parkinson disease on August 18, 1999 at age seventy-four, eleven years after he retired. Emma Jean retired from her position at Bradford High School, and is still going strong at age ninety, with no plans to slow down. Although Norman is gone, his family continues to honor his legacy of maintaining a moral compass based on Christ's teachings. They remain a close-knit, happy family and do many things together.

In those allotted two minutes I was pleased to tell my fellow breakfast-clubbers why my brother-in-law, Chaplain Norman Redding, who spent twenty-five years at, not in, Raiford Prison, had a significant influence on my life as a Christian.

Some of the Redding Family
Left to Right: Shelley, Christie, Carl, Emma Jean, Butch and Mary

Photos, articles, and biographical information courtesy of Emma Jean Redding.

20

My Cushman Scooter

I was in Clubbs Junior High and Pensacola High during the Cushman scooter craze, or at least there was a demand for the popular scooter among my age group. It was in the late 1940s when I bought my Cushman scooter, a Model 52 of the 50 Series Cushman Motor Works introduced in 1946. It had a centrifugal clutch, more like an automatic drive. The Model 54, which came out in 1949, had a 2-speed transmission and clutch, had more power and wider tires, and,

My Cushman scooter

of course cost more. My Model 52 was purchased used, and cost me in the neighborhood of one-hundred-fifty dollars. I was a paper-boy at the time, and figured it would be much better than my bicycle for throwing papers on my route. It was, but it didn't last, because the Pensacola News-Journal forbade me to use it after my customers complained about the noise it made in the early morning hours.

Owning a scooter at age sixteen opened up a whole new world for me. I was used to going everywhere on my bicycle, but it had limitations. My friend, Billy Miller, owned a motorcycle, manufactured by the Indian Motorcycle Company, and he would pick me up when we went out at night to Pensacola Beach, or elsewhere. In the 1940s, most families owned only one automobile, not like today where it's normal for everybody in the family who has a driver's license to have a car. I was allowed to use the family car as long as it was convenient and necessary. My dad didn't hesitate to determine if it was necessary, even when it was convenient.

A year earlier, when I first turned sixteen and obtained my driver's license, my brother Bill made a deal for a 1926 Model-T Roadster. It was a beauty, red, with a rumble-seat, and a black convertible top. He allowed me to keep it for a few months. I was hot stuff and suddenly had more new friends than the Model-T would hold. I drove it to school each day, stopping after school at Carl's Bakery where the Pensacola News-Journal dropped off the bundle of afternoon papers. It was tempting to spend half my profits on doughnuts and cookies, while folding my papers there. I would then return home, get on my bicycle and throw my route. Later, I was back on my bicycle for good when Bill decided it was time for me to return Mr. Ford's Model-T to him. I felt grounded after being a gad-about in that roadster, so that's why I decided to purchase a Cushman motor scooter.

The scooter was much cheaper to operate, but allowed for only one additional passenger, and we were always at the mercy of the weather. It seemed like it rained more often right after I bought my scooter. I was a paperboy for almost four years, so I was used to riding my bike in the rain, but it was a lot different driving a scooter in the rain, especially when a date was riding on the back, squealing about her hair getting wet. I finally got smart and bought two army surplus rain jackets with a hood and kept them in the storage compartment.

The model 52 was designed for only one person, the driver, but it was common to scooch up for a passenger. It was always disappointing, and it happened occasionally, that parents wouldn't allow their daughter to go out at night on the scooter. So, I'd have to leave the scooter and we would walk somewhere or catch the bus to town to a movie—not as exciting as going to the Scenic Terrace for a beer. On one occasion, my date's father suggested I take his car. I did and I'm glad he never figured out where I took it.

During the high school years, there were several nightclubs in and around Pensacola that sold beer to minors without any hesitancy, and many guys and gals my age drank beer. One such place was the Scenic Terrace on Scenic Highway in East Pensacola Heights, and it was the favorite hangout for high school and college age students. It was not uncommon to see several scooters and bicycles parked under the portico at the front door in the daytime or evenings.

The Scenic Terrace closed years ago, but Jerry's Drive-In, only a couple of blocks away, was also a popular hangout for all ages. As the name implies, the Drive-In section in the rear of the building was always busy, day and night, during the 1940s and 50s. As I recall, "Foster," a black guy, was the only "car hop," and he was there for years. Many of us became good friends with "Foster." On occasions, if my friends and I were going fishing or to the beach, I would ride up on my scooter, order beer and whatever else we needed. "Foster" would ice the beer down in the storage compartment in the rear of the scooter. I don't know if the owner, Ray Cranford, was aware of all the goings-on in the "Curb Service" area, but I don't recall that there was ever a problem.

The scooter was particularly helpful to me during the 1948 elections in Escambia County. My dad had been elected the Supervisor of Elections sixteen years earlier, and was running for County Tax Collector. I remember stuffing the storage compartment of the scooter with as many of his campaign posters and cards as I could cram in it, plus a hammer and nails. I spent several days in the northern part of the county nailing posters up at the many country stores throughout that part of the county. I was impressed at how friendly the people were, and how many already knew my dad. It was a great experience.

I'm surprised that I don't remember how I disposed of that Cushman scooter, but I'm certain I either traded it in when I purchased my 1936, four door, Ford with a V-8 engine, or sold it for cash to help make the deal. I have fond memories of owning that scooter, and I'm proud to say, I never had an accident or received any citations while operating it. Some might say it was because I was a careful driver and observed all the laws.

Naw—that ain't it. I was lucky.

21

My Friend Carter

I don't remember Carter's first name. It was like that in the military. You got to know someone pretty well, but quite often, you never knew their first name. I did know it at one time, but after sixty-two years it's beyond recall. I met Carter in 1952, during the time of the Korean War, which was not going too well for our side. His misery began, when five of us, four white guys and Carter, a black from Baltimore, traveled by train, under the same set of military orders from Bainbridge, Maryland to Parris Island, South Carolina. All five of us had recently graduated from Dental Technician's School and had been assigned to the U. S. Marine Corps Recruit Depot at Parris Island. Carter had never been in the south, and had no idea what life was like, off base, for a young black person in a segregated society. What he experienced over the next several months, was more than he was willing to accept, and in a desperate attempt to escape the humiliation of segregation, he proved himself a hero, but unfortunately his efforts ended tragically.

For Carter, the unexpected came soon after we arrived at the train station in the small town of Yamessee, S. C. The five of us, in U.S. Navy uniforms, disembarked from the train and entered the small station, typical in appearance of the many train stations throughout the south. We were immediately greeted with a man's loud, high pitched voice, shouting, "Hey, Nigger, get your black ass over there where you belong! "Over there", in the direction he was pointing, was an empty room with rows of benches, and above the entrance, the words, "Colored Waiting Room. " The guy doing the shouting was a short, wide, middle aged, man, attired in what looked like a railroad conductor's uniform, but I suppose it was the proper uniform for somebody who worked in a train station back in 1952. We were all shocked, especially Carter. I was pissed. I had seen bigots like him all my life, but I believe we had a better class of "rednecks" in Pensacola. I shouted right back at him, saying something like "Can't you see he's in uniform?" That didn't impress him one bit, and he threatened to put me in jail, if I didn't back off. It was like we had arrived in some foreign country.

Carter didn't know what hit him. He was totally humiliated and embarrassed, and I was embarrassed and humiliated for him. He was summarily escorted to the "Colored" section, where he waited, like we did in the "Whites Only" section until the military bus from Parris Island arrived. Carter was literally afraid to exit the waiting room, until he discovered the door leading to the outside area of the depot. The short, fat "station master" was outside also, and continued to be obnoxious and belligerent as he bellowed unnecessary instructions to us about boarding the bus. There were also about a dozen young guys in civilian clothes who streamed out of the station at the same time, and walked toward the bus. A sergeant, who arrived with the bus, quickly assumed the posture of a Drill Instructor, and ordered them to "line up in a single file." They were new Marine Corps recruits, arriving for boot camp. Their training had just begun.

The sergeant, aware of our presence, and seeing that I was carrying the set of orders, looked at me, smiled and said, "Doc, you guys go ahead and get on board." The five of us boarded the bus, shouldering our heavy seabags. Our romance with the Marine Corps had just begun.

During the short trip to the base, Carter was quiet, and spoke only to the M.P.'s as they checked our I.D.'s and the military orders. Although I was still embarrassed about what he had just experienced, I didn't attempt to put him at ease or apologize for the way my "homeland," the south, had just treated him. Except for the three months in boot camp and three months in Dental Technician School, I had spent my entire nineteen years in the south. I loved the south, and I was proud of my heritage. The real truth was that the south was all I knew. Except for two weeks reserve duty at the Great Lakes Navy Base, a recent vacation out west with my family and six months on active duty, I had never been out of the south. I had been just as ignorant about the north as Carter was about the south. However, what a white southern boy had to learn about the north was nothing compared to what a black northern boy had to learn about the south in the years prior to the Civil Rights movement. Carter's hell had just begun, and his experience at the depot that night was a precursor of more to come. I regret that I didn't try in some way to comfort him, or to make light of the experience, just to cheer him up. I did nothing, but I wanted to, and in retrospect, I wish the hell I had.

The early 1950's was a time in our history when the terms, "Blacks" and "Afro-Americans" were not identifying terms used in the south or the north. Instead, we normally used the descriptive terms of "Negros" and "Colored," and to have referred to someone as "black," I assumed, would have been an insult. "Black" was used more as an adjective in a derogatory manner. To use the term "Nigger" would have been intentionally hurtful. However, I honestly believe there were many people in the "old south," who said "Nigger" without intending to be hurtful, although I can't believe that anyone in the south, or the north, did not know that the use of the term was an insult and demeaning to the black citizens.

I knew and still know many people who are good people, but still use the word "Nigger" in conversation, but wouldn't think of using the term in the presence of a black person, out of respect. Many people curse a lot, and some can't open their mouths without uttering some sort of curse word; yet, those same people never say anything close to a curse word in some situations, such as in church, or at gatherings where cursing wouldn't be tolerated. It's due to their respect for the church and others. It's all a matter of establishing bad habits. Someone whom I loved very much, who was as close to being an "angel" as a human can get, and would never intentionally hurt anybody, at her age ninety-three, said, in speaking of a black person she admired, "He is such a nice Nigger." She was speaking privately and honestly, from her heart and mind how she felt about the individual, even though her choice of words could have made it seem otherwise. She was of a great generation of Americans who knew hardships, wars, depressions and unbelievable progress in science, technology, economic justice and social changes. It was her generation that changed the laws to provide equal opportunities to all Americans. However, fifty-eight years ago those laws had not been enacted, and Carter was a victim of a segregationist society that was held together by state and local laws that deemed a segment of our society inferior. He was not afforded equal protection and opportunities, which we four white sailors enjoyed. There was no question of the

"Stationmaster's" intent and belief when he ordered Carter to "Get your black ass over there where you belong."

In the months that followed, Carter's situation didn't get any better as far as he was concerned. He believed he wasn't accepted by the black's in Beaufort, S.C., a beautiful little, coastal town near the base. I suggested he attend their black churches, which he did, but for some reason, he still believed the people were unfriendly, and he didn't feel welcomed. This went on for months, and because he was willing to confide in me, I felt an obligation to help. I thought at the time he was being hard on himself, and believed that he was expecting too much from the churches and the black community. Whatever the real situation was, he was one miserable human being. I knew he had a battle going on within himself, because more than once he shed tears and got a bit emotional about his predicament. Unfortunately, he was the only black sailor in our unit.

On one occasion, my friend and fellow shipmate, Hudson Delmas, of Pascagoula, Mississippi, and I were sitting on the steps of our barracks, just talking and idling the time away. Carter joined us. At some point, a platoon of marines marched by, and the two drill instructors, D.I's, were both black, and all the marines in the platoon were white. Delmas, forgetting that Carter was sitting with us, made an unkind remark, which I believe was, "Look at that, they put two Niggers in charge of that all-white platoon." Delmas, immediately realized his mistake, and apologized to Carter. For some stupid reason, I felt I should apologize to Carter also, and I did. We were all three embarrassed, especially Delmas and Carter. I knew it hurt Carter, and it was obvious. Delmas continued to apologize. I also knew that it was one of those things that you can never undo, no matter how hard you try. I knew Delmas well, and I knew he wouldn't intentionally hurt or embarrass Carter, especially over something that sensitive. Delmas and I stayed in touch after the service, and forty years later, he mentioned to me how bad he felt about that incident. It wasn't long after that incident that Carter managed to get transferred to a Navy base in Virginia, which was closer to his home, and not as volatile, race wise, as South Carolina was. It was the right decision for him to make, but I wish he had not done so.

The decision he made was to take the Navy up on a deal whereby he could extend his enlistment time in return for a transfer. He did this and was transferred to Little Creek, Virginia. While traveling to his new duty station, he was involved in a very serious train wreck. As I understand, he was not injured, but he heroically helped a lot of people escape from the train, and was credited with saving lives. I believe it was written up in the

Navy Times, but I'm not sure about that. A former shipmate, who also was transferred at the same time returned to the base for some reason, and told us about Carter's heroic deeds. Needless to say, we were proud of him.

A short time later, perhaps only weeks later, we learned that Carter had gone to the beach in Virginia with friends from the base, fell off a jetty into the water and drowned. It was news that upset all of us who knew him. There are many ironies of his death, not the least of which is the fact that he was deathly afraid of water. How ironic it is that he should lose his life in an area where he would not have been, if he had not been so miserable because of the injustices he had to endure. I think of Carter often, and I don't know why, but I experience feelings of guilt regarding his death. I know I had nothing to do with his dying, nor could I have prevented it. I didn't make the laws that created the discomfort, humiliation and unhappiness he experienced. In my prayers, I have asked God many times to hold Carter to His bosom, and give him the peace he deserves.

The true story, "My Friend Carter" was first published in the West Florida Literary Federation's *The Emerald Coast Review, XVII*, 2013 Courtesy of WFLF

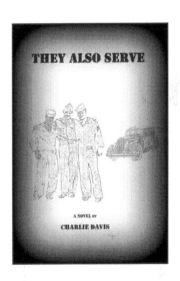

"My Friend Carter" is the basis for the novel by Charlie Davis, They Also Serve, 2013

22

My Friend Charlie

*A true friend is someone who thinks you're a
good egg even though he knows that you're
slightly cracked.*
Bernard Maltzer

 Looking back at past years, I realize I've
been fortunate to have had (and still have) a lot of
friends. Some, like me, are long-time senior
citizens; others, unfortunately, have passed away,
as has my friend, Charlie Evans. This essay is a
fond remembrance of that longtime friendship.

Charlie and I attended Pensacola High School at
the same time. We were in the class of 1951 when the
high school was at the top of Palafox Hill. Unlike today,
very few students had automobiles so when school let out, most students
boarded school buses. Some of us had bicycles or Cushman Motor Scooters,
others joined the parade of students walking down Palafox Street towards
town, some of

whom stopped at Hoppy's, next door to the YMCA, for hamburgers or milkshakes served by E.W. Hopkins, Jr. Charlie lived miles away, west of town, in the Warrington area; I lived in East Pensacola Heights, in the opposite direction. We had some classes together, had a friendly relationship, but didn't socialize other than at school functions. After high school, we didn't see each other until 1953, when we unexpectedly became college roommates at FSU's West Hall. We became good friends.

In 1953, I was released from active duty in the U. S. Navy, stationed at Parris Island, and a few weeks later enrolled as a freshman at FSU. I had raffled off my old 1939 Packard at Parris Island, so my parents drove me to Tallahassee and helped me lug my stuff up to the tenth floor of West Hall. When I unlocked the door and ushered Mom and Dad into my room, we discovered Charlie Evens, clad only in his drawers, stretched out on the top bunk. We all laughed and my mother quickly excused herself while Charlie got dressed. In the weeks and months that followed, we became known as, "the two Charlies from Pensacola." We attended many of the fraternity rush parties and pledged Sigma Alpha Epsilon; the following semester we moved into the SAE fraternity house. It's hard to believe that was sixty-three years ago.

Betty Willis and Charlie Evans ca. 1952

What I remember most about Charlie during that first semester, was how he always talked about a girl named Betty, his girlfriend back home in Pensacola. After a few weeks, I felt like I had known Betty Willis, for years, although I had never met her. Charlie and Betty had been sweethearts since high school days, even though Betty attended Catholic High School. Now I know where Charlie disappeared to each day after school; he must have made a bee-line to Catholic High School, which was only a few blocks away (Garden Street, between Baylen and Spring Streets), to protect his interest. I learned later, after getting to know Betty, that ole Charlie spent as much time with the Willis family at their beach house on Innerarity Point as Betty and her sisters did. That's what I admired about my friend, Charlie Evans—he planned ahead.

I'm not sure why, but Charlie dropped out of college and joined the U.S. Marine Corps. Some of my old buddies in the Post Dental Detachment at Parris Island did what they could, which wasn't much, to make his stay at boot camp more tolerable. All the old wars were over and the new ones had not yet begun, so Cpl. Charles R. Evans, USMC, voluntarily relinquished his dangerous assignment as the general's chauffer, and returned to FSU. This time, he was not alone; the two-hundred miles between Tallahassee and Pensacola must have been more than they could stand, so Charlie and Betty got married and moved into university housing. I too became a married student and, as couples, we enjoyed frequent social visits.

CPL Charles Evans, USMC

An extracurricular activity Charlie and I indulged in while at FSU was making several successful batches of home brew. A former Pensacola Junior College professor, who was working on his doctorate, joined us in the project. As a biologist, he had the formula down pat. We had many fellow students and fraternity brothers volunteering to taste-test the product. Somehow, we "comshawed" (a good ole Navy-Marine Corps term) bottling equipment and supplies, and to the chagrin of my tee totaling neighbor in the duplex, we stored under the apartment building, dozens of cases of twenty-ounce coke and pepsi bottles of Tallahassee's finest home-made beer. Charlie was known to be conservative in more ways than one, so was not exactly pleased when each night, two or three of the bottles exploded. Thus, we decided to drink more frequently to avoid waste. Our friends were willing to help. My neighbor and his wife, both working on their masters, claimed they couldn't sleep.

The years went by and we wound up living in Atlanta at the same time. Our families had grown. We enjoyed visiting with each other and went on occasional camping trips together in the mountains. I was transferred to Tampa and a few years later moved to North Carolina, where I became a realtor. As has been the case with many of our friends from Pensacola who moved away, but eventually returned home, Charlie and Betty did the same. They moved back home and started new careers. When I returned home in 1979, Charlie was a Licensed General Contractor and held a management position with one of Pensacola's larger construction companies. Betty was an established homebuilder, owned her own construction company, and became president of the Homebuilders Association of West Florida in 1987. What was really unique, but surprised nobody, is that in 1990, Charlie also served as the Association's president.

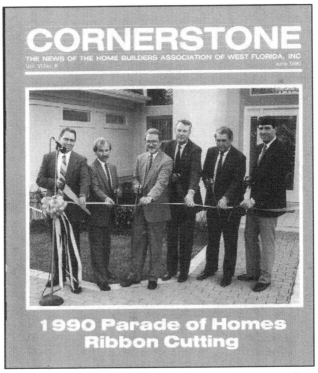

L to R: Home Builders Association, President Charles Evans, John Harold, David Riddle, Mike Underwood, Wilson Robertson and Buzz Ritchie

Charlie and his friend, Josh Carpenter, established Carpenter & Evans, Inc., a successful construction company. In the ensuing years, Charlie and Betty's business ventures in commercial and residential construction, land development, and rental properties flourished, and they enjoyed a well-earned good life with their children, Chuck Evans and Teresa Evans Walsh. Charlie and Betty retired to enjoy their beautiful waterfront home on Innerarity Point to count their blessings and grandchildren.

One of Charlie's pride and joys, in addition to his family, was his yacht, a Trawler, on which Sandra and I enjoyed being dinner guests. I was amused that Charlie seemed to be mostly impressed with the large, shiny, new, diesel engine. It was a beautiful boat, engine and all.

Betty and Charlie on their sailboat

In 2007, Sandra and I joined a large group of Charlie and Betty's family and friends to celebrate their golden wedding anniversary at The Oaks Restaurant on board Pensacola Naval Air Station. As a contractor, Charlie built the club house and restaurant structures years before. It was a great gathering for a great couple.

Charlie and Betty celebrating their daughter, Teresa's wedding in 1985

They were enjoying their retirement years, but unfortunately Charlie's health began to fade. At age 76, he lost his life to cancer on January 18, 2011. He and Betty were married fifty-four years. I was honored to be one of his pallbearers. A proud former marine, Charles Reed Evans was buried at Barrancas National Cemetery aboard NAS Pensacola.

23

The Old County Court House

A few years ago I was invited, along with several other local writers, to read from our individual works that shared a similar theme. I read a short memoir I had written, which was subsequently published in the Emerald Coast Review. The large meeting room in the Bowden Building was filled to capacity, and the crowd showed their appreciation for our readings with loud applause.

When the program ended, some of us lingered to answer questions and share opinions; it was then I noticed the large photograph mounted on one of the walls. It depicted the old Escambia County Court House and Annex, which was situated at the northeast corner of Chase and Palafox Streets. The two buildings, typical of the beautiful architecture of the 1800's were torn down in 1938. What captured my attention, other than the striking beauty of the buildings, was the lineup of county officials in front of the building; actually, they were standing in the parkway across the street from the buildings. Upon

BEN L. DAVIS
CANDIDATE FOR
SUPERVISOR OF
REGISTRATION
ESCAMBIA COUNTY
COURTESY   EFFICIENCY
ACCURACY
I ask your assistance in the Primary
of June 7. Thank you.

close inspection, I recognized my father as one of the officials. At the time he was the Supervisor of Registration. I was mesmerized by the photograph, which was part of the T. T. Wentworth, Jr. Museum collection, and was determined to obtain a copy for myself.

I should include, first, that it was difficult to recognize any of the men in the picture, but I was able to immediately recognize my dad, Ben Davis, because of his big ears. He suffered a lot of ribbing when he was younger because of his ears. I recall hearing that one of his friends told him he looked like a car coming down the street with both doors open. Second, the two buildings were torn down in 1938 to make room for a new federal building that housed the federal courtrooms and post office. The county deeded the property to the federal government in exchange for the U.S. Customs House and Post Office building at the corner of Palafox and Government Streets, which thereafter became the Escambia County Courthouse.

A short time after that meeting, I purchased a copy of the photograph from the Pensacola Historical Society. The back side of the photo listed the name of each of the nineteen county officials and other information. For example, the picture was taken on December 21, 1937 at 2:25 P.M. by "Carter," a notation that the picture was "the only one in existence," plus the identifying number "W.83.84.971." The individuals, reading from left to right, as noted, are:

Frank Parise, T.C. McCoy, E. B. Creighton, H. A. Brosnaham,
J. N. Rauscher, Langley Bell, Bennie Davis, H. E. Page, Forsyth Caro,
T. T. Wentworth, Jr., W. J. McDavid, J. Lawrence Mayo, John Cole,
J. L. Robbins, W. B. Strickland, Sam Rosenau, J. H. Varnum,
John Lewis Reese, and C. B. Fields

Granted, I purchased the photo because it included a picture of my dad, but after learning the identity of the others I was even more pleased. I knew most of them personally, or knew about them through my dad. In fact, E. B. Creighton was my uncle. After all, I was only five years old when "Mr. Carter" took the picture, but many of them were still in office, including my dad, long after I served in the military and graduated from college. I considered writing about this photo and its contents several times before now, but hesitated, knowing just because I've always had a real interest in local politics and those who participate in it, doesn't mean others share that interest.

Running for an elected office in the early years of the last century as the above county officials did, was

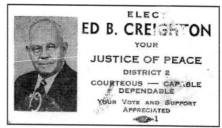

ELEC
ED B. CREIGHTON
YOUR
JUSTICE OF PEACE
DISTRICT 2
COURTEOUS — CAPABLE
DEPENDABLE
YOUR VOTE AND SUPPORT
APPRECIATED
1

much simpler than what's required of an aspiring office seeker today. The cost of running for a local office was mostly borne by the candidate and his family. My parents "hocked the house" every four years when re-election time came around. The majority of campaign expenses went for posters and cards. The posters were put up in grocery stores, businesses, yards and on the automobiles of friends and families. Television didn't exist in those days, and very little money was spent on radio advertising. The cards were handed out to individuals by the candidate and his supporters.

The big draw were the "political rallies," held in schools, churches, parks, and various other locations throughout the county. There was, of course, an occasional fight. Shouting, hissing and booing were normal, but I don't remember anything being thrown. I remember several fights, especially one that occurred at Plaza Ferdinand, about one-hundred feet from the police department. One of my cousins was involved. My maternal grandfather, Capt. William E. (Ed) Brown was running for reelection as the County Harbormaster. It was always a highly contested race between my grandfather and Capt. Bennie Edmundson, a former harbormaster. As a popular song goes, "somebody done somebody wrong," and that's all it took.

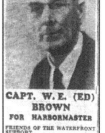

CAPT. W. E. (ED) BROWN
FOR HARBORMASTER
FRIENDS OF THE WATERFRONT

The rallies at the schools were big money-makers because many folks showed up only for the food. My favorite rally was the one held at the East Pensacola Heights Community Center where the ladies served gumbo and fried mullet and grits. I don't remember any fighting there because everybody was too busy eating while the candidates spoke.

When television came along, the old time rallies disappeared because they were being televised from the T.V. stations. I remember holding the prompter for J. B. Hopkins who was running for State Senator; he had written his speech, which I followed okay, but he included a couple of arrows and notes, which I didn't understand so couldn't follow with the prompter causing me to lose him. He had to finish extemporaneously. I was embarrassed and J. B. was a little upset. The "TV Rallies" gave way to individual candidate commercials on both television and radio. This type of advertising ate up a big chunk of the candidate's campaign funds, which came mostly from solicited contributions rather than from the candidate's own pocket.

As the late Tip O'Neill, former Speaker of the U.S. House of Representatives, said: "All Politics is Local." That was true with all the officials in the photo, including those holding office as a state representative. It's been almost eighty years since the picture was taken, but I have researched the voting records in the archives of the Escambia County Supervisor of Registration, known today as the Supervisor of Elections office. I had planned to include a short bio with a political history of each of the officials, but realized it would be too lengthy to do so, however, I have listed each as their name appeared on the ballots and the position they were elected/reelected to. They are from left to right:

1. Frank L. Parise—Escambia County Commissioner—District #1
2. T. C. McCoy—Escambia County Commissioner—District #5
3. Eddie B. Creighton—Escambia County Commissioner—District #4
4. H. A. Brosnaham—Escambia County commissioner—District #3
5. John N. Rauscher—Escambia County Commissioner—District #2
6. Langley Bell—Clerk, Circuit Court
7. Ben L. Davis—Escambia County Supervisor of Registration
8. Harvey E. Page—Escambia County Judge
9. Forsyth Caro—Escambia County Solicitor
10. T. T. Wentworth, Jr.—Escambia County Tax Collector
11. Wiley McDavid—Escambia County Tax Assessor
12. J. Lawrence Mayo—Clerk, Court of Record
13. John W. Cole—Florida House of Representative—Group #1
14. J. L. Robbins—Member, Escambia County School Board—District #3
15. W. B. Strickland-Member, Escambia County School Board—District #1
16. Sam Rosenau—Member, Escambia County School Board—District #2
17. J. H. Varnum—Florida House of Representative—Group #2
18. John Lewis Reese—Escambia County Solicitor
19. C. B. Fields—Unknown—No information available.

(Note: I found no record of a C. B. Fields having been elected to a public office between 1926 and 1940. It's possible he held an appointed position with the county. I suspect this was Clifford Bryant Fields, who later became a well-known Pensacola automobile dealership owner.)

We often hear people speak or react negatively when the subject of politics or politicians comes up. Some have adopted the attitude found in the following quote attributed to Aristophanes, a comic playwright of ancient Athens: "You have all the characteristics of a popular politician: a horrible voice, bad breeding, and a vulgar manner." We've all known politicians that fit that description, and some get elected, but most candidates of that ilk are eventually eliminated at the voting booth. I'm fascinated with politics—I had to be, since a great-grandfather, both grandparents, my dad, my brother, my uncle, and other relatives ran for and were elected to public office. I'm certain as hell that none of them were accustomed to reading the works of Greek philosophers, so that other Greek, Aristotle, must have been right when he wrote, "Man is by nature a political animal."

It's good that we are political animals, because our form of government requires it . . . you know, that "Of, For and By" the people idea. It requires hundreds of thousands of aspiring politicians every two, four, or six years, regardless of their education or status in life, to put their name in the pot, and agree to help run their city, county, state, or federal government, subject to the approval or disapproval of their fellow citizens. It's a simple look at democracy: our form of government. Winston Churchill said, "Democracy is the worse form of government, except for all those other forms of government." This takes us back to those nineteen county officials standing in front of the old county courthouse at 2:25 p.m. on December 21, 1937. They, like thousands and thousands of other elected officials, are the epitome of democracy in action. There are symbols of democracy, in the eyes of the beholder, which was my reaction that evening in the Bowden Building after exercising a couple of amendments to our democratic constitution: freedom of speech and expression.

24

Old PHS Tigers

I knew about the large group of guys, all former Pensacola High School students in my age group and older, who had been getting together for lunch at Hall's Restaurant. Don Allen "Crick" Reynolds, a fellow PHS student, class of 1951, mentioned the group to me and suggested I join him at a future gathering. I put it off, but while researching a story about paperboys for the 2009 publication of *Growing Up In Pensacola,* I met with Robert "Pee Wee" Mackey, and he also mentioned the old PHS group. In fact, he gave me a group picture that was taken a few years earlier. I recognized about half of the guys and most of the other half after Pee Wee told me who they were. Well, what the heck, we all change after a few years—that is, the guys who graduated in the 1940s—those of us in the class of 1951 and later have maintained our youthful images.

Pee Wee promised to remind me about the next luncheon, and he did. I showed up and was pleased to see a lot of guys I hadn't seen in years, some older and some younger. There were only a few I didn't know; I was impressed. They were the movers and shakers of the past and present, representing many different professions and businesses. Most were retired, some long ago, others still working. Several came from out of town; all were glad to see each other. The usual bantering continued to the end of the luncheon. I've been attending the luncheons regularly for the past six years or so, and I'm so glad I have. I wish I had known about it earlier.

I asked George Bokas, (PHS class of 1947), a retired Gulf Breeze pharmacist, how the luncheon got started. He explained that he, Dwight Morrow (known to everyone as O'Malley), and Wiley Bratcher met at the Aegean Breeze Restaurant for lunch, and "decided it would be nice if we could meet every other month with our classmates and close friends and discuss how each of us were getting around in our old age, instead of meeting at funerals." Their first luncheon was on October 30, 2001, when only a few showed up. Eventually the list of those attending grew to around eighty or more. Today, fifteen years later, many classmates have died, so the number of attendees every other month is about half that number.

If I had read the *Pensacola News Journal* article by Taris Savell on January 31, 2004, titled, "Bringing Back Old Memories," I wouldn't have had to ask George Bokas how the luncheon got started. In the article she wrote:

> The idea started as a get-together for just the class of '47. But word spread, and now the luncheons include graduates from about 1942 to 1951. Dr. Reed Bell, class of 1944, is one of the 'older' fellows. 'It's a wonderful get-together,' said Bell, 77. 'It's exciting to see how different we all look, and it's fun renewing old friendships.

Taris Savell quoted George Bokas:

> The men discuss everything from blood pressure and cholesterol levels to the best fishing and golf scores. We rarely talk about politics, and we've never invited the wives because they can start their own club. This is a men's group.

Rudy Twitty, Don Allen "Crick" Reynolds and Tom Psaltis featured in Taris
Savell's article, "Bringing back old memories."
(Courtesy of the *Pensacola News Journal*)

By the time I started attending the luncheons, O'Malley had died and Gordon MacKenzie joined George and Wiley as hosts of the bi-monthly luncheons. They worked hard at reminding the "Old PHS Tigers" about the next gathering. Sadly, Wiley Bratcher died and Tommy McVoy stepped up to the plate. Those of us who have been in similar situations know it's a time consuming and thankless task getting people to a meeting, even when they want to be there. When the reminders are intended for old codgers like us, the job becomes even more difficult, because after all, our schedules are not as flexible as they were when we were working. For example, there's golf and mid-day naps, doctor appointments and morning-naps, and golf and late- afternoon-naps. When you throw in all the honey-do's, trips to the pharmacy, grocery stores and Lowes, we're damn lucky to be at home when George, Gordon, or Tommy calls to remind us. Fortunately, they've gotten up-to-date by reminding us via email, which is good, but some of us have to wait for a grandchild to drop by to read them for us, which may be too late to make the luncheon.

Hall's Restaurant closed, so the gathering place moved down the street a couple of blocks to Franco's Italian Restaurant. We all know it's not the place that counts, it's the people in the place, and that's why it's so enjoyable when we can reminisce together about past similar experiences in that big brick building at the top of the hill. The building's gone, but the memories remain. Can any of us drive past the old high school site without

230

remembering an experience, good or bad, that places us right back inside that old building? I doubt it. On the other hand, there may be one or two of us who won't be able to remember what it was we used to remember.

All kidding aside, all of us who attend the bi-monthly luncheons share a healthy comradery and thoroughly enjoy the many amusing stories, especially when they are told at the expense of another in the room. For some, high school was seventy years ago, but they can recall incidents as though they just happened. What struck me the most about getting together with thirty-five or forty guys at a time who attended the same high school sixty to seventy years ago is how each one has maintained the same personality he had while in high school. Of course, there's been a lot of water under the bridge for all of us, and each one has an interesting and exciting story to tell about his life experiences from the time he graduated from Pensacola High School until now. How great it is that we're still around to add to those life experiences.

As I wrote above, there are many wonderful recollections and stories that develop during the luncheons. I would like to share with you one such story that T. A. Shell, class of 1948, a retired, prominent Pensacola attorney told at a recent luncheon: The PHS Tigers football team was playing archrival, Jesuit High School, in New Orleans. Danny Cunningham was the quarterback and T.A. was the second string quarterback. During the game, Danny had his pants practically ripped apart. Time was called, and Danny had to come out of the game. "Shell," shouted Coach Hugh Blessing, as he looked over at the bench.

"Yes, sir," shouted, T.A., strapping on his helmet, excited that he was finally going to get in the game. Reaching the Coach, he said, "Yes, sir?"

"Give Cunningham your pants," said the coach.

Charlie Davis & T. A. Shell

First row: (kneeling) L to R: Toby Hertz, Tommy McVoy, George Bokas, Roland Brown, Wiley Bratcher, Dwight "O'Malley" Morrow.
Second row: Dwayne Osborne, unnamed, John Kramer, Vic Bokas, Robert "Pee Wee" Mackey.
Third row: Stan Rabin, Tom Psaltis, Earl Lee, Bob Young, Bob LaBounty, unnamed, Ellis Davis.
Fourth row: Ed Allen, Bill "Red" Vickery, Bill Crooke

232

Pensacola High School
Class of 1947 ...
(and there abouts)

Presents To
George Bokas

The hallowed title of ...

P.H. S. Ambassador at Large

And To His "Side Kicks," ... **Wiley Bratcher,
Dwight O'Malley and Gordon MacKensie**

The Almost Hallowed Title Of ...

P.H.S. "Side Kick" Ambassadors

For Their Unfailing Leadership Through The Years, Which Has Provided Us The Unworthy But Grateful, Who "Muddled Through" And Some How Got A Diploma, With Countless MEMORIES ... According To Our Lords Commandment In John13: 34, 35 ...

"A New Commandment I Give Unto You, That Ye Love One Another; As I Have Loved You, That Ye Also Love One Another. By This Shall All Men Know That Ye Are My Disciples, If Ye Have Love One To Another."

... AMEN!

Henry Baggett & Tommy McVoy

Bill & Gerald McArthur

Bill Red Vickrey, Paul Daniels, George VanMatre

Vic Bokas, Larry Scott, & Stan Rabin

George Bokas, Charlie Davis & T. A. Shell

Wiley Bratcher & Gordon MacKensie

Ed Chadbourne, Bill Pennewill, Bill "Red" Vickery, & Dan Walker

Ed Chadborne, Raymond Weekley

Charlie Crooke, Ken Weekley, & Ed Chadborne

Charlie Crooke, Robert "Pee Wee" Mackey, Rudy Twitty & Jerry Hattaway

Dick Mead, George & Vic Bokas

Dick Mead

235

Earl Lee, Jack Gardner, Gene Rosenbaum, and Bob Gaines

Don Rushing

E. W. Hopkins & F. E. Booker

Vic Bokas & Dick Mead

Vic Bokas, Dick Mead & Dan Barberi

Gene & Joe Rosenbaum

Gene Bridges & George VanPelt

George & Vic Bokas

Dan Barbari, Doug Bonifay, Johnny Kramer & George Bokas

George Butler

George Bokas & Roland Brown

Harry Kastanakis, Smitty Nix, Gordon MacKenzie, et. al.

Don McLeod, E. W. Hopkins, Rip Cobb & Skippy Edwards (in background)

Henry Baggett

Hugh Weekley, Johnny Kramer & Roland Brown

Jack Smith

Jimmy & George VanPelt

Bill "Jack" Lay

Bill "Jack" Lay & George Butler

Joe Rosenbaum & Johnny Laritz (in background

Johnny Kramer & Roland Brown

John Broxson

Johnny Kramer, George Bokas, Frank Milstead, & Dan Walker

Gerald & Bill McArthur

239

Charles Butler, Ken Weekley & Henry Baggett

Tommy McVoy, Reed Bell, Billy Renfroe, and Wiley Bratcher

Billy Merritt, Don McLeod & E. W. Hopkins

Monte Barrow & Jake Hammond

Monte Barrow

Bill Pennewill, Bobby LaBounty, Ed Allen, Tommy Crooke, Bill Crooke, & Robert Bruno, et.al.

Dan Walker, Rudy Twitty & Jerry Hattaway

Larry Scott & Monte Barrow

Wayne Sturdivant, Fred Busic & Billy Merritt

T. A. Shell & Billy Renfroe

George VanPelt, Gerald McArthur & Vic Bokas

Gene Booker (left), Dick Mead (right).

241

James Wheeler, Frank Buchanan, Skippy Edwards & Adrian Blanton

George VanPelt, Tom Psaltis, Gerald McArthur, Vic Bokas, & Harry Kastanakas (in background)

Bill "Red" Vickery & Dan Walker

Frank Milsted & Johnny Kramer

Tom Psaltis, Paul Daniels, Robert "Pee Wee" Mackey & George VanMatre

242

January 20, 2003 Luncheon at Hall's Restaurant:
Robert Burke, Bob LaBounty, Ed Chadbourne, T. A. Shell, Billy Renfroe, et. al.

Billy Renfroe Marvin Beck, Bobby Harris, Don Sims,
Bobby Martin, Wayne Sturdivant et. al.

John Stanton, Henry Baggett, & James Wheeler

Earl Lee, Ken Weekley, Bobby Wells &, John Stanton

Marvin Beck, Bobby Harris, Don Sims, Bobby
Martin, Wayne Sturdivant, et. al.

243

Ed Chadbourne, Ken Weekley & Raymond Weekley

Frank Buchanann

Gene Booker

E. W. Hopkins (right)

T. A. Shell (left) &Gerald McArthur (right)

Smitty Nix, Gene Rosenbaum & Eaarl Lee

Jake Hammond & Monte Barrow

Smitty Nix & Earl Lee

NAME	CLASS	NAME	CLASS
Allen, Ed	1947	Davis, Ellis	
Baggett, Henry	1950	Driskell, Jimmy	
Barberi, Dan		Edwards, Skippy	1947
Barrow, Monte		Ellis, Bob	1949
Beck, Marvin		Gaines, Bob	1952
Bell, Reed, Sr.	1945	Gardner, Jack	
Biggs, Walter		Hammond, Jake	
Blanton, Adrian		Harris, Bobby	
Bokas, George	1947	Hattaway, Jerry	
Bokas, Fotios Vic		Hayes, Bill	
Bonifay, Doug		Herring, Frank	1952
Booker, F. E.	1948	Hertz, Toby	
Booker, Gene		Hopkins, Elbert (E. W.)	
Bratcher, Wiley	1947	Humphrey, Lucius	
Bridges, Gene		Johnson, Chris, Jr.	1951
Brown, Jim		Johnson, Henry	
Brown, Roland		Kastanakis, Harry	1947
Broxson, John		Kramer, John	
Bruno, Robert		LaBounty, Bob	1947
Buchanan, Frank	1949	Laritz, Johnnie	
Burke, Robert		Lay, Jack "Bill"	
Busic, Fred	1952	Lee, Earl	1947
Butler, Charles		Lewis, W. T. "Bill"	
Butler, George		MacKenzie, Gordon	1947
Cassimus, Angelo	1950	McVoy, Tommy	
Chadbourne, Ed	1952	Mackey, Robert"Pee Wee"	
Cobb, Rip		McArthur, Bill	1951
Cosson, Harold		McArthur, Gerald	
Crooke, Bill	1948	McCauley, Clyde	
Crooke, Charlie		McLane, Scooter	
Crooke, Tommy	1951	McLeod, Donald	
Crooke, Butch	1957	Martin, Bobby	1952
Crooke, George	1958	Mead, Dick	1945
Daniels, Paul	1951	Merritt, Billy	
Davis, Charlie	1951	Milstead, Frank	

246

NAME	CLASS	NAME	CLASS
Morain, Barne	1953	Smith, Milton	
Morrow, Dwight "O'Malley"		Smith, Richard	
Myers, Edward		Stanton, John	1947
Nass, William H.	1949	Sturdivant, Wayne	
Nix, Smitty		Tringas, John	
Osborne, Dwayne		Twitty, Rudy	1949
Pearlman, Ben		VanMatre, George	
Pennewill, Bill	1953	VanPelt, George	
Pitts, Harvey		VanPelt, Jimmy	1951
Psaltis, Tom	1949	Vickery, Red	
Rabin, Stan		Villar, Emanuel II	1948
Renfroe, Billy		Walker, Dan	1948
Renfroe, Larry	1945	Weekley, Ken	1952
Reynolds, Don Allen		Weekley, Hugh	
Rogers, Larry		Weekley, Raymond	
Rogers, John, L.		Weller, Jack	
Rosenbaum, Gene		Wells, Bobby	1947
Rosenbaum, Joe		Westmark, Ed	
Rushing, Don		Wheeler, James	1950
Scroggins, Jim		Williams, Paul	
Scott, Larry		Yarbrough, Ray	
Sellers, Acy Vance	1945	Young, Bob	
Semmes, Oliver			
Shell, T. A.	1948		
Sherrill, Dick			
Sims, Don	1949		
Smith, Donnel			
Smith, Jack			

25

Pensacola Boxers
& Golden Gloves

Imagine a group of retired, local, good-ole-boys, around a table at the Coffee Cup Restaurant, arguing over who was considered the best local boxer, ever, amateur or professional, from Pensacola. Roy Jones would probably be the first name mentioned, and understandably so, but suppose whoever brought up the subject said, "Before Roy Jones was a household name." Well, then, that would be a whole new ballgame, because over the years Pensacola has produced some great boxers. There was boxing in a big way in the twenties and thirties for a small town like Pensacola. Promoters and their stable of fighters came and went, challenging the local talent in the smokers put on by the Pensacola Athletic Club and other groups. Amateur Boxing grew at the same time, especially after 1923, when Arch Ward, Sports Editor for the Chicago Tribune, conceived the idea of city-wide amateur boxing tournaments sponsored by the newspaper. The concept led to the formation of "Golden Gloves" tournaments around the world.

Row 1: Ralph Chaudron, Billy Cutts, Ernest Kinsley, Terry Olson
Row 2: George Lockwood, Charles Kinsley, Unknown
Row 3: Bill Chavers, Robert "Knub" Kimmons, Others unknown.
Courtesy of Bob Davis

In the mid-1920s and early-1930s, bouts scheduled at the American Legion arena, and the Woodsmen of the World (WOW) arenas included bantam-weight to heavy-weight classes. At the time the contenders were referred to as "prize fighters," which is a familiar term, but I don't believe that description is used today in the boxing world. I've been unable to determine what the "prize" consisted of, but can only assume it was a trophy, a belt, or an amount of money, determined by a "won" or "lost" decision and the amount of gate receipts. One of the most popular local fighters was "Buck" Buchanan, a real scrapper who won most of his fights. Promoters wanted him on the card because he was a crowd-pleaser.

BOND LOSES TO LAWRENCE IN LEGION FIGHT

Benefit Card Is Staged For Buchanan And Large Crowd Attends

By WESLEY CHALK

Nookey Lawrence, 155, won a judges' decision over Joe Bond, 155, in the main bout of a benefit fight card given for Buck Buchanan, Legion fight promoter, last night at the American Legion Arena.

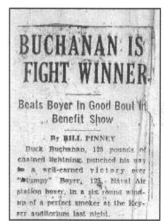

BUCHANAN IS FIGHT WINNER

Beats Boyer In Good Bout In Benefit Show

By BILL PINNEY

Buck Buchanan, 125 pounds of chained lightning, punched his way to a well-earned victory over "Stumpy" Boyer, 125, Naval Air station boxer, in a six round windup of a perfect smoker at the Keyser auditorium last night.

Following is a partial list of local professional boxers during the 1920s and early 1930s:

Charlie Ard	Louis Bond	Nooky Lawrence
Bennie Barberi	Raymond Bond	Charlie Miller
Frankie Barberi	Buck Buchanan	Walter Lagergren
George Bond	David Gafney	Red Shelton
Joe Bond	Len Herring	Sammie Stearns
		Dillon Touart

As written in an April 23, 1926 article in the Pensacola News Journal, regarding the previous night's fights at the Garden Theatre (American Legion Arena):

> The fans were well pleased with the fights last night, and it is believed that boxing is now on its way to popularity again here. B.S. Gillman, promoter, stated during the fights that he is to bring some of the best boxers in the South here to box in some of the future "smokers."

In an undated (1930s) Pensacola News Journal article about local Promoter Victor Kalfus' first boxing card of the season, three of the professional bouts at the American Legion are reported on:

> The semi-final, scheduled for eight rounds, was stopped in the fifth by Referee Charlie Miller, who awarded the decision to Marlin Springer of New Orleans over Pensacola's favorite, Buck Buchanan, who was clearly outclassed.
> Al Powers of the Naval Air Station had no problem with Joe Bond, young Pensacolian making his professional debut. After the local boy had been knocked to the floor several times in the third and fourth rounds, the referee halted the fight in the fifth, giving it to Powers.
> The opening preliminary was a fast go between Red Shelton of Pensacola and Louis Bond, also of this city, with the latter gaining the decision at the end of the third round.

In an October, 1932 article by Pensacola News Journal's popular sports writer, Wesley Chalk, the sub-heading was: "Benefit Card is Staged for Buchanan and Large Crowd Attends." Wesley Chalk elaborates on each bout at the American Legion arena, but to save space I will list only the participants and the results:

1. Nookey Lawrence, 155 lbs. won over Joe Bond, 155 lbs.
2. David Gafney, 148 lbs. won over Charlie Ard, 145 lbs.
3. Sammy Stearns, 128 lbs. and Raymond Bond, 126 lbs. No decision.
4. Sailor Leavery, 128 lbs. won over Norman Smith, 130 lbs.
5. Norman Gonzalez, 118 lbs. won over John Rogers, 118 lbs.
6. Frankie Barberi, 110 lbs. won over Dagny Matis, 118 lbs.
7. Cyclone Boone, 109 lbs. won over Buster Geri, 107 lbs.
8. George Williams, 82 lbs. won over Dempsey Bilbra, 85 lbs.
9. James Kucas, 81 lbs. won over Bert Ard, 86 lbs.

At the end of the article, Wesley Chalk explained the reason for the benefit card:

> The card was given for the benefit of Buchanan whose small daughter* was seriously burned last week and only yesterday was removed to her home from the hospital. The funds from the card will help pay the hospital and doctors' expense and Buck announced last night that he thanks all his friends for their attendance in his behalf.

Buck's daughter, Earlene "Neenie" Buchanan was a personal friend. She also grew up in East Pensacola Heights with her parents and sister, "Nell." She survived her burns, and spent most of her working life as a waitress at Jerry's Drive-In, along with her good friend, Faye. (See chapter on "Miss Faye & Jerry's Drive-In.") Buck Buchanan retired after many years at Muldon Motor Company. He was also into horses and owned a successful riding academy during the WWII years. He, like "Neenie," was well liked and respected.

In 2001, John Appleyard wrote an informative book, titled, Pensacola's YMCA, A Story of Faith, Service, & Community. It is an excellent book, as are all his books. In Chapter 13, "YMCA—Fun and Games," page 58, John explains how Golden Gloves competition became part of Pensac

> Depression years (and radio) encouraged a new sport for the Y: boxing. Clem McCarthy's snarling radio accounts

of big-time fights, and creation of the annual Golden Gloves competition by the Chicago Tribune, attracted a lot of local attention, and the Y found a natural addition to its programs. Training and sparring took place in the gym, and when the Bay Bridge opened, beach promoters got the idea of staging fights there during summer months. Those bouts were scheduled on Tuesdays, and fight fans willingly paid $1 each to make the round trip from Pensacola to the sands.

A lot of good boxers came out of this Y, names like Herb Lockwood, Pete Falzone, Frank Barberi, and Walter Lagergren. Dick Merritt was the coach. Once the Golden Gloves really got going, Pensacola had its own fight team and traveled to other cities or hosted squads from Montgomery, Mobile or Dothan. Pensacola almost always did well, and in 1943, several team members made it to the New York semi-finals. (There they met some fighters who would become big names in the professional ranks; the local boys came home sadder but wiser battlers). Jimmy Butler met and was defeated by Sugar Ray Robinson (the latter's last amateur bout) in the finals of the New York Golden Gloves competition.

Golden Gloves competition in Pensacola and towns along the Gulf Coast grew rapidly, and I recall the crowds at the American Legion and Pensacola High School's gym. The Pensacola YMCA did a great job of promoting the sport, especially after Herbert Lockwood became the boxing coach. Prior to becoming the coach, Herbert and his two younger brothers, George and Frank captured many Golden Gloves titles, and never failed to bring excitement and pride to the matches.

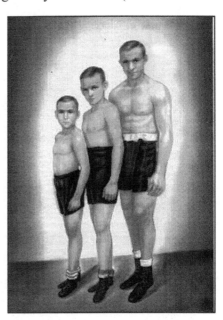

Frank, George and Herbert Lockwood

Herbert Lockwood was a boxer for twenty-three years, and twenty of those he fought as a professional. He was known in the fight game as "Ironman Lockwood," In Golden Gloves competition, he won two Southern lightweight titles, defeated his opponent in the semi-finals in Atlanta, and fought in the Golden gloves finals in Chicago. He was a big asset to the YMCA boxing team, and later, as the YMCA boxing coach, he earned the admiration and respect of hundreds of young men and the community. Herbert also coached boxing at the Police Athletic league, where several of the young boxers later became members of the Pensacola Police Department. The Pensacola YMCA, like most other organizations, had difficulty surviving during the Depression years of the 1930s, as evidenced by the following letter from Julian Olsen of the YMCA to Herbert dated July 2, 1937:

Dear Herbert,-

Your request for the amount of money expended for laundry and dry cleaning amounting to $2.65 was received and I regret that I cannot help you at this time.

Whatever is done will have to be done personally by me and since it has been many years since I have paid fifteen cents for cleaning a shirt it is also difficult for me to dig up the $2.65 to help you out. However, I will make every effort to do something for you soon.

Sincerely,

Julian Olsen

July 2, 1937

Note: Julian Olsen, instrumental in the growth of the Pensacola YMCA, later became the Superintendent of Recreation for the City of Pensacola.

George Lockwood

George Lockwood was one of Pensacola's great amateur fighters, second only to his big brother, Herbert. George won the Southeastern A. A. U. 90 and 100 pound titles, and later won the flyweight crown. He also won the southern Golden Gloves flyweight title, and fought in the New York Golden Gloves finals. Later, he won the Golden Gloves featherweight title. He was on his way to a promising boxing career, which unfortunately was

Herbert Lockwood and the George Lockwood Memorial Bench

cut short by World War II. George joined the U.S. Navy two days after Japan attacked Pearl Harbor, and subsequently scored six knockouts in fleet competition.

Nine months after joining the Navy, George Lockwood, age 18, was killed in action on August 9, 1942, when his ship, the heavy cruiser, USS *Vincennes* (CA-44), was attacked and sunk in the Battle of Savo Island (Solomon's Group) in the South Pacific. George survived the initial attacks by torpedoes and heavy gunfire from Japanese ships, but after abandoning ship as ordered by the captain, he swam back to help rescue a wounded shipmate; a torpedo struck the ship's magazine and George died, along with 332 fellow crewmen. He was the first serviceman from Pensacola to be killed in World War II.

The City of Pensacola established a memorial to George on the parkway near the intersection of Gregory and Palafox, in the form of a marble bench bearing his name, which was donated by Mr. and Mrs. Gene Trader. At the memorial service, Pensacola's City attorney, Churchill Mellen, made the following comments:

George made the supreme sacrifice, and by doing so set an example of courage and valor for coming generations of the city of Pensacola. His valor and courage in returning to the ship to rescue a mate will be one of the outstanding memories for we in Pensacola to carry for the rest of our lives in referring to World War II. As we pass this corner in years to come we will be reminded of the courage and valor of George Lockwood.

On August 9, 2003, sixty-one years after George's death, the memorial bench was replaced with an exact replica and installed near the World War II Memorial at the Veterans Memorial Park. The original bench was placed in the Holy Cross Cemetery near the gravesites of George's parents.

Industrial School Boxers Lose to YMCA Mitters, 6-4

By JERRY DOCK
Staff Sports Writer

The local YMCA boxers defeated a game Florida Industrial team from Marianna last night at Legion Arena, six matches to four.

The Marianna fighters were often outboxed, but all gave a good show.

Probably the best bout of the evening was between James Mitchell, 95-pounder from the YMCA, and Delma Blackburn, 95, from FIS. The boys slugged hard throughout the three rounds, Mitchell getting an unanimous decision.

Roy Grund, clever 118-pound "Y" boxer, felled 124-pound Pete McClellan for a count of nine in the first round with a left to the body, but was unable to KO the less experienced FIS fighter.

LOCKWOOD WINS

Veteran Frank Lockwood, 146-pound YMCA slugger, gained an unanimous decision from Franklin Edwards, 142. Lockwood staggered his FIS opponent several times, but he refused to go down.

Throwing lefty left jabs, Lucian Mitchell, 126, gained an unanimous decision over Lucious Layton, 130, FIS slugger.

Huey Courtney, 92-pound local boy, gained a clear split decision over James Burk, 88.

Long-armed Roy Norton, 98, gained a split decision over Charlie King, 95, of YMCA. Norton swung a wicked left jab and kept King away from him.

Jack Melvin, 112-pounder from FIS, gained an unanimous decision over Charlie Peterson, 112. Melvin was given the first two rounds, but Peterson fought back in the third but it was not enough for a win.

MANN WINS AGAIN

Larry Mann, 177, from FIS, gained an unanimous decision over Tommy Hatcher, 134, carrying the fight all the way.

Ralph Travis, 183, gained an unanimous decision over 160-pound Irvin Schultz, FIS.

Officials were: Timekeeper, Bennie Barbieri; referee, Fritz Are; and Henry Cohron; judges, Jack Fusell, Henry Thorsen and Fred DeFranco; announcer, Jack Petric.

Frank Lockwood, the youngest of the three brothers,
made his own mark in amateur boxing.
Source: Pensacola News Journal

257

Following is a partial list of local Golden Gloves boxers in the 1930s through the 1940s

Bob Archambeault	Lewis Edwards	Billy Miller
Fritz Ard	Nino Falzone	Lamar Miller
Grady Baker	Peter Falzone	James Mitchell
Bennie Barbari	Joe Fields	Lucian Mitchell
Frankie Barbari	Jimmy Fortune	Dwight "O'Malley
Marcus Bartlett	Johnny Fortune	Morrow
S. J. Bell	Maurice Frye	Peck Norris
Bill Butler	Billy Gregory	Terry Olsen
Clem Bonifay	Ray Grund	Lent Peaden
Earl Bonifay	J. C. Hatcher	Eddie Pericola
Harry Bonifay	Tommy Hatcher	Charles Peterson
Cecil Bragg	Ray Johnson	Gene Pfeiffer
Jimmy Butler	Robert Kimmons	Lester Pooley
Billy Byrd	Charles King	JimmyReese
Homer Cantrell	Charles Kinsley	Alton Robbins
George Catches	Ernest Kinsley	Ralph Rogers
Johnny Catches	Walter Lagergren	Ellis Starkie
Bill Chavers	George Lockwood	George Starkie
Ralph Chaudron	Frank Lockwood	Don Strickland
Roy Cooke	Herbert Lockwood	Carlos Sweeney
Huey Courtney	Pratt Martin, Jr.	Melvin Sweeney
Billy Cutts	Terry McCall	Pugh Tidwell
Bill Davis	Johnny McGrath	Ralph Travis
Raymond Davis	Carlton Melvin	Tom Ward
Freddie DeFranko	David Meredith	Sam Whitwell
		Eugene Yuhasz

Golden Gloves Boxing has continued to grow in the United States and around the world, and includes a female division, but has diminished in activity in Northwest Florida. Today, National Golden Gloves of America, Inc. has thirty franchises, which sponsor hundreds of programs competing in local and regional tournaments throughout the United States, and a National tournament of Champions each year.

Florida Golden Gloves, one of the thirty franchises, is owned by Lou Martinez, who also owns the Palm Beach Boxing Center. I spoke with Lou and inquired about the possibility of having Golden Gloves competition in Pensacola again sometime in the future. He assured me that he would welcome sponsors from the area. Perhaps the leadership at Pensacola area once the new YMCA is completed. Many of my friends and I have fond memories of when Golden Gloves was well represented in Pensacola. You'd be surprised how many of our current and former civic, business, and professional leaders duked it out for three rounds at the American Legion Arena and Pensacola High School's gym during those locally sponsored Golden Gloves tournaments.

We'll never know who that local group of retired, good-ole-boys, sitting around the table at the Coffee Cup Restaurant selected as the best local boxer from Pensacola, but I wouldn't be surprised if they chose Herbert Lockwood. He would be my choice.

Above Left: Herbert and his father, Charles
Herbert Lockwood

Above Right: Herbert & George
Lockwood

THAT'S IT, FELLERS!—Herbert Lockwood, coach of the Pensacola "Y" boxing team, watches two of his protegee work out in the "Y" gym for Golden Gloves tournaments. Billy Gregory (left) will defend his title in the Pensacola meet, while George Catches (right) is going to the Jacksonville tournament. (Photo by Sam Carlos Studio.)

"Y" FIGHTER GETS INSTRUCTIONS—Herbert Lockwood, left, former Southern Golden Gloves champion and YMCA boxing coach, gives Roy Cooke, "Y" featherweight, last minute instructions before a recent fight. On the right is Carlton Melvin, another "Y" fighter.

Above: Billy Gregory vs. George Catches

Left: Herbert Lockwood instructs Roy
Cooke. Assisted by Carlton Melvin.

260

GOLDEN GLOVES NOVICE CHAMPIONS—Pictured above are the 11 winners of novice championships in the Gulf States Golden Gloves boxing tournament completed last week at the Legion arena. Reading from left to right, front row: Hughey Courtney, "skeetersweight," YMCA; Billy Byrd, "paperweight," unattached; Tom Ward, "netweight," Molino FFA; and Gene Pfeiffer, "goosesweight," YMCA. Back row: Eugene Tabaas, flyweight, Molino FFA; McGrin Sweeney, bantamweight, Bagdad; Allen Robbins, featherweight, Walnut Hill FFA; E. J. Bell, lightweight, YMCA; Terry McColl, welterweight, Walnut Hill FFA; Carlos Sweeney, middleweight, Okaloosa county, and Lem Braden, heavyweight, Bagdad.

BOXING CHAMPS—Here are the champions of the Gulf Coast Golden Gloves boxing meet staged last month at the Pensacola "Y." Left to right, kneeling, Ralph Rogers, Pensacola Y, novice 126-pounder; Jimmy Fortune, Laurel Hill, novice 135, Lionel Valdez, of Florida Industrial School, member of the Panama City team, open 112, Roy Cooke, Y, open 118, Ellis Starkie, Walnut Hill, open 135, and Cecil Bragg, Y, open 126. Standing, Bob Archembault, Fort Barrancas, novice 147, Wallie Tarranto, Biloxi, Miss., open 147, Marcus Bartlett, Walnut Hill, novice 160, Raymond Davis, Walnut Hill, novice 175, Homer Cantrell, Y, open 175, George Catches, Y, open 160 and Price, Y, runner-up, novice 175. (Edal's Studio Photo)

Golden Gloves Boys at the YMCA

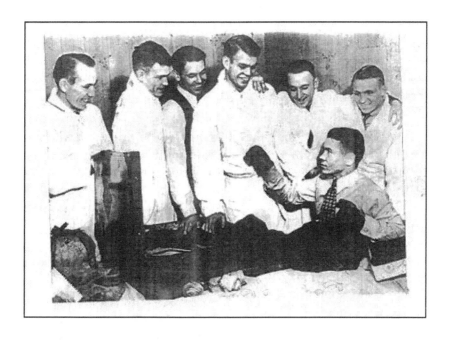

★ ★ ★ ★

S. J. BELL
... novice performer

Bell Is Hopes For New Title

YMCA Boxer Offered As Threat to Crown

Of the many novice fighters working out three times each week at the YMCA in preparation for the coming Gulf Coast Golden Gloves Boxing tournament, Coach Herbert Lockwood believes S. J. Bell, a lightweight, to be one of the most promising.

Only five feet, six inches tall, Bell is solidly built and tips the beam at an even 135 pounds. Although he has had little previous experience in the ring, Bell boxes well and packs a hard wallop in either hand.

Bell was graduated from Catholic high school last year and was a standout lineman on the Crusader football team. He is 18 years old.

This year's tournament, to be held Feb. 24-26 at Legion arena, is expected to attract a large number of simon pure mittmen from Northwest Florida and the gulf coast.

Approximately 30 entries already have been received, Oscar Brock, tournament secretary, said Monday. Included among the entries received are 10 from the FFA chapter at Walnut Hill.

Jim Barrineau, Walnut Hill coach, will bring down a number of good fighters including Ellis Starkie, defending lightweight champion in the division. Ellis is one of four Starkie brothers who will perform for the Future Farmers.

Ellis Starkie's entry brings to three the number of defending champions who definitely will be back to defend their laurels. Others are Roy Cooke, bantamweight champ, and Cecil Bragg, featherweight ruler, both of the YMCA.

BEST SPORTSMAN AND COACH — Pratt Martin, Jr., (left) received the West Florida Sportsman's trophy for outstanding sportsmanship in the Golden Gloves tournament. On the right is Herbert Lockwood, Pensacola "Y" coach. (Edal's Studio Photo)

"Old Timers" Trade Blows For Boys Ranch

"Old Timers" included (from left) Nemo Falzone, Sheriff Bill Davis, Fritz Ard, Sgt. O. V. Regan and Herbert Lockwood

The Pensacola Journal   Saturday, December 19, 1970

LOCKWOOD RETIRES — Fellow employees of Herbert Lockwood (center) at the City Parks and Recreation Department Friday presented the long time city employee with a mechanical chain saw. The occasion was retirement ceremonies for Lockwood with the city. Looking on as Lockwood examines his gift is Vic Odom, left, Superintendent of Parks and Jimmy Hitzman, right, Pensacola Parks and Recreation Director. Lockwood is retiring to go into the landscaping business. Lockwood is a former heavyweight

News Journal
PENSACOLA

Thursday, December 7, 1995

SNAPSHOT

Know someone to spotlight in a snapshot? Call us at 435-8519

HERBERT LOCKWOOD

Age: His 80th birthday is today. Family and friends celebrated his birthday Dec. 2 at Sanders Beach.

Family: Lockwood has four children — Charles Lockwood, Sharon Fletcher, Connie Fell and Doris Falzone. He also has eight granddaughters and six great-grandchildren.

My hometown is: Pensacola, born and raised here.

Career: He worked for the City of Pensacola for 30 years and was foreman of park department. After he retired in 1970, Lockwood worked in landscaping.

Boxing history: Lockwood was a boxer for 23 years and was a professional for at least 20 years. He was known as Ironman Lockwood. His son says in all those years he was never knocked out. He coached boxing to young boys for a number of years with the YMCA and the Police Athletic league. The boys ranged in age from 10 to 21. At one time he was training about 180 boys at YMCA. He was well known by members of the police department through his work. Some of those boys he coached have grown up to become policemen.

*Photographs, newspaper articles and biographical information courtesy of Ms. Barbara Lockwood

26

The Pensacola Interstate Fair

Eighty years ago, in 1935, the Pensacola Interstate Fair began on the corner of Cervantes Street and "O" Street (now Pace Boulevard). It was, as some would say, in the heart of Brownsville, the same corner where the Barnum & Bailey Circus erected their Big Top each year. It wasn't the first fair in Escambia County; there were county fairs as early as 1913 at the popular Kupfrian Park, located near where Baptist Hospital is situated today. I recall how my mother, who was born in 1902, spoke of the good times she and her young friends had at Kupfrian Park after riding the trolley there and back. Unfortunately, the fair had problems and eventually stopped.

John E. Frenkel, Sr.

It was several years before the citizens of Pensacola and surrounding communities had a fair of their own to attend, but thanks to the late

Aerial view of the Pensacola Interstate Fair

John E. Frenkel, Sr., a man of vision, who, like on other occasions, saw an opportunity to be of service to his community.[1] Through his foresight and leadership the Pensacola Interstate Fair has progressed, uninterrupted, for eighty years as of this year, 2015.

In 1935, John E. Frenkel, Sr. was the City Clerk for the City of Pensacola and the City Permitting Agent. At the request of Mr. Whittie Weis of Royal American Shows, he began the Pensacola Interstate Fair. The Royal American, a railroad carnival that moved from location to location by rail, was the largest traveling carnival in the United States. According to current fair officials, it seems Mr. Weis and Royal American Shows ended their tour somewhere in Alabama each year. He believed Pensacola would be the ideal location to have one more show before spending the winters in Florida and prevailed upon Johnnie Frenkel to assemble a group of citizens to start the Pensacola Interstate Fair. Mr. Weis was aware of Johnnie Frenkel's experience in promoting Pensacola's first radio station, WCOA, Mardi Gras and other local events and believed he was well equipped to take on the fair. He was correct.

In 1936, the fair's second year, it moved a few blocks south to the corner of Garden Street and Pace Boulevard. With experience and the community's support, the Pensacola Interstate Fair grew. In 1940, the Fair

John Frenkel, Sr., T. T. Wentworth, Jr., Ms. Fairest of Fair, Mr. Blount, Governor and Mrs. Leroy Collins, Charlie Curler and John Frenkel, Jr.

purchased its first permanent location on Pottery Plant Road, later known as Fairfield Drive. My fondest memories of the Fair are while it was at this location; first with my parents and siblings, then with my friends, and later with my wife and kids. As I write this essay, I occasionally, nostalgically remember the dust, the loud noises, the aroma of cooked food mixed in with the odors from the livestock barns. I enjoyed the rides like any other kid or grown-up, but I mostly enjoyed watching the people enjoy the fair, especially the children.

In 1942, the Fair was reorganized as a non-profit organization. It's charter was locally incorporated by the Board of County Commissioners and verified by County Judge Fabasinski, rather than through the State of Florida.

In 1963, as a member of the Northwest Florida Zoological Society, I worked alongside other members for several days while developing our exhibit of zoo animals at the Fair, most of which we borrowed from the Audubon Park Zoo in New Orleans. We were seeking support from the public in our effort to start the Pensacola Zoo.[2] I was amazed at the amount of work that was required prior to opening day from all Fair participants, including Fair officials, ride operators, food vendors, and exhibitors from fields in Agriculture, Education, Entertainment, Science, Livestock and Poultry, Culture, Commerce and Industry. It wouldn't be a stretch to say it was like "Old MacDonald's Farm," in the middle of a gigantic construction site under the watchful eyes of the "Keystone Cops." Some might consider the whole operation a "Chinese Fire Drill," for truly it was a major operation, yet the Pensacola Interstate Fair has continued to grow in each of its eighty year history.

The Fair progressed for over twenty years at the Fairfield Drive location until that property was sold for a local development (Builder's Square). In 1968, the Fair purchased property at 6665 Mobile Highway in Pensacola. (Highway 90). Construction began immediately on the fairground, which was built from the ground up. The Fair was held at the new location in 1969. The Fair currently owns over one-hundred-seventy acres at the site.

John E. Frenkel, Sr's extraordinary life came to an end on February 17, 1988. He was ninety-four years old. His two sons, John, Jr. and Don already had management positions at the Fair, in addition to their own demanding personal careers. John E. Frenkel, Jr. joined the Fair in July of 1963 as Assistant General Manager, Secretary, and Treasurer. He helped develop the fair as the years passed and became the General Manager, Secretary, and Treasurer in 1975. During those years he also served as City Councilman from 1967 through 1977, and County Commissioner from 1978 through 1982. Sadly, John died in 2008. Don E. Frenkel is currently the Fair's General Manager and member of the board of directors. He is retired from Fisher-Brown Insurance.

Following are some additional facts about the Pensacola Interstate Fair which I believe the public would appreciate knowing:

1. The Fair is a licensed business operating 365 days a year and serves the useful purpose of providing the facilities for the development of Agricultural, Educational, Scientific, Livestock, Cultural and Commercial resources of the community and surrounding area.

2. Every year the Fair generates over $8 million dollars of consumer spending in the local economy and is proud to be a major part of Pensacola's economy.

3. Of the Fair's $2.5 million budget, 80% is spent and stays in our local economy.

4. The Fair operates SOLELY and ONLY from the proceeds derived from its annual Fair. It does not receive any subsidy or any financial aid from any source: City, County, State, Federal or Business Organizations.

5. The Fair generates over 300 jobs each year for our local economy.

6. The Fair gives $30,000 a year in scholarships to local students and since 1983, has given over $955,000 to more than 1,016 students to further their education. In addition, the Fair has endowed scholarships through the Pensacola State College Foundation.

7. The Fair awards over $100,000 in prize money to exhibitors every year.

8. The Fair provides an atmosphere of entertainment and fun for the Whole Family.

9. The Fair provides an opportunity for local citizens to showcase their talents and hobbies each year.

10. The Fair is actually a non-profit corporation run by a Board of Directors representing all walks of life and residential areas of Pensacola.

Officers, Directors and Members of the Pensacola Interstate Fair:
Officers:

Gil Bennett	President
Gene Rosenbaum	Vice President
Don Frenkel	General Manager/Director
Felecia Chivington	Assistant Manager
John Frenkel III	Operations Manager/Administrative Assistant
Natalee Brooks	Concessions Manager
Dondi Frenkel	Webmaster and Front Gate Supervisor

Officers

Gil Bennett,
President

Gene Rosenbaum
Vice President

Don Frenkel
General
Manager/Director

Felecia Chivington
Assistant Manager

John Frenkel III
Operations Manager
Admin Assistant

Natalee Brooks
Concessions Manager

Dondi Frenkel
Webmaster and
Front Gate Supervisor

Directors:

Dr. John B. Webb	President Emeritus/Veterinarian
Charles Carlan	Pres.-Hatch Mott McDonald, Arch., Eng. & Surveyors
Ashton Hayward	Territorial Manager, Southdown, Inc.
Harry Kahn	President (Retired), Kahn Entertainment
Edward R. Mills	President, Langford and Mills
Lewis Bear, Jr.	President, The Lewis Bear Company
Bill Farinas, Jr.	Horticulture/Instructor, George Stone Center
Lesa Morgan	Principal, West Florida High School

Members:

Walter F. Biggs, Jr.	Sun Trust Bank (Retired)
Pat Mills Benjamin	President, Gulf Coast Paving & Grading (Retired)
William "Bill" Bond, Sr.	CCPO, Pensacola Naval Air Station
H. Miller Caldwell, Jr.	Architect, Caldwell Associates
E. J. Gowen	County Extension Director (Retired)
Jeff Rogers	Corp. Communications Mgr., Gulf Power Company
Fredrick G. Levin	Attorney
Dr. Philip J. Levine	Forensic Dentistry
Kathryn Errington	Program Attorney, State of Florida, Guardian Ad Litem
George VanPelt	VanPelt Brothers, Dairy and Food Mart
Danny J. Cobb	President, D. J. Cobb Construction Co., Inc.
Andy Peterson	Small Business Owner/Rancher
Ellis W. Bullock III	President, E. W. Bullock and Associates
Dr. William Spain	Chiropractor

Directors

Dr. John B. Webb
President Emeritus
Veterinarian

Charles Carlan
Pres. Hatch Mott
McDonald, Arch., Eng.
& Surveyors

Ashton Hayward
Territorial Manager
Southdown, Inc.

Harry Kahn
President (Ret.)
Kahn Entertainment

Edward R. Mills
President
Langford and Mills

Lewis Bear, Jr.
President
Lewis Bear Company

Bill Farinas, Jr.
Horticulture Instructor
George Stone Center

Lesa Morgan
Principal
West Florida HS

Members

Walter F. Biggs, Jr.
Sun Trust Bank
(Ret)

Pat Mills Benjamin
President, Gulf Coast
Paving & Grading
(Ret.)

William "Bill" Bond
CCPO, Pensacola
Naval Air Station

H. Miller Caldwell, Jr.
Architect, Caldwell
Associates

E. J. Gowen
Count Extension
Director (Ret.)

Jeff Rogers
Corp. Communications
Mgr.,
Gulf Power Company

Fredrick Levin
Attorney

Dr. Philip J. Levine
Forensic Dentistry

Kathryn Errington
Program Attorney,
State of Florida,
Guardian Ad L

George VanPelt
VanPelt Brothers,
Dairy and
Food Mart

Danny J. Cobb
President
D. J. Cobb
Construction Company,
Inc.

Andy Peterson,
Small Business Owner
Rancher

Ellis W. Bullock, III
President
E. W. Bullock and
Associates

Dr. William Spain
Chiropractor

The Pensacola Interstate Fair is unique in many ways. It not only provides entertainment, but also supports important community organizations and businesses. Without the Fair, some of these causes might go unnoticed or even cease to exist. For local Future Farmers of America (FFA) chapters, the Fair is a vital part of the curriculum, as well as a place for competition and exhibition. The local economy benefits, since the Fair offers small businesses an inexpensive way to exhibit their products and services in their own community; thus the hometown folks can recognize the resources that exist in their own backyards. The phrase, "something for everyone," hangs true at the Pensacola Interstate Fair as there's something for all ages. "Multi-generational Entertainment," is what the professional

Fair Managers call it, because there aren't many other events that can pull a community together like an annual fair.

No one can dispute that the Pensacola Interstate Fair is a monumental success story. Much credit is due the many Frenkel family members who have worked tirelessly over the years to assure the Fair's success. Equal credit is due others who devoted their time and efforts as managers, officers, board members, and members in an advisory capacity. One only needs to review the caliber of the above list of individuals to understand why the Fair has been so successful. Those who knew Johnny Frenkel know he's proud of the Fair's success. If you listen real good, and use a little imagination, you might hear "the breezy boy from the gulf" singing his theme song, *Down Pensacola Way.*

Pictures and information courtesy of Mr. Don Frenkel
[1] See chapter in this volume titled, "John F. Frenkel, Sr."
[2] The Pensacola Zoo became a reality. See Chapter 36 in <u>Growing Up in Pensacola,</u> Volume I, titled, "The Old Pensacola Zoo."

T. T. Wentworth, Jr, John Frenkel, Sr., and other dignitaries break ground
for the Fair's new location on Mobile Highway

Above: Mr. & Mrs. John Frenkel, Sr. and Bob Box

Below: Miss Eglin 1960, Marta Weitling and John Frenkel, Sr.

Above: T. T. Wentworth, Jr., John Frenkel, Sr., Governor Ferris Bryant, Roy Philpot and others open the Fair.

Below: John Frenkel, Jr. and John Frenkel, Sr.

27

PHS Class of 1951 Reunions & Luncheons

The Korean War was raging when the 392 students in Pensacola High School's Class of 1951 graduated, and it wasn't long before most of the guys were scattered around the country, attending military boot camps, basic training or enrolled in some distant college ROTC program. As for the gals, some married their high school sweethearts; others went off to college or to work. With the nation at war, it was difficult to plan a future, which had turned more uncertain a few months before graduation when Communist China entered the conflict on the side of North Korea. In

Pensacola High School

1953, when the fighting stopped, most of us returned home to resume our future plans.

I wasn't the smartest kid in Mrs. Priest's math class, but I believe I'm correct about it being 65 years since graduation. I feel safe with that assumption, especially since we recently had our 65th class reunion. Like many of my classmates, I left my beloved hometown for a few years of military obligations, college attendance and employment. It may not be a phenomenon, but it sure is unique how so many of us who moved away eventually moved back. We were like the swallows of Capistrano, or perhaps more appropriate, the sea turtles that return to Pensacola Beach. The late Vince Whibbs, Mayor of Pensacola, was correct when he described Pensacola as, "The city where thousands live and play and millions wished they did." A recent count shows about one-third of our class lives somewhere other than Pensacola, but we're always glad to see them, especially when they return for a reunion or one of the quarterly lunches.

I didn't start attending the PHS Class of 1951 luncheons until sometime in the late 1990s, so my first Reunion was the 50th in 2001. I was amazed at the number of alumni in attendance. Most impressive was the large number of out-of-town classmates who returned for the festivities. I thought it was great that only a small percentage of classmates had died at that time; one of them, sadly, my good friend, John Browder.

Dan and Evelyn Thaxton McLeod

As of 2016, according to Evelyn and Dan McLeod, who have worked tirelessly along with the committee members to co-ordinate the luncheons and reunions, the known number of classmates who have died is 136. The committee members are still in contact with 183 classmates. With these figures, we can safely assume that half of our classmates are alive today. Not bad, considering the life expectancy for both male and females born in the early 1930's was about age 62, and all surviving classmates of the 1951 senior class are in their early 80's today. Mrs. Priest is probably up there smiling at my brilliant calculations and assumptions, but I hope she's forgotten that I barely passed her class.

We were fortunate to have had good teachers, administrators and coaches at PHS, and I'm grateful, as I'm sure my classmates are, that we

2016 Reunion Committee

Ann Thames Bennfoy
Chairperson

DeLane Floyd Ackerman

John Eichelberger

Tom & Evelyn Thaxton McLeod
Secretary/Treasurer

Josmine Miller Pritchett

Duane Jones Ingram, Sunshine Chairman

-4-

2016 Reunion Committee

Avis & Tom Tolbert

Jackie Boggett Patterson

Carolyn Brooks Jones

Pat & Nicholas Hutchings

-5-

281

didn't have the many non-classroom problems and concerns that our own children, grandchildren and great-grandchildren have experienced. Thank God we didn't have a drug problem back then; however, the teachers, preachers, principals, school board members and our parents told us we were going to hell for smoking those nasty ole cigarettes. They might have been nasty, but they went well with the beer we could often purchase illegally at our favorite hangouts such as the *Scenic Terrace, Nob Hill* and *Jerry's Drive In.* I look back on those places with fond memories and many reasons to smile.

Okay, so we would sneak a beer or two, which was not so bad when you consider the things that go on today with teenagers. We had our share of bars and clubs that would serve us young adults in those days. Occasionally groups would gather at *Carpenter's* in Warrington for cocktails, a delicious meal and dance to a great band. That would have been a special date. However, a typical Friday or Saturday night date during our senior year would have been to attend a movie at one of the local theaters downtown, like the *Florida, Rex, Isis* or the *Saenger.* Afterwards, we would probably "Drag the Main," then go to one of the many "Drive-In's" for a hamburger before heading to the "Terrace" (The Scenic Terrace in East Pensacola Heights) to meet up with friends. By then, George Jordan's popular place would be crowded with guys and gals from PHS, Catholic High School, and Tate High School, plus college students home for the weekend. In addition, there were older friends who had graduated from high school and college years earlier. For some, there was the side-trip to places like "Ski-Jump Road" near Bayou Texar to watch the moon for a while before taking their dates home.

In 1951, Pensacola High School was a huge, classic red brick building at the top of Palafox Hill, a block south of Cervantes Street. I didn't think much about it then, but the building took up almost the entire square block; there was no campus, with barely enough room for the teachers to park their cars. I attended Pensacola Junior College when it occupied the building after PHS moved into their new location, and I get a bit confused about some of the teachers who taught at PHS and later at PJC, like Miss Virginia Tyler. I often think about Miss Tyler, who was a good English teacher. I know she's up there somewhere with Mrs. Priest, admiring what her former students have accomplished over these past sixty-five years. I suspect, however, that she's also shaking her head in wonderment that I am actually capable of writing a complete sentence. She was a wonderful person, and patient with me, because as a paperboy I never got enough sleep and was always nodding off in her class. I suspect I passed her class only because while at Clubbs Jr. High, I was particularly fond of her niece, Patsy Tyler. I'm kidding, of course—not about my fondness for Patsy, as I have a small box of love letters my mother secretly saved for me as proof—but I'm sure I passed on my own, in spite of those incomplete sentences.

When I reminisce about PHS, I usually picture in my mind the football games at Legion Field and later at the new stadium. Sometimes I also think about Mr. McCord, the Principal, and how he was always standing out in the hall and kinda sliding along the wall. Now, these remembrances were not exactly the highlights of my high school career. There were some highlights, but frankly I'm reluctant to write about them. I should mention that I often visualize the hordes of fellow students walking down the sidewalks of Palafox Hill towards the downtown area minutes after school "let out". Everybody seemed to be in a hurry to get to where they were going, but some would stop at "Hoppys," a favorite after-school hangout about halfway down the hill known for its hamburgers and milkshakes. Aside from the good food, it was a place where kids were welcomed to just be there with their friends, either inside or outside under the huge oak trees. I always thought of "Hoppy's" years later when watching the TV sitcom, *Happy Days.* We alumni of PHS could relate to that program perhaps more than others, because we had our share of characters like "Fonzi" and "Richie".

Except for real close friends, I never thought much about how others in our class fared in their chosen careers, but it became obvious over the past few years that they did well for themselves. Our class produced a fair share of doctors, lawyers and Indian chiefs, plus salespersons, business owners, farmers, military professionals and a great bunch of educators. I believe it's safe to assume all our faculty members made it up there with Miss Tyler and Mrs. Priest, however, I can think of a couple who might have been required to take a few make-up tests first. All would have congratulated each other for a job well done for their part in preparing us to meet the challenges of an uncertain world in 1951.

It wasn't the best of times, or the worst of times, but we didn't let a good cliché get in our way. The war ended, we got married (some of us more than once), we had kids, our kids had kids, and now those kids are having kids. What happened? We got old—that's what happened, but ain't it wonderful? So, what if we are in the last act of some play, as the bards would say, yet we're glad we're here. The late Ogden Nash wrote:

One day a bachelor, the next a grampa.
What is the secret of the trick?
How did I get so old so quick?
                    And
Here lies my past. Good-Bye I have kissed it;
Thank you kids. I wouldn't have missed it.
                    Ogden Nash
            You Can't Get There From Here

I began taking pictures with a cheap camera at the fiftieth reunion, and continued to do so at all subsequent meetings of our class. It's obvious I'm a poor photographer, but I wish to share the photos anyhow. To my fellow classmates, if I missed you or the picture was too fuzzy to use, I apologize.

Ann Thames Bonifay, Dorothy & John Eichelberger,
and George VanPelt

Ann Thames Bonifay

Avis Tolbert, Delane Floyd Ackerman & Dot
Merchant Gilmore

Bernie & Maripat Haven Oyaas

Bill & Lenora McArthur

Bernie Oyaas & Walton Owens

Bill & Sarah Howarth Hayes with George VanPelt

Bill McArthur & Hugh Wright

Bill McArthur & Joe Ackerman

Bob & Pat Black Gehrke

Bud & Mary Padgett

Chris Johnson, Doc Bailey & Ron Nursey

Dee Summerall

Delane Floyd Ackerman

DeWayne & Dorothy Hall Robideaux

Donna Layman, Hugh Wright & Evelyn
Thaxton McLeod

Dot Merchant Gilmore (right) & Family

Duane "Dee" Jones Ingram

287

Evelyn Thaxton McLeod & Ann Thames
Bonifay

George & Lorraine Johnson Dawson with Betty Clopton

Walter Spivey & Guest

George VanPelt & Earline Cooper O'Toole

Mary & Ted Peaden with Charlie Davis

Janie Mitchell Scott with Eddie & Faye Heath Conger

Jeanne Perdue Layman & daughter, Donna

Jeanne Perdue Layman & Charlie Davis

Jeannine Miller Pritchett, Dorothy Eichelberger & Avis Tolbert

Jack Eichelberger & Dan McLeod

Joe & Jewel Grimes Partridge

Jerry & Lelia Roche' Hattaway

Jeannine Miller Pritchett, Jackie & Bill Vickery with Tom Tolbert

Jeannine Miller Pritchett

Jim & Jackie Baggett Patterson

Jim Gregory

Joe Ackerman & Carly McFall

JoAnn McKay

John & Barbara Ellis

Joan & Ron Mitchell

Bernard & Judy Howell Parker

JoAnn Owens Doman, Jim & Jackie Baggett Patterson, with
Evelyn Thaxton McLeod

Ken Scruggs & George VanPelt

Myra & Ken Scruggs

Lance & Ruth Lodge

Louis (Bear) Godwin with Lew & JoAnn Owens Doman

Larry & Janie Mitchell Scott

Mary & Ted Peaden

Ted & Mary Peaden with Eddie & Faye Heath Conger

Mary Peaden & Judy Howell Parker

Myra Scruggs, JoAnn Owens Doman, & Jackie Baggett Patterson

Nathan & Myra Orden Kahn

Monroe Matheny, Louis (Bear) Godwin & Bob Scrip

Pat & Nicholas Hutchings

Rameth & Walton Owens

Rex & Lola Vanderford Berry

Russell (Rusty) Scott & Clyde McCauley

Robert & Jackie Calhoun Saxon

Robert & Rosemary Currie Blackington

Robert & Vivian Scrip

Russell (Rusty) & Marcia Howay Scott

Russell (Rusty) Scott & Ron Nursey

Marilyn & Charles McDade

Susan Crooke with Bernie & Maripat Oyaas

294

Avis & Tom Tolbert

Walton & Rameth Owens

Tom Tolbert, Evelyn Thaxton McLeod, with Jackie & Robert Saxon

Wilmer Mitchell

Ron Nursey, Hugh Wright, Ted Peaden & Charlie Davis

Ron Nursey

Ron Nursey, Hugh Wright, Ted Peaden, Charlie Davis & Louis (Bear) Godwin

Walton Owens

Will & Joan Henderson Murray

Warren & Almeada McClanahan

Tom Tolbert & Ken Scruggs

Charlie & Sandra Davis

296

Bob & Barbara Barnes Douglas with their daughter

Harold & Barbara Morris

Don Allen "Crick" Reynolds
With Frank & Jackie Warren Rush

JoAnn McKay & Joanne Jones String

The Reunion Committee: John Eichelberger, Ann Thames Bonifay, Avis & Tom Tolbert, Nicholas & Pat Hutchings,
Duane (Dee) Jones Ingram, and Evelyn Thaxton McLeod

297

28

Sandra's Quarter Horse

Over twenty years ago, when my wife, Sandra, was a department head at Pensacola Junior College, now Pensacola State College, she purchased a raffle ticket from a fellow employee. She obviously paid no attention to what was being raffled off, but knowing the raffle was sponsored by the local Montessori School, Sandra was glad to purchase the raffle ticket, considering it a worthwhile contribution. With no thought of winning, she thought no more about it until several weeks later when she received a phone call from someone informing her she had won the raffle. "Congratulations," the lady said, "you are the grand prize winner."

Sandra assumed it was one of those sales calls with an opening "hook" to whet your interest enough to keep you on the telephone. "I'm really not interested," she said.

The lady hesitated before saying, "I'm serious Dr. Davis. You won the horse."

"What horse?" she asked.

"A beautiful quarter horse colt of impeccable bloodlines from the

Sandra, proud owner of a Quarter Horse from Kings Ranch

King Ranch in Texas, and we need to know when you can arrange to pick him up?"

That's the gist of their conversation, but the immediate thought was, what do we do now? The reality was, Sandra finally had an opportunity to look a gift horse in the mouth.

Owning a horse was never one of our goals—we already had two dogs, a golden retriever and a Heinz-57 variety from the pound. We also had a blind cat and a pet possum. As a small child, Sandra and her siblings did have a one-eyed, pinto pony named "Billy" when they lived in their hometown of Parkersburg, West Virginia. A few years later, after her father was called to active duty and stationed in Albany, Georgia, he bought them a buckskin pony named "Bucky." Thus, she had a lot more experience with horses than I did. In Volume I of Growing Up In Pensacola, I wrote about my family owning a hard-headed, white mule named "Frank" when I was a kid. Our combined childhood experiences of two ponies and a mule was not much, but as adults, it was enough to know that big animals are expensive to feed, shelter, and care for.

299

Situations like this make some of us appreciate the wisdom of our parents. As a youngster growing up in East Pensacola Heights, where several of my friends had horses, I tried desperately to get my dad to purchase a young filly from a family in the neighborhood. I had helped break her in, and imagined what it would be like to own her. He refused, of course, even after I rode the beautiful, spirited horse by the house for him to see. Although I was very disappointed at the time, I fully understand today. He knew the cost.

Sandra and I quickly learned how right he was. It would have been much better if she had won a boat, which we could have parked in the garage. The meter was ticking at the local horse ranch where the colt was boarded. It was like getting into a taxi—the charges began once Sandra was notified.

We made a big mistake—we went out to the ranch to see her new grand prize. He was beautiful. I expected to see a small colt, but he was probably three-quarters grown. We admired him; I think Sandra fell in love with him. We began talking about why we should keep him. We were nuts. Fortunately, the ranch owner told us about a local business woman who would be willing to buy the colt for her autistic son. We learned the raffle was conducted to raise funds for the local autism association.

We hesitated initially, but once the ranch owner detailed the cost of maintaining such a beautiful creature, we decided we would rather the businesswoman have that privilege. We agreed to sell. We learned quickly that owning a horse was like owning a boat; the best two days are the day you got it and the day you got rid of it. We used the money to purchase a video player and a stand-alone Benjamin Franklin fireplace. We really enjoyed both, but I still wish he had been a boat.

Ginger

Rosie

Ms. K, a blind kitty and Sandra

Sandra and Opie, her Opossum friend

29

Seminole Friends Revisited

As a pre-dental student at FSU in the early 1950's, majoring in Zoology, I began to have doubts about making it to Dental School. I looked into Journalism as an alternative, met with the Dean and talked to several journalism students, but I must not have been too impressed or motivated. There's a strong possibility the Dean wasn't too motivated either. It saddens me today, sixty plus years later, when I realize I had a genuine interest in writing back then, but wasn't smart enough to recognize the opportunity even though it was staring me in the face.

The FSU School of Journalism must have been outstanding, because several of the journalism students I knew, later attained prominent positions in the newspaper industry. One in particular was the late Jesse Earle Bowden, who graduated from FSU before I arrived, served in the military, and had recently been hired by the Pensacola News-Journal as a sports writer. Earle became a much respected editor of the Pensacola paper.

I didn't change majors at that time, but discussed my interest in writing over a beer or two with my old Navy buddy, Bodie McCrory, a sports writer with the Pensacola News-Journal. I attribute my unexpected interest in writing to my equally unexpected friendship with Bodie. I knew who he was because I always read the sports pages, and he showed up at the practice field when I was a star benchwarmer with the Pensacola Alumni Football Team. Four years earlier (1951), during the Korean War, Bodie and I, along with a couple hundred other Pensacola men, were ordered to Boot Camp when our U.S. Navy Reserve unit at Ellison Field was activated. We traveled aboard the train together to the U. S. Navy base at Bainbridge, Maryland. During that slow trip, Bodie purchased every newspaper he could find—just for the sports pages. He was a rabid sports-junky, which is why he was such a great sports writer. I learned the stats on every baseball team in both leagues, plus a detailed account of how, only two weeks earlier, the Giant's Bobby Thompson hit that famous homer in the bottom of the ninth, with two outs, runners on second and third—and the Giants beat the Dodgers for the pennant. In the club car, with help from a few beers each, he explained why the Giants then lost to the Yankees a week later in the 1951 World Series.

Recently, my son, Frank Davis, was disposing of old letters and papers from his mother's estate and ran across the following letter addressed to me, dated January 14, 1955, from Marion T. Gaines, Editor, *Pensacola News-Journal*.

Attached to the letter by rusty paper clips were two poorly constructed articles intended for a weekly column under the heading, "THE FSU POW WOW" By Charlie Davis. One of the articles had the date 2/23/55 written at the top. (Apparently it was written after receipt of the

Marion T. Gaines (on right) at the Florida State Capitol Building with Secretary of State, R. A. Gray (left)
Source: www.floridamemory.com, 10/9/2016

letter of the 14th from Mr. Gaines.) They were my attempt at becoming a writer. Opportunity appeared to be knocking but for reasons unknown I chose not to follow through. I've now decided, however, to share bits from these two articles—with apologies for their quality—assuming some would find it interesting to learn what became of the well-known FSU students from Pensacola and others identified in the articles written over sixty-one years ago.

With respect for space, I include only a copy of the first page of one of the articles, since most of the campus events covered would be of little interest to readers today. I do include material that pertained to specific students. It should not be a surprise, but is definitely a disappointment after these many years that I have been unable to locate or obtain information about every student mentioned in the articles. I include what information I could assemble from personal knowledge, the students themselves, friends, family members and public records.

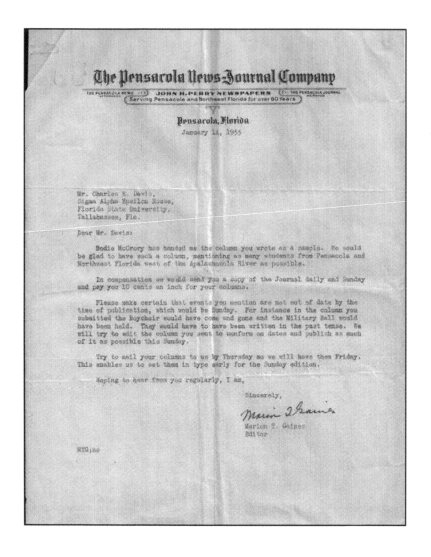

THE FSU POW WOW

BY

CHARLIE DAVIS

At the dedication of the new Wescott Auditorium last
night, the president of the class of 1954 presented the
university with a portrait of President Dosk S. Cambell. The
dedicatory address for the new auditorium was given by Governor Leroy Collins preceding a duo-concert by faculty members
Dr. Ernst von Dohnanyi and Edward Kilenyi. The two distinguished F.S.U. musicians were heard by an overflow crowd of
students, faculty, and guest.

The oil painting of President Cambell is a gift of the
class of 1954, and was painted by Fredrick Roscher of Palm
Beach.

The Sigma Chi Fraternity recently elected new officers
for the coming semester, and Chris Johnson, 1020 E. Brainard
St., was elected Treasurer.

Another interesting feature for this week will be the
famous Columbus Boychoir, who will present two concerts tuesday
and wednesday, January 11, and 12, at 8:15 PM in the newly
dedicated Wescott Auditorium. The program will be the same
both evenings, and will include The Apothecary, an opera in
one act, by Joseph Haydn. Choral selections will include
works from Leisring, Groce, Handel, Pergolesi, Mozart, and
Lowell Riley.

Under the direction of Hebert Huffman, founder-director
of the organization, the celebrated choir is expected to
draw a capacity crowd.

Sixty-one years later— I include brief summaries of interest about those students and others included in the articles whom I've been able to contact personally. For those who have passed away during the interim years, I've depended on information from loved ones, friends and public records. It is a list of outstanding citizens, and I'm proud to include them in this book.

Jesse Earle Bowden, as written previously, graduated from FSU where he majored in journalism and minored in political science. He was the

J. Earle Bowden
Courtesy of the J. Earle Bowden Family

sports editor and then associate editor of the FSU *Florida Flambeau,* where he also drew cartoons for the student newspaper. While a student, he supplied freelance sports feature stories and cartoons to regional weeklies and the daily Panama City News Herald. When the Korean War ended, the U.S. Air Force second lieutenant moved to Pensacola, where he spent the next forty-three years as a newspaper editor/cartoonist for the Pensacola News Journal. He retired in 1997.

Earle was more than an outstanding newspaper man and cartoonist; he championed liberty and patriotism, crusaded for Pensacola's historical heritage, and campaigned vigorously for protecting the natural environment and much more. He wrote volumes about his love for Northwest Florida, and volumes were written about him and his accomplishments. Highways and buildings were named in his honor. He died on February 15, 2015.

Bodie McCrory became the Sports Editor at Pensacola News-Journal, and later the Publisher and Editor of the Monroe News-Star in Monroe, Louisiana, a city in which he became active in many civic organizations and community affairs. He died in 1993 at age sixty-three.

For additional information about Bodie McCrory, I refer you to volume one, *Growing Up In Pensacola,* Chapter 11, titled "Bodie," pages 73-79.

Marion T. Gaines was the editor of the *Pensacola News-Journal* from 1939 until 1965, and was previously the editor of the *Mobile Press Register.* Mr.Gaines had a distinguish career as a journalist and editor, and received accolades for his professionalism as well as his community involvement, especially his time with the City of Pensacola Human

Relations Commission (also known as the Biracial Committee). A collection of the Marion T. Gaines Papers, 1939 – 1975 are on record at the UWF University Archives in the UWF History Center. Mr.Gaines and his wife, Howie, had four children, Helen Gaines Hunter, Edmund P. Gaines, Marion T. Gaines III, Robert P. Gaines and Harry T. Gaines. Note, Harry married **Gail Jackson,** one of the students covered in the articles, and whom I write about below.

Article 1, Page 1:
     The Sigma Chi fraternity recently elected new officers for the coming semester, and Chris Johnson, 1020 East Brainard St. was elected Treasurer.

Article 2, page 2:
     Chris Johnson is a senior, and was recently elected Treasurer of Sigma Chi fraternity. That is right along his line, for he is majoring in accounting. Chris is also a member of Alpha Kappa Psi, a national business fraternity.

Chris Johnson
Source: Legacy .com
8/15/16

Chris Johnson was a member of Sigma Chi fraternity, graduated from FSU in 1955 with a degree in Accounting, earned his CPA designation and became a partner with the CPA firm of Saltmarsh, Cleveland, and Gund. At some point in his active life, Chris became a Navy Officer and served aboard destroyers in the Pacific Fleet. In 1960, Chris married Susan Jane Scheuer of Warrington, and four years later, he, Susan and three-year old son, David, moved to Fort Walton Beach, Fla. where Chris opened a new office for the firm. As expected, he became active in the community and his church. In addition to the Rotary Club, he served as president of the Greater Fort Walton Beach Chamber of Commerce, and as a long-time member of the Krewe of Bowlegs, he served as Capt. Billy Bowlegs XXIX. In addition to their son, David, Chris and Susan had two daughters, Ginny Scheidt and Suzy Gavin, plus four grandchildren. Chris died on April 21, 2015, and is buried at Holy Cross Catholic Cemetery in Pensacola.

Article 1, Page 2:
Janie Cornwell has returned to FSU after completing her internship in Pensacola. Janie is a senior, majoring in Elementary Education; a member

of Pi Beta Phi sorority and as a pledge was president of the Pledge Class; a member of the Village Vamps, of which members are chosen on looks, poise, and personality; and was a member of the University Singers for three years. She is the daughter of Mrs. Z .W. Cornwell, 1224 East Lakeview Avenue. Janie plans to teach at one of the elementary schools in Pensacola after graduation next June.

Article 2, Page 2:
"Janie Cornwell is spending her last semester at FSU. She will graduate in May, and plans to teach in Pensacola. Janie is a member of Pi Beta Phi sorority.

Janie Cornwell Schwab
Source: 1954 Tally Ho

Janie Cornwell Schwab graduated in 1955, with a degree in Elementary Education. She taught school in Escambia County before her marriage to Golf Pro, George Schwab. They moved to Central Florida where George passed away on August 4, 2000. They were the parents of daughter, Mary Stokes of Belair, Maryland, and two sons, David of Jacksonville, Fla. and Robert of New Smyrna Beach, Fla. Janie is the proud grandmother of six grandchildren, and currently lives in New Smyrna Beach, Florida. Her son, Robert followed in his dad's footsteps, and is a Golf Pro in New Smyrna Beach, Fla.

Article 1, Page 2:
Last Friday night, the Cavalier and Cotillion, men's and women's dancing honorarias, presented their annual dance, which was held in the Women's Gymnasium. Music was furnished by the "Universals," a Negro combo. Nancy Mayer, High Point Road, Gulf Breeze, is a member of Cotillion. She is a senior with a major in education. Also, she is a member of Delta Delta Delta sorority.

Article 2, Page 3:
Saw Nancy Mayer and Eloise McGirr walking across campus the other day. They are both graduating seniors, and members of Delta Delta Delta sorority. I understand that Nancy is planning on 'Wedding Bells' in the near future.

Nancy Mayer Young
Source: Legacy. Com
8/23/16

Nancy Mayer Young, graduated from FSU in 1955 with a degree in Education. She married Richard Young, who also graduated from FSU, having received a doctorate in zoology. Dr. Young was recognized as a pioneer in space biology. A *New York Times* article stated, "Dr. Young was chief of life sciences exploration for the American space program, which sent men to the moon and unmanned spacecraft to Mars in the 1960's and 70's. In 1979 he became vice president of Rockefeller University in New York.

While living in New York, Nancy was active in real estate sales. In the late 80's, Nancy and Richard moved back to Cape Canaveral when he became the chief science consultant to NASA's Life Science Division. Nancy and Richard were the parents of Dee, Sandy and Mark; and the grandparents of Kyle, Megan, Ian and Sam. On October 6, 1996, Richard died, and on March 3, 2016, Nancy died while living in Merritt Island, Florida. Her obituary stated, "Nancy was a Native Floridian who was passionate about her art, bridge, travel and gardening."

Article 1, Page 3:

A new organization on campus, The Student Fashion Institute, was recently organized and officers have been elected for the coming year. The newly organized club has been founded to provide facilities in meeting the educational needs of the group.

One of the charter members is Eloise McGirr, daughter of Mr. and Mrs. L. D. McGirr, East LaRua Street. Ellie is a senior, and is majoring in Fashion Illustration and Commercial Art. She is a member of Delta Delta Delta sorority. Also, she is pledging Gamma alpha Chi, which is advertising honorary for women.

Eloise McGirr Bills
Source: 1954 Tally Ho

Eloise McGirr Bills Graduated from FSU in 1955 with a degree in Commercial Art and Fashion Illustration. She was a member of Tri-Delt sorority, along with Nancy Mayer. Ellie married soon after graduating and moved to Maryland, where she became successful as a graphic artist. She was eventually responsible for all advertising for five major department stores in the Baltimore-Washington D C area, where she produced thousands of T.V. Commercials for her clients. Ellie is the mother of two sons and a daughter. Her first marriage ended in divorce early on, but she and her current husband, Don Bills, have been together for over forty years. Don retired after many years with U. S. Navy Headquarters in Washington D C. After his retirement they moved to Stuart, Florida, where their home overlooks the ocean. Currently, Ellie resides in a nursing home not far from their family home and Don visits often.

Article 1, Page 2:
Susannah, a new two-act opera, written by Carlesle Floyd of the music faculty, will make its world premiere at Florida State University, February 24, 1955. Two prominent New York opera stars have agreed to come to Tallahassee a week in advance of the premiere to rehearse with the cast.

Included in the cast is Kenneth Nelson, 2715 West Lakeview Avenue. Ken is a senior, and he is majoring in music. He is a member of Phi Kappa Tau fraternity.

Article 2, Page 2:
Months of preparation came to a climax last Thursday night when Carlisle Floyd's "Susannah" was world-premiered in Wescott Auditorium. Ken Nelson was one of the supporting members of the cast.

Kenneth Nelson: I have been unable to locate Ken, or learn any information about him or his whereabouts since his graduating from FSU in 1955.

310

Osmond "Bo" Sharpless, a
fellow Penascolian, and
Kenneth Nelson, members of
Phi Kappa Tau.
Source: 1954 Tally Ho

Article 1, Page 2:

Gail Jackson, 1724 N. Magnolia Avenue is a new member of Cotillion, and she was presented at the dance. Gail is a member of Sigma Kappa sorority. **Gail Jackson Gaines** married **Harry Gaines**, a fellow FSU student, also from Pensacola, and the son of Marion T. Gaines, editor of the Pensacola News Journal. Gail and Harry settled in Seminole, Florida. Harry died a few years ago; Gail died on May 4, 2014.

Gail Jackson Gaines
Source: 1954 Tally Ho

Harry Gaines
Source:
1954 Tally Ho

Article 1, Page 4:

I had the surprise of my life this morning, which under the circumstances I was glad to have. I was about to drive through Wescott Gate, when I almost collided with a ford convertible. The driver of the car was none other than fellow Pensacolian, Bill 'Jug' Harrison, who is here at FSU for the purpose of registering for the Spring Semester. Billy recently returned from Korea, and he is to be discharged from the Marine Corps this month {February, 1955}. I last saw him at Parris Island, the U. S. Marine Corps base where we were both stationed in 1952.* He said, 'It will be quite a change from Korea to college,' but, he added, 'I think the parties will be much better.' I didn't have time to talk with Bill, for he was in a hurry to meet Sherry Cobb at the Amber House for a coke.

Bill Harrison
Parris Island, S.C ca, 1952

Bill Harrison had only recently returned to the states, after his second tour in Korea, when I ran into him in 1955. He had been in a U. S. Military hospital in Yokosuka, Japan as a result of getting banged up pretty bad in Korea. He never got around to registering at FSU, but decided   instead, to enter the automobile sales business in the Dothan, Alabama/Blakeley, Georgia area, where he enjoyed great success. He retired from ownership of an auto dealership business in Dothan, Alabama, and he and his wife settled in Blakeley, Georgia. Bill suffered a painful loss when his wife died in 2011. She was a graduate of LSU, and Bill had promised her he would someday get a college degree. After her death he made good on that promise by not only earning a bachelor's degree, he also qualified for a master's in economics, both from the University of Alabama.

* I wrote about meeting up with Bill at Parris Island in my first book, *Growing Up In Pensacola,* and in my novel, *They also Serve,* I featured him as a tap-dancing marine. In about 1949 or 1950, Tex Beneke and his orchestra performed in Pensacola, and Bill, an accomplished tap-dancer, and a student at PHS, was invited to perform with the "Big-Band" group.

Article 2, Page 1:

I saw Sherry Cobb last week; all dressed in white, and smiling from ear-to-ear. The reason: she was on her way to the Pi Beta Phi house for pledging ceremonies. Congratulations, Sherry.

Sherry Cobb Snead married fellow Pensacolian, **Howard Snead.** * I located Sherry and Howard in Signal Mountain, Tennessee with help from mutual friends, Roy and Myrth Tummler. After contacts via snail-mail, email and a telephone call, Sherry emailed me the information I asked for, which is written so well and concise I decided it would be better to quote her, rather than rewrite, so, here's Sherry's story in her own words:

312

Sherry Cobb Snead

"Howard and I met after FSU and he graduated from GA Tech and then 2 years in the Air Force. Funny thing you mentioned Janie Cornwell. I had been to a party, I believe for her wedding, and we went to Trader Jon's, and I met Howard there. We married in 1959, and he went to work for Chemstrand for a year in Pensacola until we were transferred to Charlotte, N.C. Stayed there for 10 years and then moved to Atlanta for 2 and then back to Charlotte for 2 more years until we ended up on Signal Mountain and he worked in Dalton, GA in the carpet industry. I retired from the Hamilton County Department of Education after 28 years there. Not as a teacher but at the central office. We have three children, Renee, Kevin, and Doug. Renee is in Vero Beach, Fla., Doug in Germantown, TN, and Kevin lives in Chattanooga. We have been blessed with 7 grandchildren."

* See chapter this volume, "Eugene 'Razzi' Rasponi" for Howard Snead's testimony.

Left: Howard and Sherry Snead Courtesy of Sherry Snead

Right: Roy and Myrth Tummler Courtesy of Roy Tummer

Article 2, Page 1:
Ralph Atwell has returned to FSU after having been called away for two years in the Army. Ralph, a sophomore, is a member of Sigma Nu fraternity.

Ralph Atwell graduated from FSU & the University of Florida School Of Law. While at FSU, Ralph and I shared an apartment near the campus for a couple of semesters.* At that time, he was involved with the FSU Circus as a partner in an "Adagio Act," an acrobalance performer. He was good. Ralph practiced law in Bradenton, Florida for a short period following law school, before returning home to Pensacola. While managing his private practice, he also served as an attorney for the City of Pensacola. He was an avid golfer, and a rabid Seminole football fan. Ralph suffered major health problems, and retired early from the practice of law, but succumbed to his illnesses on May 17, 2012. He is survived by his wife, Linda; two sons, Chris and Mike and daughter, Ashley.

Ralph Atwell
Courtesy of the Atwell Family

* See chapter titled, "Beach Buggies," this volume.

Article 2, Page 2:

> Ed Threadgill, having pledged last semester, will be initiated into Sigma Alpha Epsilon fraternity sometime in the very near future.

Judge Ed Threadgill, a graduate of Pensacola High School, class of 1950, spent three years in the U. S. Army prior to attending FSU. He married fellow Seminole student, SuzannTope. They transferred to the

Judge Ed Threadgill
Source: Legacy..com
8/23/2016

University of Florida where Ed received an undergraduate degree in industrial engineering (1959) and a law degree in 1962. After several years in private practice in Winter Haven, Florida, Ed served as a City Judge, then as an assistant county solicitor and assistant state attorney before being elected several times as a Polk County Judge. In 1981, he was appointed as a judge to the 10 th Judicial Circuit Court, after which he was appointed to the 2nd District Court of Appeals, where he served until retirement. On March 2, 2016, retired Judge Edward F. Threadgill, Jr. age 84, died from complications of multiple myeloma. He and Suzanne were married 57 years.

Article 2, Page 2:

I went to see the Dublin Players the other night and saw Joan Cunningham there. Joan is a sophomore and a member of Alpha Gamma Delta sorority.

Joan Cunningham
Source: 1954 Tally Ho

Dr. Joan Cunningham graduated from FSU with not just one degree, but three degrees, a Bachelor's, a Master's and a Doctoral, all in education. She was also affiliated with Sigma Tau Delta and Phi Kappa Phi. Her teaching career spanned forty-one years, and included being on the first faculty at the opening of Escambia High School in 1966. In 1986, Joan was among the small group of teachers who brought the International Baccalaureate Program to Pensacola High School. A true professional, she was inducted into Delta Kappa Gamma and Phi Delta Kappa, professional education societies. Joan died on February 26, 2011

Article 2, Page 2:

Raymond Weekley is now a 'Seminole of Florida State.' He attended Pensacola Junior College before entering the service. Now that he is back in school, he plans to continue his studies in engineering.

Raymond Weekley has been involved with civilian airplanes since he was a teenager. After FSU, he moved to Virginia, got married, bought an airplane (maybe not in that order), and developed a successful business transporting sky-divers to an appropriate altitude. In the process he leased a strip of land from a man in the sod and grass business. They became close friends, and when the man died unexpectedly, Raymond bought the business from the family, and grew it into a large, successful enterprise, situated in

Raymond Weekley
FSU

the suburbs of the nation's capital. He is also the co-owner of businesses related to the sod and grass industry. Recently, after attending a mutual friend's funeral, I had an opportunity to ask him about his business successes. Raymond's response was:

"Charlie, I'm a farmer, and I can't wait to get home and climb up on my tractor—it's seed planting time." Those are words of a happy man in his chosen field.

Ray Weekley
Owner of Chantilly Turf Farms, Inc
Source: FaceBook
10/9/2016

Article 2, Page 2:

Bill McArthur, a senior, will intern sometime this summer. Bill said, 'Upon graduation, I plan to teach until Uncle Sam gets me.' He is a member of Sigma Alpha Epsilon fraternity.

Bill McArthur
Source: 1954 Tally Ho

Bill McArthur is from a family of educators. He graduated from FSU with a degree in education, and after teaching for a few years, he became the Personnel Manager (Human Resources Director) for the Escambia County School System. He remained in that position for many years, but he and wife, Lenora, are enjoying their retirement. Bill's brother, Gerald McArthur, also graduated from FSU with a degree in education. Like Bill, he taught for a short while before becoming the Human Resources Director at Monsanto. Their father, L. D. McArthur was on the Escambia County school Board for many years, and the L. D. McArthur School was named in his honor. Bill's sister, Annette, is the former principal at the L. D. McArthur School.

Bill McArthur,
Director of Human
Resources,
Escambia County School
System

Article 2, Page 3:

Leroy Boling is back in school, after dropping out for a semester. He left school temporarily, so he could take a cruise in the Merchant Marines. While he was in South America, his ship got involved in a civil war of some sort. He said that the only fighting he wants to do is fighting his way from one class to the other.

Leroy Boling graduated from FSU where he was a member of Phi Kapa Tau fraternity. He subsequently graduated from Emory University Law School. He practiced law in Pensacola for several years, but

Leroy Boling, Bill Ames and Dale Werhan, fellow Pensacolians in Phi Kappa Tau
Source: 1954 Tally Ho

returned to the Merchant Marines for a few years. He resumed his law practice, but after a few more years, he retired and became the owner of a one-man trucking business. One can only admire Leroy's independent nature. He explained to me several years ago how he had a special truck built to his specifications. It was a combination truck and Recreational

317

Vehicle. Leroy was a licensed driver and traveled thousands of miles, hauling freight, accompanied by his family. He said, 'We traveled the United states, Canada and Mexico, all-expense paid, with some profit at the end of the year. Leroy died May 22, 2006.

Article 2, Page 3:

> If a contest were held to determine who has the most beat-up car on campus, I am sure that Ronnie Jutila would win with his old "Olds." Ronnie, who is now known as the "Guatemalan Kid" is a member of Sigma Nu fraternity. Also, he is a senior and will graduate in May.

Ron Jutila
Source: 1954 Tally Ho

Ron Jutila graduated from FSU in 1955 and although a Pensacola native, he settled in Panama City, Florida. He had a successful career as an independent agent with Prudential Life Insurance Company. He was member of the Seminole Boosters and an avid supporter of Florida State University. Ron died in Panama City at age seventy-seven and is survived by his son, Rev. John Jutila, his daughter, Cindy Terrell, his brother Andrew, and six grandchildren.

30

September 11, 2001

Hayden Davis

September 11, 2001, my grandson Hayden's eighth birthday, and the day after my wife Sandra's big "Six-O", is a date that represents what some consider the worst tragedy our country has ever experienced. Previously, December 7, 1941 had that distinction. Sadly, the death toll of Americans at the World Trade Center, the Pentagon and the hillsides of Pennsylvania were comparable to the number of deaths at Pearl Harbor. A big difference, of course, is that the attack on "Nine-Eleven" took place on our homeland against civilians. Once again, our president declared a national emergency. Like all previous national emergencies, our men and women were called to arms to help defeat an enemy, who, like our previous adversaries was also possessed with a fanatic ideology and hell-bent on seeing our freedoms, our way of life and our religion destroyed.

Dr. Sandra
Lockney Davis

The World Trade Center, September 11, 2001.
Source: www.history.com 8/25/16

Many of our young men and women, all volunteers, lost their lives or suffered horrendous injuries in our recent war, which was the longest war we've ever been engaged in. It's the price of liberty. So, what else is new? We have always made sacrifices, on the battlefield and at home. The message and lyrics in a popular WWII song are, "We did it before and we can do it again." The men and women in uniform are in harm's way and although the way wars are conducted changes with each war, the one thing that remains the same is the family's anguish and concern for the safety of their loved ones.

In World War I, my grandparents worried about my father and his brother until they were safely home from Europe. My mother had to wait until the war was over before she and my dad could marry. In World War II, my two oldest brothers, Ben and Bill, volunteered for duty; their young wives and babies were left behind with parents and relatives. Before Bill completed enough missions to be furloughed home, the entire family kept close count of his combat missions, knowing the next one could be disastrous. I was only ten at the time, but I well remember how upset my sister-in-law got. She came to live with us while my brother flew missions over Germany from England and Africa. We were proud of the two stars in the window, but I was too young to fully realize the sleepless nights that my family, like thousands of other parents, wives, children, relatives and friends experienced.

Above left: to right: Ben L. Davis, Sr., U. S. Army, WWI, Ben L. Davis, Jr. U. S. Army Air CorpsWW II

Below left to right: William "Bill" Davis, U. S. Air Corps, WWII, Charlie Davis, U. S. Navy, Korean War

The Korean War, first dubbed as a "Police Action," and now often referred to as the "Forgotten War," was a different kind of war and against a different kind of enemy. It was fought by some of the same who fought in World War II, along with their younger brothers, and the families had the same kind of fear. I remember well, the Chief telling us in boot camp, "This war will last for years, so kiss your girlfriends' goodbye, boys." We and our allies were winning that conflict until the Chinese entered on the side of North Korea. Many young Americans died or became P.O.W's, and for months and even years in some instances, the families back home did not know if their loved ones were dead or alive. In contrast, modern warfare with its technology allows the military to notify a family within days of a loved one's death, injury or capture.

Tom Davis.
U. S. Navy
Reserve,
Berlin/ Cuban
Crisis

My youngest brother, Tom, was called to active duty aboard the USS *Tweedy,* a ship home-ported in Pensacola during the Berlin Crisis and the lead up to the Cuban Missile Crisis. Fortunately, President Kennedy and Congress made the right moves and the Russian Communists backed down, as both sides were aware that the world was on the brink of another major war. Both sides shared a sigh of relief when the Russian missiles were removed from Cuba, but it was several years later before world leaders and historians realized how close the world came to having a nuclear holocaust.

The USS *Tweedy*

322

Following the Korean War, another younger brother, Jack, joined the Navy. He served aboard the battleship, the USS *New Jersey*. He travelled the world, the Mediterrean, Europe and visited relatives from Wales in London. Upon discharge he became a banker in Stuart, Florida, a Realtor in Pensacola before purchasing B & M Generator Service. Jack died in 1983 at the age of 47.

Jack Davis

The Vietnam War was fought by a whole new generation, mostly the sons and daughters of those who fought in World War II. My wife, Sandra, served in Vietnam as a civilian employee of the Army, and her father, Bill Lockney, an Air Force fighter pilot, served in World War II, Korea and Vietnam. Sandra's mother, Gracie, had more

than her share of worry and concern while her highly-decorated husband did his duty in three separate wars and her oldest daughter, although not a combatant, was in the war zone. Thus, my wife, her siblings and her mother underwent what other families experienced while her father was away in two wars, and her mother and siblings had the same anxieties while she and her father were away during the Vietnam War.

Many of the men and women who served and who are currently serving in either Iraq or Afghanistan are children, grandchildren, and, in some cases, great- grandchildren of veterans of World War II, the Korean War and the Vietnam War. Because there have only been a few years between the several more recent wars, there are more generations of loved ones at home to be concerned about the family members who are away in dangerous situations.

Sandra Lockney
US Army,
Special Services,
VN 1968

LTC William "Bill"
Lockney, USAF, WWII,
Korea, & Vietnam
Veteran

323

The Iraq and Afghanistan wars have only recently ended. Like the Vietnam War, our countrymen disagreed on whether or not we should have been involved in either war, but we were involved in both, longer than any other wars. At one time, well over one-hundred thousand American military personnel, plus a large contingent of non-military, all in jeopardy, were in a conflict with a culture many of us don't understand. It seems wrong to compare the smaller number of our men and women killed and injured with the numbers for World War II, the Korean War and the Vietnam War because only one death or only one injury is too many.

The one thing that remains constant in all our wars is the families' painful concern for the safety of their loved ones in dangerous circumstances. They are an immeasurable casualty list of loving souls. It has been written that "truth is the first casualty of war," but if the truth were known, the loving families, faithfully "keeping the home fires burning" become casualties of war before the first shots are fired.

As I finish this essay on September 11, 2016, fifteen years after the dastardly and cowardly acts that took place in New York City, Washington, D.C., and on the hillsides of Pennsylvania, I'm reminded of President Roosevelt's words in reference to the attack on Pearl Harbor. September 11, 2001 was also a "Day of Infamy." We know the consequences suffered by the attacker on December 7, 1941; with America's strength and resilience, we are confident of eventual, similar results due to the "Nine-Eleven" attack.

To conclude on a much lighter note, I find it interesting how so many people proudly boast about having been born, married, retired, etc. on September 11th. It's a "badge of honor," and rightfully so. It's a date that's embedded in our memories and our nation's history.

Last year, at this time, we received an invitation to attend a birthday party from our next door neighbor, Aubrey Fulford. He's a WWII veteran who served as a bombardier on a B-29 and turned ninety on September 11, 2015. It's a "double" birthday party because his great granddaughter, also named Aubrey, turned one year old September 11, 2015. Many more Happy Birthdays to both of them, and may God bless them, us, everybody else, and this great nation of ours.

Aubrey Fulford and great
granddaughter, Aubrey Hooke,
September 11, 2015

LT. Aubrey Fulford, US Army Air
Corps., WWII June, 1945

31

So, You Got A Speeding Ticket, Huh?

When I turned sixteen in 1948, my dad used his influence as a county official to get me a driver's license without taking the tests. That couldn't happen today. He would be crucified by the press and it would be all over the radio and TV news. It would be fodder for his political opponents' in the next election. Well, let's be realistic, life was much simpler in those days around governmental offices. Driver licenses were issued by the county judge, and Judge Harvey Page's office was just down the hall from my dad's office. Now, don't get me wrong, I'm not implying that just because their offices were close made it right. The truth was I only needed a restricted license so I could use my recently purchased Cushman Scooter to "throw" my paper route.

Charlie Davis

I figured it must have been a misunderstanding by one of the clerks in the Judge's office, because when my dad brought the license home to me, it wasn't restricted to scooters, it was a regular operator's license. I didn't mention the clerk's mistake right away. I did get the usual lecture he had given my older brothers on safe driving and threats about getting a speeding ticket. Our only sister didn't get that lecture. The clerk's error was a blessing, because The Pensacola News-Journal stopped me from using the scooter on my paper route when a customer complained about the noise so early in the morning. I was glad to have the unrestricted license so I could drive a car. My brother-in-law, Norman Redding, taught me to drive in his Model-A Ford; he wound up with a bent front bumper as a memento.

Ben L. Davis

I learned later that the Judge's clerk didn't make a mistake. My dad, aware that I knew how to drive, had requested unrestrictive license for me. I suspected he was having second thoughts because he was always cautioning me about driving carefully.

A short time later, while a sophomore at PHS, my brother, Bill, who owned a service station, allowed me to use a Model-T Roadster he had acquired in a trade.[1] Mr. Henry Ford's little red Model-T had a fold-down canvas top and a rumble seat. I used it several months like it was my own, and I thought I was hot stuff when I drove it to school each day. The steep Gadsden Street hill at the west end of the old Bayou Texar Bridge was always a problem; I had to get up a lot of speed to make it up the hill. More often than not, I usually had to turn around in the middle of the bridge and back up the hill because the Model-T's reverse drive had more power than the two forward drives. (Model-T's had bands, not gears.) Residents in the Mirador Apartments and that part of East Hill probably wondered what all the horn-blowing was about each morning while I held up traffic as I slowly backed up the hill on my way to school. (The old bridge was replaced, and the current bridge connects to Cervantes Street today, eliminating the steep Gadsden Street hill)

Before returning the Model-T to my brother Bill, I did what my dad had been cautioning me not to do—I got a ticket for speeding and running a red light, at the corner of Palafox and Wright Streets. I was coasting down Palafox hill too fast and couldn't stop in time. My dad was not pleased. On the morning of the day I was to be in court, he instructed me to stop by his office at the court house before going to court. I hoped that meant he was willing to pay the court cost and fines, even though I was prepared to pay the fine from my paperboy earnings. But that wasn't the case; he suggested I go by Chief of Police Crosby Hall's office on the way to court, which was in the same building as the city jail. As I walked through Lee Square on the

Chief Crosby Hall

way to the police station I wondered why my dad wanted me to talk to the Chief. I hoped it meant he was thinking the Chief might put in a good word to the Judge about me.

At the station, I was directed upstairs to the Chief's office. He was talking to a couple of uniformed officers when I entered, but he acknowledged me and told me to take a seat, which I did as several more policemen walked into his office. I remember it got real quiet as the Chief asked me my name.

"My name's Charlie Davis," I said. All the officers instantly started mumbling to each other and stared at me like I was some surrendering, escaped murderer. I never got a chance to tell him my dad sent me.

"You the boy that got caught speeding and running a red light?" asked the chief in a gruff voice.

"Yessir," was about all I could say before he started in on me, telling, not explaining, how I could have killed somebody or myself. I'm sure his tirade must have lasted only a few minutes, but it seemed like a long, long time. He was interrupted, only briefly, when one of the officers handed him a pair of handcuffs and said, "You might need these, Chief." I was relieved when the chief waved him off. I don't remember everything he said to me that morning, sixty-seven years ago, but I do remember he got my attention. Neither do I remember saying anything beyond "Yes, Sir," which I must have uttered a record number of times. Suddenly he was through giving me hell, and all the policemen filed out of his office.

"Aren't you supposed to be in school today?" he said.
"Yessir."
"Well, get out of here. I don't want to see you back here, you understand?"
"Yessir," I said. I started toward the door when he surprised me, smiling and coming from from behind his desk to shake my hand.
"I'll talk to the Judge; you go to school," he said, patting me on the back.
I'm sure I thanked him before heading down the stairs and out of the building, which I exited much faster than I entered. As I recall, a couple of the officers who had been upstairs in the Chief's office, joked with me as I left the building.

The Chief was a good man. I appreciated what he did and I've thought about him and that incident many times over the years. Perhaps I didn't listen well, since I've had more than my share of additional speeding tickets. However, I believe I've always had a healthy attitude and respect for law enforcement due to that early meeting with the Chief and his officers.

My dad knew what he was doing, although I never learned what he asked his friend, Chief Crosby Hall to do. I'm sure it was something like, "Get on his butt," or "Scare the hell out of him," or maybe something worse. Unfortunately, I never thanked my dad, but I should have.

[1] See chapter titled, *"My" 1926 Model-T Ford* this volume.

32

The Ten Kids

In the mid-1970's, I visited my brother Bill aboard his commercial snapper boat, the *Native Dancer,* which was docked at William's Seafood across the slip from Joe Patti's Seafood. As we enjoyed a freshly brewed cup of coffee, we heard the huge diesel engine start up in one of the larger shrimp boats tied up at Joe Patti's dock. This may sound strange to some folks, but to me a diesel engine is just a noisy machine in a truck or some other land equipment, but in a boat it's a great sound.

As the beautiful, Biloxi style shrimper pulled away from Joe Patti's dock; the captain and crew acknowledged us as they passed close by heading out of the slip toward Pensacola Bay. The large boat was impressive with her out-riggings upright and net and "doors" in position. The crew appeared anxious to get out to the Gulf to start dragging for the popular Gulf Coast Shrimp. The captain turned her to port several degrees, lined up with the channel marker and advanced the throttle. As the stern came into view, I saw her name: *Ten Kids, Pensacola, Florida.* Turning to Bill I said, "That's an unusual name for a boat." His response was, "Not really, that's Captain Sidney Clopton's boat, and he has ten kids."

The *Ten Kids*

I don't know why I found it so fascinating that a man with ten kids would name his boat after his number of kids, but I suppose it makes perfectly good sense if he loved his ten kids, or was proud of the fact he was the father of ten kids. He couldn't name the boat after all of them, or just one of them, so no one got their feelings hurt. The *Ten Kids* was just one of many boats that Sidney Clopton owned and operated throughout his career in the bays and the Gulf of Mexico. He and wife, Agnes, spawned the local Clopton dynasty of commercial fishermen. All six boys of their ten kids grew up to become men of the sea, owning their own commercial boats. The Clopton Clan of commercial fishermen has been a major factor in Pensacola's commercial fishing industry for almost one-hundred years.

Captain Sidney Clopton

Captain Sidney Clopton, born in 1910 into an old, established Pensacola family, began his long career in commercial fishing at age thirteen after his father, Nathaniel Clopton, a railroad man, was robbed and murdered. He operated all types of commercial fishing boats out of Pensacola, including seine boats, shrimp boats and snapper boats. He net fished for Spanish mackerel, bluefish, skipjack, hardtails, mullet and "LY's" (alewives) in his early years. Later, he captained the *Buccaneer,* a 102 foot

331

The *Buccaneer*

sailing schooner, the largest of Saunders Fish Company's fleet of "fishing smacks," fishing the Campeche Mexico snapper banks for Red Snapper.

He used the sexton to get the longitude and latitude readings before modern navigational equipment was available. Later, he owned eight fishing and shrimping vessels throughout his career and acquired the *Ten Kids* in the mid-sixties. In a Pensacola News Journal article, Troy Moon referred to him as the "legendary fishing captain Sidney Clopton." He further described the Cloptons as, "the first families of Northwest Florida fishing and shrimping, along with the Patti family, of Joe Patti Seafood fame."

The famous Frank Patti and Joe Patti's Seafood

Captain Sidney, as he was addressed by locals who knew him, was also well known as a boat builder, a shipwright, and he built, and repaired, many boats for local fishermen. Troy Moon, a reporter for the *Pensacola News Journal,* quoted Frank Patti, owner of Joe Patti Seafood, in an article he wrote about Captain Clopton:

> Sidney is one of the pioneers, and The Cloptons' legacy is secure in Northwest Florida. That boat in front of Joe Patti's—Captain Sidney built that for my daddy. It was a beloved vessel for my daddy, dating back to the 1930s. It was a joy to him until the last days he lived. Now, it's on

display. It will be there as long as I'm alive. That family gave a lot.

The *Sammie* built by Captain Sidney Clopton for
Joe Patti still on display at Joe Patti's Seafood

I remember how it was growing up with six of us boys and one girl in our home in East Pensacola Heights, especially when it was crowded around the dinner table, so I appreciate how it must have been for the Clopton family with six boys and four girls. When both parents and an occasional house guest were added, space must have been a premium at the Clopton family home on Pine Street, however, the Captain always felt that there was always room for more. I suspect the Cloptons look back on those crowded days with fond memories like we Davis siblings do, and they probably wonder, like we do, where the heck did everybody sleep?

Captain Sidney's six sons didn't have much choice but "to go down to the sea in ships," as a famous poet wrote, and it wasn't only because they grew up admiring their father as he attained success in commercial fishing and boat building. There was another force that helped guide them to the sea. Their maternal grandfather, Charles Herbert Lockwood, [1] was a cabin-boy on a "square rigger" from Australia. He jumped ship in New Orleans, wound up in Pensacola, married, and raised his large family in downtown Pensacola on Zarragosa Street, close to St. Joseph's Catholic Church. Members of the Lockwood and Clopton families were longtime members of St. Joseph's Church.

[1] See Chapter about Golden Gloves and Pensacola Boxers

Above: Capt. Chip Clopton and his *Mystical Rose*

Below: Capt. Jeff Clopton and his *St. Christopher*

Above: Capt Chip Clopton and his *Mystical Rose*

Below: Capt. Jeff Clopton and his *St. Christopher*

335

David Clopton's *Brit n Shane*, named for his two children

Below: Capt. Jerry Clopton and the Angela Kay

Thus it was the marriage of the railroad man's son and the cabin boy's daughter that produced enough kids to name a boat after. Those "ten kids" are: Chipley, Loice, Sheila, Jeff, Johnnie, Joyce, Tommy, Gail, David, and Jerry. Sidney and Agnes Clopton are responsible for the Clopton family being a major player in the commercial fishing business, leading to a flotilla of Clopton family fishing boats over many decades. Their son, David Clopton, continues the family tradition today aboard his wooden hull bay shrimp boat, *Brit-n- Shane,* in search of shrimp in local bays and along the Gulf Coast. Jerry, the youngest of the ten kids, died at age thirty-nine from a heart attack; prior to his death he was captain of the *Little Flower.* The remaining nine siblings are doing well; all live in the Pensacola area except Gail, who lives in Houston with her family.

I learned recently that the trawler, *Ten Kids,* I saw in the mid-1970s was the second shrimp trawler by that name owned by the Clopton's. The first *Ten Kids* was a seventy-two-foot wooden-hull trawler combination snapper/trawler built in the mid-1960s. She was sold to a local family in the 1970s, but unfortunately, she was run aground near Ft. Morgan on the new owner's maiden voyage. The boat's name was changed to *Sailor's Choice.* The second *Ten Kids,* a ninety foot, steel-hull trawler was built in the mid-70s, and jointly owned by Sidney and son Johnnie. She was a vessel to be proud of, with the latest in equipment, and all the modern conveniences, such as: central heat and air, television, showers, individual cabins, comfortable beds, and a complete kitchen. She was the *Ten Kids* I saw while having coffee aboard the *Native Dancer* with my brother Bill. Anyone would have been impressed.

The steel-hull *Ten Kids* was sold around 1989, exclusive of its name, to a Vietnamese six-member family. The name was changed to *New Horizon* and shrimped out of Bayou La Batre. Later, the family converted the rigging to long-line fishing for yellow fin tuna. Her last known location was in Hawaii. After meeting with several of the Clopton family members, I learned they survived many dangerous and life-threatening situations during their many years as commercial fishermen and shrimpers. Their stories are reminiscent of the current reality television programs like "The Deadliest Catch" and "Alaska Fish Wars." In 1964, Jeff was trawling for shrimp aboard his boat, the *Al-Don,* when his right leg was caught in a cable wench. It was several minutes before he and his brother's, Tommy and David, were able to free his leg, but too much damage was inflicted and doctors had to amputate it above the knee. After being fitted with an

The First *Ten Kids*

artificial limb, Jeff went back to shrimping on the *Al-Don* until around 1969. He then purchased the seventy-five-foot plus, steel hull, *St Christopher*.

David related a story to me recently about a near tragedy while on the *Ten Kids* when he was jerked overboard at night in stormy, below-freezing weather while shrimping in fifty-seven fathoms in the Gulf of Mexico. He accidently stepped onto a coil of rope as the net was being let out. Visibility was bad, and by the time he surfaced, the lights on the boat were no longer visible. Fortunately the captain turned the boat around, followed the bubbles created by the prop wash, and located David. He recalls waiting for a shark to get him since he was too cold to grab the rope thrown to him. His cousin, Alfred Black, grabbed a rope, dove in and reached him. Both were pulled safely back aboard the *Ten Kids*.

Captain Sidney Clopton died on January 25, 1978, at age sixty-eight, and is buried in the Clopton Cemetery in Brent, an area in north Pensacola where he was born. It is the cemetery where my paternal grandparents are also buried. Beside his traditional headstone stands a miniature lighthouse inscribed: "With this Light and the Grace of God May his Soul Rest in Peace." His headstone features a fishing boat and the inscription: "The Heart is Bigger than the Body."

338

Troy Moon was correct in describing the Cloptons as the "first families of Northwest Florida fishing and shrimping," as was Frank Patti in referring to Captain Sydney Clopton as "one of the pioneers."

Above: Capt. Sidney and his wife, Agnes Clopton

Below: The Clopton Family, Nine of the ten kids: Gail, David, Jeff, Tommy, Sheila, Joyce, Loice, Johnnie, and Chipley.

Above : Chipley Clopton and Sidney Jeff Clopton

Below: David Clopton with grandson, Shane Clopton

Above: Jerry Clopton

Below: Johnnie Clopton

33

Uncle Cousin D. L. Johnson

When God made D. L. Johnson, He didn't just throw away the mold, He destroyed it. He knew then, and we know now, that the world didn't need but one David Levy Johnson. Somehow I have the feeling that God places someone like D. L. on this earth to make up for those quiet, tender souls who never make a ripple, and are hardly remembered after they are gone. The word "quiet" just didn't fit D. L., unless he was helping someone or some family in dire need. Otherwise, if he was around, you knew it. And, if you wanted his opinion, or, if you didn't want his opinion, it didn't matter, because you were probably going to get it anyhow.

Uncle Cousin D.L. Johnson

342

Uncle Cousin D. L. as a little boy, with his siblings

He was born in 1903, in Brent, a community just north of Pensacola, and lived there his entire life, except for the few years he spent in the Merchant Marines. Mostly, he's remembered as the owner of Johnson Pump Company, and the Hunt Master at D. L. Johnson's Deer Hunting Camp. He was a jack-of-all-trades, and in his younger days he worked as a truck driver, carpenter, maker of whiskey stills and good boot leg whiskey. As an avid sportsman, he was known far and wide for his knowledge of hunting dogs and cock fighting. As an entrepreneur, he developed and marketed a product directly and through local veterinarians called "Johnson's Mange Magic."

D. L. was my mother's first cousin. My dad was very strict on how we kids should address adults, so my brothers and my sister and I called him "Uncle Cousin D. L." Later, he acquired the moniker, "Guvnor," used by close friends and family.

As a teenager on my first deer hunting trip with D. L.'s hunting club, I was impressed by all the stories that were told around a campfire. I've forgotten most of them, but I do remember D. L. talking about being in Germany several years prior to World War II. I don't remember which city, but he was with crew members from his ship, as he was in the Merchant Marines at the time. They were attacked by a group of thugs who mistook them for Englishmen. D. L. was convinced that Adolph Hitler was part of

343

the group. He got a little flak from some of his fellow hunters, but held to his conviction, and described the future Fuhrer in detail. The campfire became a thing of the past, because he constructed a building with a large bunk room and kitchen, complete with all modern facilities and appliances. I missed the campfires.

Now, the good book says God made each of us in His own image. I'm not so darn sure that's true, because if you will just look around, you'll realize that not too many people look alike . . .which is a good thing. Also, I'm not so sure that God made D.L. in his image either . . . but he could have. Why not?

Well, for one thing D. L. was always looking different when he was alive. It just depended on where you saw him, and what time of the year it was, and whether or not somebody who was kin or friend had died. If you had seen him at work in his well drilling clothes, he would have probably been wearing khaki pants and shirt, and I don't believe God dressed like that. If it were hunting season, he would be wearing a pair of tall hunting boots, laced up over his khaki pant legs. In the meantime, if someone he knew well died, he would be the first to offer help, and would be at the funeral, dressed in his "Sunday best."

DL as a young man

If politics was in the air, look out! He had his opinions, and his mind was usually made up, and he made dang sure that everybody knew how he felt about a certain candidate. If you didn't agree with him, well, forget about changing his mind. It wasn't that he was wrong, he usually had good judgment, but he wanted the world to know, so he was always happy to share his opinions.

In his retirement years, D.L. was still a quick thinker. His doctor had strongly encouraged him to stop smoking, and his son, Henry, reluctantly became the bad guy, since he found it necessary to fuss at his dad when he suspected he was sneaking a smoke while in the garden or his workshop. Henry described one such occasion: "He must have heard me coming, because when I got to him, he was propped up against the tool shed, feeding the last of his cigarette to one of his goats."

D.L. had a large garden and grape orchard that was the envy of his neighbors and friends. A preacher of one of the local churches lived on property that adjoined D.L's property, and they usually had long conversations "across the fence." I understand that one particular conversation went as follows:

"Mr. Johnson, I would like to invite you to come to our church services next Sunday."

"No, I don't think so," answered D.L.

"Why not?"

" 'Cause I don't want to, that's why."

"Well, don't you want to go to heaven, Mr. Johnson?"

"No."

"Why not, Mr. Johnson?" asked the preacher, who was shocked at D. L's answer.

"Well, preacher, I'll tell you why. I grew up in the country, when every family had cows. As a kid, I was the one who had to milk those dang cows, so I grew up to hate milk. My daddy had several bee hives on the property for the honey, so I didn't care much for honey either. Now I keep hearing you preachers talk about all that milk and honey up in heaven. Well, I think God just wants somebody up there to milk all those damn cows and rob all those damn bee hives."

That was typical D. L. Johnson, but I believe he's up there where the good guys go. Perhaps God would do better to use him to help provide meat and vegetables for his fellow angels.

34

USS *Pennewill* (DE 175)

During the WWII years and later, I attended school with a bunch of so-called military brats, who were children of a parent or parents serving full-time in the U. S. Armed Forces. That's the way it's always been in Pensacola, ever since the Navy Yard was established in 1825, and expanded as the base evolved into a large Naval Air Training Center. Identifying the

Chris and Bill Pennewill

children as military brats is a term of endearment in U. S. military culture, and refers to both current and former children. My wife is a military brat, and I'm proud to have had many friends over the years who fit that category. Two such friends, Bill and Chris Pennewill, who as military brats returned to Pensacola in 1941 with their mother, Lucie Reilly Pennewill, and their father, LCDR William Ellison "Bill" Pennewill, Sr., a U. S. Navy pilot reassigned to Pensacola Naval Air station.

346

LCDR Pennewill, Sr., born in Dover, Delaware in 1907, was appointed a Midshipman in 1925. Upon graduation from the U. S. Naval Academy in 1929, Ensign Pennewill reported to Pensacola Naval Air station for flight training and received his wings as a U. S. Navy aviator in 1931. He met, fell in love with and married Pensacola native, Lucie Reilly. Bill and Chris were born during the years their father was attached to several land bases as well as four ships: the USS *Chicago* (CA-29), USS *Ranger* (CV-4), USS *California*(BB-41) and the USS *Idaho* (BB-42). About the time the Pennewill family arrived in Pensacola, the United States entry into WWII was only a few months away.

Once the nation joined the conflict, tragedy struck. While away on assignment, and in command of Escort Scouting Squadron Twelve, Lieutenant Commander Pennewill lost his life on June 23, 1942, when his plane, a Grumman F4F Wildcat crashed in the Aleutian Islands.

LCDR William Ellison "Bill" Pennewill, Sr.

Lieutenant Commander Pennewill was posthumously awarded the Distinguished Flying Cross for outstanding achievement in aerial flight in contact with the enemy, for leading his inexperienced squadron in a series of remarkable flights over strange terrain and through most severe weather conditions, and for gallantly giving his life in the service of his country. He was also awarded the Purple Heart.

USS *Pennewill* (DE-175), a destroyer escort, was named in honor of Lieutenant Commander Pennewill. Her keel was laid on April 26, 1943 at the Federal Shipbuilding & Drydock Co., Port Newark, New Jersey. She was launched on August 8, 1943, sponsored by Mrs. Lucie Reilly Pennewill of Pensacola, and commissioned on September 15, 1943.

USS *Pennewill* (DE-175) Destroyer Escort

Mrs. Lucie Reilly Pennewill launching the USS *Pennewill*
with an explosion of champagne.

After shakedown the *Pennewill* saw active escort service in World War II, until she was decommissioned and leased to the Government of Brazil in 1944. In 1953, she was transferred to Brazil and struck from the U. S. Navy List. Her Brazilian name was CT *Bertioga* (BE-1). After twenty-one years of service to two nations, she was scrapped in 1964.[1]

348

LCDR Pennewill (center) and fellow squadron members. 1942

The old cliché, "the fruit doesn't fall far from the tree," is applicable in this story, because Lieutenant Commander Pennewill's sons followed in his footsteps by serving their country as officers in the U.S. Military.

Commander William E. Pennewill, Jr., USNR, (Ret), served aboard the USS *Tweedy* (DE-532) as the ASW Officer and Navigator. The *Tweedy,* a naval reserve training ship equipped for anti-submarine warfare (ASW) was activated in the 1960s during the Berlin Crisis and the lead up to the Cuban Missile Crisis. Bill is a

Commander William "Bill" Pennewill, Jr., USNR

retired banker, having served as President of a local Pensacola bank, and continues to be active in the community.

LTC Chris Pennewill, USMC

Lieutenant Colonel Christopher Pennewill, USMC, (Ret), was in the elite Marine Corps Reconnaissance Battalion, RECONS, similar to the Navy's SEALS and the Army's RANGERS. He proudly wore the Marine Corps Jump Wings. Chris retired from the Marine Corps and was involved in several successful local businesses prior to his death in 2002.

The death of Lieutenant Commander Bill Pennewill, Sr. in 1942 was, of course, sad and heartbreaking, but since Pensacola was the family home, his survivors, Lucie, Bill, Jr., and Chris remained in Pensacola, and became prominent members of the community. The Pennewill legacy exemplifies the uniqueness that exists between the military and Northwest Florida. Pensacola is fortunate to have many families who decided to remain or return to Pensacola after having been stationed locally with the military. Much has been written, and much more should be written about military retirees who have much to offer their adopted city by becoming active in government, business and civic organizations. In my lifetime alone, there have been at least three Pensacola mayors who were retired U. S, Naval officers.

Most families eventually move on with their life after a tragedy, and the Pennewill family did the same. Lucie Pennewill married prominent Pensacola businessman, George Cary, a widower with two daughters, Margaret "Molly" Cary (Biggs) and Marianne Cary (Beckman), giving Bill and Chris instant sisters. Over the years, the close, well-known, active siblings, Bill, Chris, Molly and Marianne blessed Lucie and George Cary with the joy of many grandchildren and great-grandchildren enhancing the Pennewill and Cary legacies.

Marianne, Chris, Lucie, Bill and Molly

Bill and Chris Pennewill

The two military brats, Bill and Chris, cherished the memory of their father and shared the pride in having a great ship, the USS *Pennewill* (DE-175) named in his honor.

[1] NAVSOURCE.org/archives or
Wikipedia.org./wiki/William_Ellison_Pennewill, 4/20/2015

35

USS *Tweedy* (DE 532): Destroyer Escort

Pensacola has been a Navy town since 1825, when President John Quincy Adams decided to build a Navy yard on the southern tip of Escambia County. The Pensacola Navy Yard soon became one of the best equipped naval bases in the country. Over the years, local officials, merchants, and residents have welcomed the officers and crews from military ships that made port of call in the city.

Like other military branches, the officers and crews aboard U. S. Navy ships have traditionally come from all parts of the country, however, the USS *Tweedy* (DE 532), a destroyer escort, first assigned to Pensacola in 1959 as a Naval Reserve training ship, didn't follow that tradition. The ship's normal complement of fourteen officers, a dozen or so chief petty officers and about one-hundred enlisted men consisted primarily of reservists from Pensacola, other near-by towns and rural areas.

USS *Tweedy* (DE-532) Destroyer Escort
(Courtesy of Bill Pennewill)

This was a new concept in Reserve training. For the first time in our nation's history a regular Navy ship was being manned by part-time reservists from one area. For over two years the *Tweedy* and her ship's compliment (Navy lingo for *personnel*) conducted training out of Pensacola and for two weeks each summer meshed with the active fleet in such places as Key West and Guantanamo.

The U. S. Navy names Destroyers and Destroyer Escorts after deceased heroes. The source for information about the naming of the USS *Tweedy* was obtained from NAVSOURCE NAVAL HISTORY, April 20, 2016:

The USS Tweedy was named after LT Albert William Tweedy, Jr., USMC, who was born on March 22, 1920 and attended public schools in Winnetka, Illinois and Hingham, Massachusetts, before enrolling at Williams College, Williamstown, Mass. He attended flight training at Pensacola, and was commissioned a Second Lieutenant in the United States Marine Corps Reserve on October 14, 1941. Early on the morning of June 4, 1942, during the Battle of Midway, LT Tweedy took off from the island of Midway in his

LT Albert William Tweedy, Jr., USMC

"Dauntless" Navy dive bomber. He began a bombing attack on the Japanese aircraft carrier, *Hiryu,* despite a fearsome antiaircraft barrage. Outnumbered by Japanese "Zeros," LT Tweedy dove his aircraft dangerously low over the enemy carrier before releasing his bombs for a direct hit. Japanese fighters, much faster than the U.S. Navy Dauntless, attacked, killing LT Tweedy. He was posthumously awarded the Navy Cross for his extraordinary heroism.

President John F. Kennedy, feeling the pressure of the Soviets, activated forty "small ships," including the *Tweedy,* in August, 1961, calling them into active duty with the fleet for a year. It began with the Berlin Crisis and melded into the run up of the Cuban Missile Crisis. The officers and men were civilians one day, and then awoke to life aboard ship, assigned to units of the Atlantic Fleet.

CDR William Moore,
Commanding Officer
(Courtesy of Bill
Moore and Kathy
Turtle)

The *Tweedy's* Commanding Officer, Lieutenant Commander (soon to be Commander) William Moore, an Executive Vice President at Pensacola Junior College, was suddenly in command of a fighting ship. My brother, Seaman Thomas Davis, was a Deputy Tax Collector; he and all others on board, had to leave their jobs, their loved ones, their civilian life style and report for duty aboard their ship.

The *Tweedy,* a 306 feet long WWII destroyer escort, was designed primarily to escort and protect ships in convoy. Secondly, the *Tweedy* was a specialist at finding and destroying enemy

Thomas H. Davis, SN
(Courtesy of Sue Davis)

submarines. After duty in WWII, she became a Reserve Training Ship. Her purpose, as written in a published brochure in 1961, was:

> . . . as a unit of the Navy's Selected Reserve Program, the Tweedy's mission is to maintain the ship and personnel in a state of training, readiness and availability for immediate employment in the active forces upon the initiation of

hostilities. In other words, *we are ready to put to sea at virtually a moment's notice and to become an effective unit of the fleet.*

The *Tweedy* arrived in Pensacola fourteen years after WWII. In the next two years, the officers and crew trained as a team in antisubmarine warfare. When the call came for activation in 1961, all hands were ready. The occasion for the activation by the President was the Berlin Crisis, an event that is barely a footnote in history and was soon overshadowed by the run up to the Cuban Missile Crisis, and then by the Missile Crisis itself.

The official commissioning ceremony was held on October 2, 1961, on Allegheny Pier, with several Admirals and other high-ranking officers in attendance. Pensacola native, Lieutenant Commander John A. Merritt, III, commanding officer of the U.S. Naval Reserve Training Center stood by. The ceremony marked the transition from "in service, in reserve" to a fully commissioned warship.

Thus, in October, 1961, the *Tweedy*, once again a commissioned warship, and her complement of local week-end warriors, honed to the task, departed Pensacola Bay to join up with the Atlantic Fleet and other recalled ships. In 1997, Homer Hirt, LIEUTENANT COMMANDER, USNR (Ret), Supply Officer aboard the *Tweedy*, reflected on the one year assignment in a letter to fellow officer, Ned Mayo, CAPTAIN, USN, (Ret):

That the Tweedy did well during the year of active duty may seem even more remarkable if one looks at the makeup of the wardroom and crew. Captain Moore and Lieutenant Commander William Maloy, his executive officer, both held doctorates in education, and in civilian life were associated with Pensacola Junior College and Florida State University, respectively. Other officers came from a variety of civilian activities: real estate, automobile sales, building supply management, and several engineering backgrounds.

The crew, even though each man was trained well in his respective naval rating, had been policemen, clerks, and teachers. The commissaryman (cook) was in "real" life an insurance agent! Regardless of background or interest, almost all, officers or enlisted, performed their duties with quiet efficiency and skill.

356

OFFICERS OF THE U.S.S. TWEEDY (DE 532)

LCDR WILLIAM MOORE, USNR .... Commanding Officer

LCDR WILLIAM L. MALOY, USNR .... Executive Officer

LT JAMES L. BURTON, USNR .... Gunnery Officer

LT JAMES E. SAPP, USNR .... Operations Officer

LT JACK N. JOLLY, USNR .... First Lieutenant

LT HOMER B. HIRT, JR. (SC) USNR .... Supply Officer

LTJG WILLIAM E. PENNEWILL, USNR .... ASW Officer

LTJG NED H. MAYO, USNR .... Communications Officer

LTJG GEORGE K. WALKER, USNR .... Engineering Officer

LTJG MALCOMB L. GILCHRIST, USNR .. Damage Control Assistant

USS *Tweedy* Officers
Commissioning Program
Pensacola Naval Air Station
October 2, 1961

CHIEF PETTY OFFICERS

JAMES W. BUSHEA, III
Machinest Mate Chief, USNR

PAUL G. MAULDIN
Boiler Tender Chief, USN

WILLIAM C. DUBOSE
Radarman Chief, USNR

EDWARD E. MARCH, JR.
Machinest Mate Chief, USN

THOMAS B. HARRIS
Radioman Chief, USNR

LABENCE T. NUNLEY
Gunners Mate Chief, USN

JACK E. HULL
Interior Communications
Electrician Chief, USN

CHARLES R. OGLE
Signalman Chief, USN

CHARLES P. LEE
Machinest Mate Chief, USNR

RAY H. RHODES
Radioman Chief, USNR

USS *Tweedy* Chief Petty Officers
Commissioning Program
Pensacola Naval Air Station
October 2, 1961

U. S. S. TWEEDY CREW (DE-532) CREW

AFFONCE, F. T. MM3
ALLAIN, Jerome V. RD3
ANDERSON, Hector A. BM1
ALLEN, Robert M. FN
ANDRE, Robert B. FA
ARMSTRONG, Roland E. SOG3

BARR, Wayne R. ETN3
BATES, Dan C. SN
BAILLY, Larry D. SM3
BARBER, Thomas W. FN
BENTON, Luther H. BT2,
BOLTON, Harry J. FT2
BROWN, Francis C. BM2
BROWN, Noland L. DC2
BURKE, Dale L. SN
BECK, Robert D. FN
BENTZ, Robert D. SN
BROWN, Hoover SD3
BURRUS, Gerald W. SFM3
BURT, James W. MR3
BRADLEY, H. L. Jr. SN
BOSARGE, Ellis J. SA
BOWEN, Dewey F. SN
BANSEMER, David C. SA

COOK, Parker M. FTM2
CORLEY, Willie E. Jr. CS1
CRAVEN, Paul W. QM2
CARR, Virgil J. SFM3
CHILDRESS, Tommy T. SOG2
COLEMAN, Arthur D. RM2
CONWAY, Robert T. SN
CHABOUDY, Robert B. MM2
CUNNINGHAM, Leroy FN
CUSHING, W. D. FN
CUSHING, John J. Jr. YNT1
CHRIST, Lee T. BM3

DAVIS, Billy C. BT2

DAVIS, Thomas H. SN
DAVIS, Vassar R. Jr. SN
DOWLING, Timothy T. M. BT1
DUNNAM, Donald W. MM2
DUBAZ, Don W. SA
DUTIL, Henry Jr. SA
DEESE, Marshall "T". BT1

EVERS, Mabrey C. SM1

FOSTER, James W. SN
FANNIN, J. C. SN
FALLOWS, Thomas ETR2
FRITSCH, Clyde F. CS2

GINDL, Joe W. SN
GLASS, Claude B. SA
GARDEN, John L. SN
GREEN, Joseph E. Jr. BM3
GULLING, Herbert E. Jr. YN1

HAMIL, Charles H. GM3
HART, Alton R. SN
HASS, Ronald P. RM2
HENDRIX, John W. Jr. ETN3
HORTON, Bob G. SN
HUTTO, Edward J. BM3
HATTON, Lester W. Jr. DC1
HEMPSTEAD, David R. GM1
HOFFMAN, Victor F. FN
HOLLIFIELD, Harold D. MM2
HOWELL, George Jr. DC2
HUNTER, Charles E. Jr. BT1
HANN, W. D. RM3
HANSEN, Daniel T. SA
HENNIG, August FN
HICKS, James O. FA
HENDERSON, Grady L. GMM1
HENDERSON, Robert M. SA
HOWARD, Hubert E. SN

USS *Tweedy* Crew Members, Page 1
Commissioning Program.
Pensacola Naval Air Station
October 2, 1961

359

HOWARD, Joseph H. SA

IRWIN, Joseph R. SN
IRWIN, Floyd L. SK3

JOHNSON, Thomas W. EN2
JOSEPH, Otto E. FN
JOSEPH, Edwin L. YN3

KERRICK, John W. SN
KLAUKA, Lawrence D. SN
KUTACK, Henry L. SK1
KING, Calvin E. EM1
KELLY, Vancil L. SN
KIERNAN, John H. SA
KING, Richard M. SH2
KELLY, Leo S. SN

LAWSON, Willie G. BT3
LEE, James F. SN
LEISER, Donald E. EM2
LAMBERT, Barnette H. YN3
LAWS, George L. BM3
LOGAN, Johnny MM3
LUNA, Angel G. TN
LACY, Kenneth D. SA

MILLER, Irvin L. BT2
MANCIL, Reginald SN
MC DAVID, Wilton H. Jr. QM3
MC DONALD, Robert O. SN
MC LEMORE, Charles H. SN
MORGAN, James O. SM1
MABERY, Clyde C. GMM2
MADISON, Ruben, Jr. SN
MYRICK, William M. FN

NAWROCKI, Richard T. ET2
NAYLOR, James L. CS2
NICKEL, Rudolph V. HM1
NIELSEN, Joseph N. Jr. RM2

OSTROWSKI, Stanley EM2

OLIVER, Benjamin F. SA

PULLEN, Horace B. MM3
PEAEZ, Anthony E. SA
PHELPS, James L. SA
PHILLIPS, Thomas H. MM2

RAY, Donald V. SN
RESEDEAN, F. R. HM3
RUPPING, James M. ETNSN
ROBERTS, Ronald F. SA

SAMS, James W. SN
SNIPES, Carl L. BT2
SULLIVAN, Clarence J. BM2
SETTLE, Robert SN
SPINKS, Chester P. EM1
SUGG, Richard P. RD3
SURRENCY, Walter M. FN
SHELLEY, James E. CS2
SIDLIK, Stanley T. RD2
STOKES, Larry W. MM3
SWANSON, John A. III YNSN

THOMAS, William G. Jr. FTMSN
THERIOT, Wilton L. SA
TARRANT, James L. SA
TAYLOR, Scott D. SA

UMLAUF, Raymond SO1

WHEATON, Charles W. II RD3
WEST, Karl G. BM3
WHITFIELD, Grady E. DC3
WHITE, Burley C. Jr. FN
WILDER, Jackson J. EM3
WILDER, Richard P. Jr. EM1
WHITING, Harvey E. MM1
WILLIAMS, Isaac W. BT1
WOOD, Robert H. MM1
WILKERSON, Samson, Jr. SA

YOST, Roderick A. SN

Six months into the one year assignment, the *Tweedy* and her crew, in company of four other similar ships, departed Norfolk Navy base. The destination of the five warships was, as Homer Hirt, LCDR, USNR, (Ret), wrote years later:

> . . . a certain spot off the coast of the United States; its purpose: to take part in a fleet antisubmarine exercise. The weather was far from calm. It was called 'destroyer weather' then. Miserable, choppy, gusts of wind and rain, but weather that never kept the destroyer types in port. But bearing down out of the cold Arctic reaches of the Atlantic Ocean, the very area through which destroyers and destroyer escorts had steamed during those convoy days of World War II, came a 'Northeaster,' the storm later labeled the 'Ash Wednesday Storm,' and the benchmark against which future storms of this type would be measured, whether on land or sea. It was later rated as the ninth worst storm to hit the eastern seaboard in the Twentieth Century.

USS Tweedy Rode Out Mighty Storm While on Active Duty

Source: Pensacola News Journal

Much has been written about the "Ash Wednesday Storm," in which the *Tweedy* and her crew were involved and became perilously close to becoming a sad statistic. According to Wikipedia:

> . . . the storm killed 40 people and injured more than 1,000. Property damage in six states was in the hundreds of millions of dollars. Its impact was so powerful that the U.S. Weather Bureau gave it a name: 'The Great Atlantic Storm.' It is also known as the 'Five High Storm' because it lingered off the Atlantic Coast of the northeast United States over a period of

five high tides. However, because the heaviest damages occurred in most areas on Wednesday, March 7, which was the Christian holiday of Ash Wednesday, the first day of Lent that year, it has become most popularly well known as the 'Ash Wednesday Storm of 1962.'

Fortunately, the *Tweedy* and her four sister ships made it back to safe harbor at Norfolk, but not before suffering heavy damages and injuries. They would have concurred with what Ernie Pyle, a WWII war correspondent wrote about their type ship from Okinawa in April, 1945:

> A DE my friends, is a Destroyer Escort. It is the answer to the problem of the tremendous amounts of convoying in a war, amounts so huge we simply hadn't the time to build full-fledge destroyers for escort. The escort was the result. They roll and they plunge. They back and they twist. They shudder and they fall through space. Their sailors say they should have flight pay and submarine pay both—they're in the air half the time, under the water half the time.
> My Three Years Aboard Destroyer Escorts,
> John J. Sheehan

Twenty-five years later, long after the officers and crew had returned to their civilian careers, some wrote of their memories of the storm, which for most was still vivid as if it had happened yesterday:

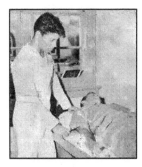

HM2 Pete Resedean with patient (Oourtesy of Mary Resedean and Gosport, NAS, Pensacola, August 21, 1959

PETE RESEDEAN, Hospitalman, 2-- (COMMANDER, USNR, RET):

I don't think other people can understand or believe what we went through. I guess our squadron would have had to sink to make it spectacular enough to impress folks. I remember being afraid to tie myself into my rack (bunk) for fear of not being able to get free if the ship started sinking. The head (bathroom) was a place to be sick because you certainly couldn't sit on the commode. The cooks and a few others were conducting prayer services on the mess deck (crews dining area). I remember Lieutenant Jim Burton receiving a bad laceration just above his eye. Nickel (Hospitalman 1) sewed him up and I assisted. It took several of us to hold him still.

CDR Pete Resedean, USNR (Ret) (Courtesy of Mary Resedean)

Pete Resedean was a Petty Officer 2nd Class during the time the *Tweedy* was activated for the Berlin Crisis and the run up to the Cuban Missile Crisis. He remained in the Navy Reserve, obtained a commission and retired with the rank of COMMANDER, an amazing accomplishment. In Pete's civilian career, he retired after becoming Chief of the Pensacola Fire Department, another great accomplishment.

LANE GILCHRIST, LTJG, Engineering-- (LIEUTENANT COMMANDER, USNR, RET):

LCDR Lane Gilchrist. USNR, (Ret) (Courtesy of Susie Gilchrist)

I recall wedging myself into the fold down rack (bunk) at a 45 degree angle and still bouncing off the rack above. (On the bridge) There was a wall of water ahead in the dark. We did not know where the other ships were—it was a miracle we did not collide. I recall being miserable for seventy-two hours, and gear being stripped off the main deck—oxygen or acetylene bottles bouncing around on deck and finally going overboard— stripped from welded steel racks. I agree with (Ned) Mayo, we were in more trouble than any of us realized at the time—Bill (Pennewill), we were a lot younger and more bulletproof in 1962.

In civilian life, Lane Gilchrist was an engineer with Gulf Power Company, having received his engineering degree from Auburn University. He served as Mayor of Gulf Breeze for seventeen years until his untimely death in 2009.

BILL PENNEWILL, LTJG, Navigator/Anti Submarine Warfare--(COMMANDER, USNR RET):

CDR Bill Pennewill,
USNR (Ret)
(Courtesy of Bill
Pennewill)

Jim Hardy, a Philadelphia lawyer on two weeks Reserve duty, reported to the pilot house for duty. Ned Mayo immediately said, 'Jim Hardy! You're just in time to abandon ship!' He dropped like a rock and had to be hauled to After Officers' Quarters, where he didn't move for two days. You, (Lane Gilchrist) slept above me the first night of the storm, yelling that your body got slammed on the overhead, and then you went to the head to throw up. (On the Bridge) knowing that chances were good that Bansemer (quartermaster seaman) was on the helm and Bill Moore (commanding officer) was always in the Pilot House captain's chair. I remember finding humor in a scenario that logically should not have evoked humor. I wondered why everyone wasn't continuously wearing life jackets. Captain Moore said he saw the inclinometer indicate a 58 roll. I watched the windgauge *slap* at 100, then fall off then *slap* and *stay* at 100 over and over (note: 100 was max reading possible). I wondered why the force of the waves did not blow out pilothouse portholes. (The Storm) were we afraid, or as somebody suggested, too young to have fear? Frankly I didn't even know where my life jacket was. I felt that as long as we had steerageway we were safe, and why worry, when I couldn't prevent it.

A graduate of Auburn University, Bill Pennewill was active in the banking community and served as president of the Bank of Pensacola. In retirement, he remains active in civic and social organizations.

WILLIAM MALOY, LCDR, Executive Officer--(CAPTAIN, USNR, RET):

Ash Wednesday, the day I should have given up for Lent. (Trying to get the loose canisters off the second deck) . . . . . The Boatswains

CAPT Bill Maloy, USNR, (Ret),
Executive Officer
(Courtesy of the Bill Maloy Family)

Mate was going to fasten a line to himself and give it a try. . . fortunately things worsened so quickly that we never had to attempt that dumb stunt. Some of you will recall the heart stopper from another ship, 'I have lost steerageway.' How she kept her head into that sea I'll never know. Several of us spoke to the rolls. Whether 58 or 56 degrees, I know not, but 10 is more than I ever want to see again. It was the heights of the sea . . . I used to say 80 feet until I noticed a number of sniggers among bored listeners. I truly believe they were not an inch under 60 feet. If I am wrong, tell me—but for God's sake don't show me.

Dr. Bill Maloy began his military service during WWII as a Navy Hospital Corpsman assigned to the Marine Corps. He earned his Bachelor's and Master's degrees in education from the University of Nebraska, and a Doctorate in education from Florida State University. He served aboard two U.S. Navy ships, but education was his career choice. As a professional educator, he served as a high school teacher, college professor, Education Advisor to two governors, and Senior Civilian Advisor to the Chief of Naval Education and Training. In addition, he was appointed to the Florida Board of Regents of the State University System and was elected Superintendent of Schools in Escambia County. Dr. Maloy died September 9, 2012.

LCDR Homer Hirt,
USNR, (Ret)
(Courtesy of Homer Hirt)

HOMER HIRT, Lieutenant, Supply and Disbursing Officer-- (LIEUTENANT COMMANDER, USNR, RET):
The storm reduced our existence to the basics—eating, trying to sleep, trying to walk from place to place, and surviving. I remember vividly the condition of the ship after we returned to port . . . paint stripped off the hull and bulkheads, life rafts gone, heavy damage to torpedo launchers and main deck fixtures. I remember sitting on the deck, holding on and eating peanut butter sandwiches. George Walker was thrown from his upper rack and landed athwart the wash basin across the room. I observed a 54 degree roll. Headlines in a Norfolk newspaper read, *'Five Old ShipsDefeat the Sea.'* We didn't defeat it . . . it toyed with us . . . and then let us go. We lost torpedos that were chained down, and, I think, some depth charges. And, no one knew where we were.

Homer Hirt resides in Sneads, Florida, and is a long time staff member with the Jackson County Times. He grew up in nearby Chattahoochee, and graduated from Florida Southern College in Lakeland, Florida. In addition to many awards for his writing talent, Homer received the Citizen of the Year award and the Wayne Mixson Economic Developer of the Year award from the Chamber of Commerce. He is a former Mayor of Sneads, and previously owned an automobile dealership. Later, Homer used his Naval experience and knowledge to successfully manage the Sneads River Port.

NED MAYO, LTJG, Communications Officer--(CAPTAIN, USN, Ret):
The isolation—I recall Bill Pennewill and I being on the open bridge. The wind was shrieking so loud that I could only see his lips move—no sound at all. In retrospect, we were in more danger than we realized. Should we have lost

LCDR Ned Mayo, USNR,
(Ret)
(Courtesy of Jan Mayo

steering through some minor failure, we would have turned broadside to the seas and probably capsized. It was the worst storm that I'd ever seen in my 23 years of active duty.

Ned Mayo was a career Navy officer. A graduate of Georgia Tech, he earned a Bachelor's degree in Physics and a reserve commission in the U. S. Navy. Following his two years of obligated sea-duty, Ned joined Armstrong World Industries in Pensacola as a research physicist. It was here that he joined the reserve crew of the *Tweedy* in the call up to the Berlin Crisis. Afterwards, he obtained a regular Navy commission, attended the Navy's post-graduate school in California, where he obtained a Master's degree in physics. After retiring as a Captain in 1988, Ned, wife Jan, and family returned to Pensacola, where he became a professor of physics at Pensacola State College. Ned died October 29, 2012 in Whitefish, Montana, the family's second home.

WILLIAM MOORE, CDR, Commanding Officer— (CAPTAIN, USNR, RET): "These are some of my memories":

Receiving the message from the admiral canceling the exercise. In it he directed each commanding office to maneuver his ship 'according to the best dictates of seamanship.' In other words, every ship for herself. Observing the inclinometer on at least one occasion swinging to the 54 or 55 degree mark. Noting that the vertical distance from trough to crest of the waves was at least 60 feet. Thanking God for the most marvelous crew a captain could ever have had.

LCDR Bill Moore makes
inspection
(Courtesy of Bill Moore
and Kathy Turtle

Dr. Bill Moore was an educator, having earned a Bachelor's, Master's, and a Doctorate in education. He resided in Pensacola for forty-two years, and worked in public schools, colleges, and universities for forty-eight years. He retired from the United States Naval Reserve as a CAPTAIN, and from Pensacola State College as a Vice President. Dr. Moore died on December 2, 1999.

In June, 1962, the USS *Tweedy* was selected as the "Visiting Navy Ship" for that year's *Fiesta of Five Flags* celebration, so her officers and crew returned to Pensacola for the event. The brief, midyear visit was one of mixed emotions. Homer Hirt, LCDR, USNR, (Ret), later wrote:

> At 8:00 (in the) morning we took in all lines, backed the good ship TWEEDY down and turned and departed Pensacola Bay. I am certain that almost everyone on her felt as I did. There was almost no talking as we sank deep into thought and perhaps some despair. We knew we were getting closer to a showdown with Castro's Cuba and possibly with the Soviet Union. We felt the uncertainty that all service folk feel in times like these.

The *Tweedy* traveled along the Florida Straits and followed the Gulf Stream currents into the Atlantic Ocean; shortly afterwards, the lookout spotted a small, open fishing boat, in which were three men, a woman, and two small children. They had departed Cuba several days earlier, bound for the Keys and freedom. The motor quit, they had no food and very little water. They and their boat were brought aboard, and the Captain ordered the *Tweedy* to turn and make for Miami. The refugees were well fed, given new clothes, and turned over to the U. S. Coast Guard at the harbor entrance. Homer Hirt, LCDR, USNR, (Ret), later wrote of the incident:

Source: Pensacola News Journal

They waved to us and cried, and I am certain that there were tears in our eyes, too. Our spirits changed and we felt renewed. We realized that our country must be something special for a mother to take her two children to sea in a boat that was unsafe in any waters, just for the possibility of an opportunity for freedom.

The *Tweedy* and her crew arrived at their destination and reported for duty, as ordered by the President and the Navy Department. The *Tweedy* participated in the run up to the Missile Crisis, which was the blockade (more properly the embargo) of Cuban ports. She was assigned out of GTMO (U. S. Navy Base, Guantanamo Bay, Cuba), to interdict Iron Curtain cargo ships that might (or might not) be carrying missiles into the island. She served well, and was on the "front" of this needed effort. Crypto was kept busy, both with incoming and outgoing encrypted messages that included secret and top secret traffic. The *Tweedy* was often near or in hostile waters.

In late August, 1962, the *Tweedy* was back in Pensacola, her mission completed. She returned to the Navy's Selected Reserve Program. The officers and crew returned to their civilian positions. Some of the many accomplishments during the year's mission were: surviving the Ash Wednesday Storm, refueling from the newest carrier, the USS *Enterprise,* patrolling Caribbean waters, encounters with possible hostile ships, rescuing Cuban citizens at sea and other individual challenges. The *Tweedy,* her officers, and her men made up a good team for her country, her Navy, and most of all, for her City of Pensacola.

The USS *Tweedy* made her final decommissioning voyage on May 29, 1969, when she arrived at Orange, Texas for inactivation. On June 30, 1969 her name was stricken from the Navy list. She was, *"on the beach,"* a Royal Navy term, meaning, *"retired from service."* In March, 1970, she was assigned to Naval Air Atlantic for destruction as a target. She was sunk as a target off Jacksonville, Florida in May, 1970. LCDR Homer Hirt, USNR (Ret) wrote: ". . . a ship that took all day to slide beneath the waves."

*Photos and Information courtesy of Bill Pennewill and Homer Hirt

The USS *Tweedy* returning to Pensacola from recall to active duty, Fall, 1962, greeted by a welcoming committee, Mayor of Pensacola, City Councilmen, Commissioners, Chief of Naval Air Basic Training and RADM Magruder Tuttle as the ship docks at Palafox Pier.
(Courtesy of Bill Pennewill)

USS Tweedy crew reunited

Reservists were called to action in response to Berlin crisis, Cuban missile crisis

Sean Dugas
sdugas@pnj.com

In 1961 many Navy reservists were called into action by President Kennedy in response to the Berlin Crisis and the escalating Cuban Missile Crisis.

Several of those men who served aboard the USS Tweedy DE 532 were from the Pensacola area. On Saturday, more than 45 years later, some those men reunited in Gulf Breeze to reminisce and reconnect.

The reunion, which was the third gathering of the Tweedy's crew, is important to

preserving the lasting bonds of friendship that formed during the men's service aboard the ship, said Homer Hirt, who now lives in Sneads.

"It's a funny thing to sit down with someone you served with but haven't seen in years," he said. "Within a minute, it's like you saw them yesterday. That's just the kind of camaraderie we share."

Hirt

The USS Tweedy was commissioned in 1944 and served as a destroyer escort until it

became a Navy training vessel in 1968, said Gulf Breeze Mayor Lane Gilchrist, who served on the Tweedy.

The ship was recommissioned in 1961 in response to the Cuban Missile and Berlin crises. The vessel and its crew, who were mostly reservists, were sent to the Windward Passage between Cuba and Haiti to photograph ships headed to Cuba from Russia, Gilchrist said.

"We were weekend warriors," he said. "But we knew what we had to do and how important it was."

Using a camera the size of a large banquet table, retired

Pensacola police Officer Joe Irwin photographed the ships entering Cuban waters and sent his analysis of the vessels to Naval intelligence officers.

"We saw all the missiles that were coming into Cuba," Irwin said. "Most of the missiles were sitting on the decks of the freighters from Russia."

Irwin

Seeing the missiles was a memorable experience for many of the Tweedy's crew, but there was another event that also deeply resonated with the

sailors — the "Ash Wednesday" hurricane in March of 1962.

According to the Weather Channel's Web site, the storm was the ninth most powerful storm of the 20th century. And the Tweedy crew rode the storm's enormous swells, which were nearly twice as high as the ship's superstructure, while traveling in the Atlantic Ocean, Hirt said.

"It was the height of the sea that I remember most," former Executive Officer William Maloy said in a letter to the crew. "I truly believe that they were not an inch under 60 feet. If I am wrong, tell me — but for God's sake don't show me."

25% OFF Cabinets*

PLUS

FREE Counter-tops*

CABINET DEPOT WELLBORN

Pensacola - R. Walton
Mobile - Biloxi - Wilcox

cabinet-depot.com
1-877-435-DEPOT

Source: Pensacola News Journal and Bill Pennewill

36

WCOA Radio Station

In the early 1940s, while attending elementary school at Annie K. Suter, my friends and I would often catch the bus from East Pensacola Heights into town to watch a double-feature at either the ISIS or Rex Theatre. The San Carlos Hotel was directly across the street from both theatres. I don't know how we kids knew that the WCOA Radio Station was in the hotel, but we did, and thought our trip to town was not complete if we didn't visit the radio station before catching the bus home. First, we avoided the elevators near the front desk and sneaked past the bellhops and managers before charging up the winding staircase to the second floor, where we then took the elevator to the top floor.

It was a big hotel, and we walked the halls, avoiding eye-contact with the housekeeping ladies who watched us suspiciously. Eventually we would find the large plate glass window that exposed the studio and equipment. We stared in childish wonderment at the announcers and disk-

WCOA Logo

jockeys at work. It was a world of high technology that we kids could not understand. All we knew about radios was that people sat in front of them at home listening to programs like *Lassie, Rin Tin Tin, The Lone Ranger,* and *The Green Hornet*. In the evenings, our family gathered around the radio; actually, we stared at the radio as we listened to *Fibber Magee &*

Molly, Charlie McCarthy, Red Skelton, Bob Hope, and many others. My favorite was *Bill Stern's Sports Legends and Tall Tales.*

My friend and fellow writer, Ron Tew, said when he and his buddies were growing up in Mississippi, they always listened to baseball games on Saturdays. They would sing "Take Me Out to the Ball Game" during the seventh inning stretch, and sang "Wabash Cannonball" with Dizzy Dean. Just think, if it had not been for radio, the world would not have heard Dizzy Dean shout , "he slud into third base."

WCOA was Pensacola's first radio station and the area's main source of entertainment and information. We kids, and probably most adults, were not curious about how, when, or by whom WCOA was brought to Pensacola; we were more concerned about our favorite programs and the

news. However, if we had inquired, we would have learned that on February 3, 1926, at precisely 8:30 p.m. WCOA began broadcasting from studios on the second floor of City Hall, since it was owned by the City of Pensacola. The station's records show that City Clerk John E. Frenkel, Sr. was placed in charge. He obtained the proper permits, figured out how to operate the equipment (which he purchased for $3,500), and came up with the call letters WCOA, which stood for, "Wonderful City of Advantages." Calling

John E. Frenkel, Sr.

himself the "Breezy Boy from the Gulf," Frenkel was the voice of WCOA for several years and even sang, "Down Pensacola Way," the original song written for the first broadcast.

I wrote elsewhere in the chapter titled, "John E. Frenkel, Sr.": "He traveled with Harvey Bayless, Mayor of Pensacola, to Atlanta and then to Washington D. C. in an effort to give WCOA and Pensacola a voice on the airways." Included in the same chapter, was an article by Celia Myrover Robinson, in the magazine, *Florida on the Gulf*:

So, Mayor J. Harvey Bayless and City Clerk John E.Frenkel made a trip to Atlanta, and there met W. Van Nostrand, Jr., supervisor for radio for the southeasterndistrict, who accompanied them to Washington, where the Florida representatives, Senator Duncan U. Fletcher and

373

Congressman J. H. Smithwick helped them to get in
conference with the powers to be. Permission was
granted to the City of Pensacola then to install WCOA.
WCOA took (to) the air during the last part of last
February (1926), on a 222 meter wave length and 500 watts
power. Mr. Frenkel volunteered as public servant to
sponsor the station as a city institution. He not only
assumed responsibility for its physical well being, but he
took charge of the programs. Having a good voice himself,
he has not neglected the musical phase of the broadcasting.

Even though it was a cool night on February 3, 1926, a large crowd
gathered in front of City Hall and spilled over into Plaza Ferdinand across
the street. The broadcast was piped over a large loud-speaker on top of City
Hall. Local citizens who owned receivers could tune into the 500 watt
signal that was broadcast from two, 250 watt, 100-foot towers located
behind City Hall.

WCOA Staff.

The City of Pensacola, Florida
cordially invites you to be present
at the opening of its
Radio Broadcasting Station
W.C.O.A.

"Wonderful City of Advantages"
at half after eight o'clock
Wednesday evening, February third
Nineteen hundred and twenty-six
City Hall

Board of Commissioners
J. H. Bayliss, Mayor
Commissioner of Finance and Revenue
Thos. H. Johnson
Commissioner of Streets and Public Works
E. E. Harper
Commissioner of Police and Fire

WCOA
222 Meters
"Wonderful City of Advantages"

MUNICIPAL BROADCASTING STATION
CITY OF PENSACOLA, FLORIDA

BOARD OF CITY COMMISSIONERS

J. H. BAYLISS, Mayor
Commissioner of Finance and Revenue

THOS. H. JOHNSON
Commissioner of Streets and Public Works

E. E. HARPER
Commissioner of Police and Fire

JOHN E. FRENKEL
Announcer and Director

Inaugural Program

MUNICIPAL BROADCASTING STATION

WCOA
ON WAVE LENGTH 222 METERS
"Wonderful City of Advantages"

CITY OF PENSACOLA, FLORIDA

WEDNESDAY EVENING FEBRUARY 3, 1926
EIGHT-THIRTY O'CLOCK

JOHN E. FRENKEL, Announcer and Director

WCOA
222 Meters

PENSACOLA, FLORIDA

INAUGURAL PROGRAM

8:30. "DOWN PENSACOLA WAY"
Miss Anita O. Villar and Mr. John E. Frenkel, soloists, assisted by Chorus of artists participating in program.

8:40. Hon. HARVEY BAYLISS, Mayor City of Pensacola
Dedication of WCOA and the truth about Pensacola—"Wonderful City of Advantages."

8:45. Mrs. S. L. LaHATCHE, Vocal Solo.
Accompanist, Miss Elizabeth Moreno.

8:55. Lt. Col. R. H. WILLIAMS, Commanding Fort Barrancas at Pensacola, "Army Activities at Pensacola."

9:00. 13th COAST ARTILLERY BAND, stationed at Fort Barrancas, Pensacola, Florida, in melodies of the Old South and popular airs.

9:10. Hon. THOS. H. JOHNSON, Commissioner, City of Pensacola, expressing his sentiments as to WCOA and Pensacola.

9:13. Mr. EMILIO O'BRIEN MOTTA, Violin Solo.
Miss Katherine Motta, accompanist.

9:23. JOHN E. FRENKEL in "Popular Arias of Today."
Mr. E. J. Johnson at the Baldwin Grand.

9:35. Hon. ERNEST E. HARPER, Commissioner, City of Pensacola, "Pensacola Topics and WCOA."

9:38. Mrs. J. P. SANDUSKY and Mr. MICHAEL DiLUS-TRO, Vocal Duet. Accompanist, Miss Marguerite Roberts.

9:48. Miss ANITA O. VILLAR, Vocal Solo.
Accompanist, Miss Frances Keen Villar.

9:58. Major W. VAN NOSTRAND, Jr., Supervisor of Radio, Atlanta, Ga., Pensacola's honor guest and representative of Department of Commerce, Radio Department.

10:00. Mrs. SYLVIA MITCHELL, "Pianologue from the Land of Jazz."

10:03. Mr. W. B. FERRISS, President Pensacola Chamber of Commerce.

WCOA
222 Meters
PENSACOLA, FLORIDA

INAUGURAL PROGRAM

10:15. Mr. DAVID LLOYD, Tenor Solo.
Accompanist, Miss Elizabeth Moreno.

10:15. Hon. GEORGE E. CRAWFORD, Mayor City of Mobile, Alabama. Honor guest City of Pensacola. Address selected.

10:18. Instrumental Trio, "Purveyors of Melody"—Mr. MAX J. HEINBERG, Violin; Miss IMOGENE JONES, Piano, and Mr. RAY C. DINSMORE, Cello.

10:28. Capt. J. J. RABY, Commandant, U. S. Naval Air Station, Pensacola, Florida. Largest Naval Aviation Station in the World. "Aviation in Pensacola."

10:30. Mrs. W. QUINTILLUS JEFFORDS, Vocalist.
Accompanist, Mrs. Paul P. Stewart.

10:40. Mr. MAX J. HEINBERG, Violinist.
Accompanist, Miss Imogene Jones.

10:50. Mrs. OLGA WHITE BARNES, internationally known expressionist. Humorous Readings.

11:00. RAINBOW ORCHESTRA, High Flyers in Melody and and Jazz. "Flyin' High."

11:12. Mrs. C. M. KELLY, Vocalist.
Accompanist, Mrs. Paul P. Stewart.

11:22. Playlet, Descriptive, By Announcer JOHN E. FRENKEL.

11:27. MT. OLIVE JUBILEE SINGERS of Pensacola. In Negro Spiritual Melodies of Olden Days.

11:40. ANNOUNCING OF WINNERS OF PRIZES offered by merchants and radio fans of Pensacola for telegrams received during broadcasting program over WCOA.

11:50. "DOWN PENSACOLA WAY," Finale, by all artists appearing on this program.

Baldwin Artist Grand Piano used and played exclusively by all artists
participating in this broadcasting program

WCOA came into being just six years after the birth of radio and operated for almost six years before John C. Pace bought the station on December 1, 1931, for a purchase price of $6,500. He indicated he would spend another $20,000 to modernize the station. The studios were moved to the top floor of the San Carlos Hotel where they remained until 1949, during which time the station increased its power to 5,000 watts. An interesting excerpt from an article about WCOA was written by Maxwell Chase and published by Pensacola Independent News. It states, "One of the most significant events that occurred during that time was the crash of the Hindenburg in 1937. Radio stations all over the country broadcast live coverage of the unlikely tragedy, but WCOA was the only one who recorded it. Engineers left the tape rolling from the previous show and inadvertently archived a powerful moment in world history."

WCOA continued to grow and operated for many years as an affiliate of NBC. In 1956, on its 30th anniversary, the station received congratulations from notables around the country, including Frank Sinatra and Nat King Cole. The station changed ownership, locations, and network affiliation several times while expanding. In 1991, the programming switched to an all-talk format. On February 16, 2006, Congressman Jeff Miller, in a speech to the U. S. House of Representatives, said, "Mr. Speaker, on behalf of the United States Congress, it is an honor for me to rise today to recognize the 80th Anniversary of NewsTalk Radio, 1370 WCOA."

On February 3, 2016, the station celebrated its 90th Anniversary. Don Parker, Jim Sanborn and Bryan Newkirk hosted several of WCOA's former personalities in an hour long broadcast that included: Gordon Towne, Dave Pavlock, John Teelin, and others. It was a lively discussion by a group of broadcast professionals who for years have entertained and informed the public.

Today, WCOA continues to run on AM 1370 under the Cumulus Broadcasting Company. While industries and businesses have been greatly influenced by the expansion of technology,   this is especially true in broadcasting. A good example is the information Gordon Towne, former General Manager at WCOA in the mid-1980s, shared in a recent talk before a group at a local church. He said he supervised over fifty employees, whereas today it takes only a few employees to run the station.

Following are a list of professional broadcasters I remember who were or are presently with WCOA. Only one of them, John Frenkel, Sr., was with the station when my young friends and I were sneaking into the old San Carlos Hotel in the early 1940s.

CURRENT BROADCASTERS	FORMER BROADCASTERS AT WCOA	
1. Brian Newkirk	1. Bern Benicks	14. Dave Pavlock
2. Don Parker	2. Ted Cassidy*	15. Don Priest
3. Jim Sanborn	3. Ellis Davis	16. Don Redfield
4. Rick Outzen	4. John Frenkel, Sr.	17. Bob Reed
	5. Don Griffith	18. Steve Remel
	6. Sally Henderson	19. John Richardson
	7. Ronnie Joyce	20. Jim Roberts
	8.. Luke McCoy	21. Arlene Sadrow
	9. Victor Land	22. John Teelin
	10.. Dan Lucus	23.Gordon Towne**
	11. Laura Lunsford	24. John Waite
	12.. Pappy Lynn	25. Marty White
	13. Rusty Menschew	26. Jim Young

* Ted Cassidy was one the most widely known of the broadcasters. After leaving WCOA, he played the character "Lurch" on *The Adams Family* TV show.
** Gordon Towne served as General Manager of WCOA and Vice President of Summit Communications of Florida. (See chapter this volume titled, *Gordon Towne).*

Rick Outzen

379

Above: John Teelin, Don Parker, Dave Pavlock, Bryan Newkirk and Gordon Towne

Below: Jim Sanborn, John Teelin, Dave Pavlock, and Gordon Towne

NEWS

RADIO

TONY GIBERSON/NEWS JOURNAL FILE PHOTO

In this 2007 photo, Florida State Sen. Don Gaetz, left, talks with the Luke McCoy.

Former WCOA host Luke McCoy dies

HANA FRENETTE
HFRENETTE@PNJ.COM

Longtime WCOA radio host and well-known Pensacolian Luke McCoy has died at the age of 76.

McCoy joined WCOA in 1993. He hosted "Pensacola Speaks" and was a prominent figure of conservative politics in Pensacola. He retired from a 40-year career in radio in 2008.

McCoy died Friday at his home in South Carolina after a year-long battle with lung cancer.

Services are pending.

37

Wayne Westmark
Sergeant at Arms,
Florida House of Representatives

Wayne Westmark

Wayne Westmark and his three brothers grew up in the Brent area, a few miles north of downtown Pensacola. All four of Sam and Alta Westmark's boys were born during the depression years. "We were poor as dirt," Wayne recently said, while my wife Sandra and I were having lunch with him in Tallahassee in November, 2015. Being poor was not uncommon in those terrible years of the Great Depression and World War II but, sadly, conditions became worse when Sam Westmark, an employee of Gulf Power Company, died of a heart attack in 1942.

David, Edward, Ronald and Wayne, the Westmark brothers

With faith, determination, and established goals, plus encouragement and guidance from their mom, the four Westmark boys excelled. Two of Wayne's brothers, Edward and David, are physicians; his youngest brother, Ronald, a graduate of Mississippi State University, is a successful businessman; and Wayne, a graduate of Florida State University, spent twenty-two years as the Sergeant at Arms in the Florida House of Representatives.

The Westmark families of Northwest Florida make up a respectable clan that has made its mark in business, politics, government, and medicine throughout the region. The Sam and Alta Westmark branch followed that tradition, and the individual successes of each of their four sons has the makings of a great story, but this story is mostly about Wayne and his family, who eventually made their home in the Tallahassee area.

FSU Tally Ho

Wayne and I were classmates at Clubbs Junior High School, Pensacola High School, and Florida State University. Prior to enrolling at FSU, he attended Pensacola Junior College and Mississippi State University. We often crossed paths on the FSU campus and, following college, we occasionally bumped into each other in airports as we traveled our respective territories as sales reps for different industries.

Wayne met his wife Joyce at East Hill Baptist Church, back when

Joyce Lambert Westmark

the church was at its original site on Gadsden Street. The youth group was sponsoring a hayride and he was smitten with the attractive blonde, a nursing student from Atmore, Alabama. "It took me three weeks to get a date with her," Wayne said. He is quick to tell everyone, "When I looked across the room and saw her, I saw the most beautiful woman I'd ever seen." Obviously, the wait was worth it because she became his bride on June 6, 1956 at East Hill Baptist Church.

Joyce graduated from Sacred Heart's Nursing School and, after their wedding, they moved to Tallahassee. While Wayne worked toward a degree in Biology at FSU, and Joyce worked as a Registered Nurse, both worked toward expanding the family. The

Joyce and Wayne enjoying life on the water

family grew, two girls and a boy: Cindy, Lindy, and Jay, each separated by two years; a timely feat, easily accomplished when the parents include a Biologist and a Registered Nurse.

Wayne earned his degree in biology in 1956, and spent the next two years in research as an employee in FSU's biochemistry department. With his family still growing he needed to make more money, so he resigned. His field of study and experience provided a natural entrée into the pharmaceutical industry, where he was very successful and the financial rewards were good. Company management moved Wayne and the family to Georgia, but with success, he gained clout with his superiors, who agreed to relocate his base of operations back to the Tallahassee area.

THE WESTMARKS
TALLAHASSEE, FLORIDA

Being an adventurous family, they moved to Oyster Bay Estates in Wakulla, County, a short distance south of Tallahassee. It was ideal since the whole family enjoyed fishing, crabbing, and scalloping on the St. Marks flats. They also enjoyed Wayne's mullet boat as well as the family's pleasure. Wayne's love for being near the water was acquired from early years on the beaches around Pensacola when he and his three brothers used to go skinny-dipping at Aunt Jenny's Hole,[1] a popular spot on Carpenter's Creek in the Brent area.

Biology, biochemistry, and years in the pharmaceutical industry were not prerequisites for a career in public service, but it worked for Wayne when his many other talents were thrown in. His numerous friends and family members in Pensacola and Tallahassee were very proud when the Speaker of the House, Don Tucker, appointed Wayne to the important

get the best of life
BRISTOL

386

and powerful position of Sergeant at Arms of the Florida House of Representatives. He was subsequently sworn in on September 1, 1976 by a member of the Florida Supreme Court. The position was for a term of two years, and Wayne was reappointed by subsequent Speakers of the House ten times. He served in that position for twenty-two years, the longest ever for any Sergeant at Arms in the House of Representatives. His last appointment was by Speaker of the House, Daniel Webster, current U.S. Congressman from Florida. Wayne retired on June 3, 1998.

One of the swearing in ceremonies of Wayne Westmark as
Sergeant at Arms in the Florida House of Representatives

While discussing his long career as Sergeant at Arms, Wayne explained that he had to break up occasional fights when heated debates on the floor of the house continued in private conferences. He recalled one instance in 1992, involving two Miami house members regarding a bill that appropriated money due to damages from Hurricane Andrew. He said, "I heard the fight going on in the Speaker's conference room; the guy that caused the fight was as slick as you know what on a doorknob." Wayne explained that the guy had slipped in an amendment to the bill that put the money into his district and not the other house member's district as intended by the original bill.

I suggested to Wayne that he should consider writing a book about his many interesting experiences as the Sergeant at Arms for a record twenty-two years. He laughed and said, "Charlie, I'm too old, I know too much, and I don't want to die." He suggested that when we get back together, he would gladly share some interesting situations that occurred during his tenure which I might want to write about. I assured him that I, too, preferred to live.

Our own Jerry Maygarden, former State Representative and Majority Leader from Escambia County, had kind comments and amusing memories about Wayne. Jerry explained that smoking was not allowed in the House chamber, so the smokers often took breaks in Wayne's office, with his approval. Jerry laughed when he said, "You had to have a knife to cut through the smoke to get into Wayne's office."

I believe I would be safe in assuming a most proud and emotional day for Wayne during those twenty-two years as Sergeant at Arms was the day the Speaker of the House, Ralph Haben, acknowledged Wayne's mother, Alta Westmark, who was in the visitor's gallery. He asked both, Mrs. Westmark and Wayne, to stand and be recognized. The ovation was loud and clear, a tribute to both of them. I am sure the Honorable Mr. Haben was aware that Alta Westmark was highly regarded as a person, a mother, and respected in her long-time position with the County Clerk's office at the Escambia County Court House.

As mentioned above, Wayne was reappointed ten times, not because he had political clout or some other form of influence, but because he did his job well, and followed the rules of the house and the responsibilities required of the Sergeant at Arms. An incident occurred that gained national attention when Wayne followed the rules, and refused to allow Jimmy Buffett of Margaritaville fame to enter the floor of the House of Representatives without a coat and tie—although he had been invited by the Representative from Miami. I don't know if he was wearing "A White Sport Coat and a Pink Crustacean,"[2] but if he was, it wasn't enough—he needed a tie. Wayne would not allow him to enter the floor as he was dressed, and it later made national news. A coat and tie was found for the singer, and he eventually entered the chamber.

Wayne and I compared notes on growing up with brothers; he had his three and I had my five. We laughed about how when we were young that fighting was the order of the day. He explained that his mother handled that problem, once she stopped the fight, by making them kiss. I can't imagine how that would have worked with me and my five brothers—it

A Westmark Family get-together

would have been worse than having to kiss our sister.

When the three Westmark children were out of the nest, Wayne and Joyce moved back to Tallahassee to Shalibeau Farm, a working horse farm, and she returned to nursing. They celebrated their 50th wedding anniversary in 2006 at the Gibson Inn in Apalachicola, surrounded by many family members and friends. Later, when both retired, they enjoyed traveling and spending time at their vacation retreat in the mountains of North Georgia.

On October 16, 2013, fifty-seven years, three months, and ten days after their wedding at East Hill Baptist Church, Joyce died, after struggling for years with COPD. At that time, she and Wayne had, in addition to their three children, five grandchildren and one great-grandchild.

Wayne currently lives on thirteen acres in Chairs, Florida, a small community east of Tallahassee. He and daughter, Cindy, recently zipped through his old hometown on their way to Mobile to visit his grandson, a professor of chemistry at the University of South Alabama. His grandson obtained his doctorate in physics from FSU. The trip probably gave him an opportunity to visit with his brother Ronald in Lillian, Alabama, and Edward, who practices medicine in Pensacola, but lives in Gulf Breeze. It's much easier to visit with his brother David because his medical practice is in Crawfordville, a small town south of Tallahassee.

Wayne and Joyce enjoying life together

I need to warn Wayne just in case he gets nostalgic and wants to visit his old stomping grounds for a beer at the Old English Tavern; it closed a long time ago, as did Aunt Jenny's Hole, just in case he has the urge to go skinny-dipping.*

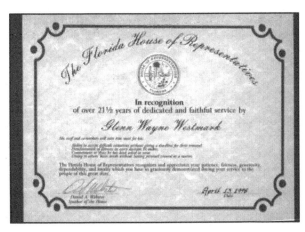

*Sadly, Wayne died unexpectedly in July, 2016

Above: Wayne, FSU Coach, Bobby Bowden and Charlie Ward, 1993 Heisman Trophy Winner and Pensacola's Washington High School head coach.

Below: Wayne and Richard Petty, NASCAR Hall of Fame Race Car Driver

[1] See chapter, "Aunt Jenny's Hole."
[2] Buffett's play on Marty Robbin's, "A White Sport Coat and a Pink Carnation
."Photos courtesy of Wayne Westmark

391

38

You're Never Too Old

You're never too old to play softball, just ask some of the "old codgers" who play serious softball on several local teams, all sanctioned by the Softball Players Association (SPA), a national organization. These granddaddies don't sit in the park and feed pigeons or rock on their porches,

Senior Softball Team sponsored by Ed's Aluminum Buildings

they travel all over the country and compete with other grandpas in their 50's, 60's, 70's and yes, some even 75 and older. Senior Softball is a major player in the American Sports scene and will continue to grow in popularity as senior citizens age gracefully through healthy habits and exercise.

The SPA is not a private men's club, there's a women's division also. The local softball playing gals are just as serious about the game as the men are, they are tough and win more than their share of the games. Whoever wrote that Christmas song, "Grandma Got Run Over by a Reindeer," didn't have those grandmas in mind. A reindeer wouldn't dare, he'd end up on the spit at one of their frequent cookouts.

My late friend, John Stanhagen, a retired local banker, was a first baseman on Ed's Aluminum Buildings team in the Gold Seniors 70s Division. John was no stranger to softball, baseball, basketball, or football. He lettered in all of them and played sports since he was a kid. He couldn't help it, his dad, known as Kenneth "Kid" Stanhagen, was selected to be on West Virginia's All-State basketball team from Keyser High School in 1929. The old cliché, "like father like son," held true when John was picked to be on the All-Florida basketball team from Pensacola High School in 1957. Sports writer, J. Suter Kegg, quoted the *Pensacola News Journal* in his column "Tapping On The Sports Keg":

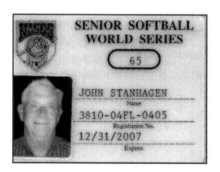

Stanhagen, considered by most Northwest Florida coaches as the best college prospect in the Panhandle, led coach Shorty Sneed's Tigers with 349 points during the regular season. Averaging 15.1 points a game, the slender PHS athlete is a deft rebounder, a strong defender and skillfully champions the Tigers' fast-breaking attack. The Pensacola High cager was one of the big guns in the Tigers'

sudden reversal of form this year. Consistently the top scorer, Stanhagen and his teammates snapped back from a 4-11 chart in 1955-56 to log 20 victories against three losses this season.

John had several scholarship offers from colleges around the country, but he chose Marion Military Institute in Marion, Alabama where, as a cadet, he excelled in basketball and baseball. Upon graduation, he entered the United States Army; following his discharge, he attended the University of Tampa and later returned home to pursue a career in banking.

JOHN STANHAGEN

Stanhagen, J. A.
1st Base

Like other players on Ed's Aluminum Building's team, John's passion for playing sports didn't end when he became a banker but continued into retirement years. He joined the team in 1990 as a first baseman when he was a vice president of a local bank.

I didn't know much about senior softball, but I knew John and our mutual friend, Ronnie Pfeiffer, an engineer and former football standout at Pensacola High School, were actively involved and traveling all over the country to play. When I heard that a couple of other gray-haired friends were also playing softball, I decided to investigate the sport. After doing some basic research, I was amazed at how big, popular, and organized the game had become. More than 1.5 million men and women over forty play Senior Softball in the United States today. Tournaments and championships are sanctioned throughout the world.

What impressed me the most was the caliber of the players; they were not a bunch of older guys out of work or retired with time on their hands. They were mostly well-known professionals or semi-professionals, some retired, others still working, who loved the comradery of competitive sports. Among the players were engineers, a vice mayor and a city councilman, the Escambia County Sheriff, the Executive Director of the Historic Pensacola Preservation Board, deputy sheriffs, a land surveyor, printer, several civil service employees, bank officials, business owners, a high school teacher and coach, and a former Detroit Tigers second baseman.

Among the several local senior softball teams, I have chosen to focus on one team, Ed's Aluminum Buildings, one of the top teams, which organized over twenty-five years ago. Ed Vignolo, owner of Ed's Aluminum Buildings, is the team's sponsor. Known affectionately as "Mr. Ed" by the players, he and his wife, Joyce, are actively involved with the team. The business was founded in 1972 and was proud to begin sponsoring the "Over 50 Senior Softball Team" in 1990. As the team members moved up in the age group, their classification changed. For example: "Over 55, 60, 65, 70, and 75." During the past twenty-five years, their team has moved up to the "Over 75 Senior Softball Team." Team members have come and gone

Joyce and Ed Vignolo

over the years, and the group has traveled all over the country and won many tournaments, including the Seniors Softball World Series in 1992.

Senior Softball has become a very popular sport in Pensacola, partly because of travel teams like Ed's Aluminum, who has hosted a Softball Players Association's regional qualifier each year and partly due to the Seniors Games Program sponsored by the City of Pensacola. Ed's Aluminum team has hosted the SPA Winter Invitational in the past, which

2001 National Softball Association Senior Division World Series Trophy

brought teams from across America to Pensacola to compete for a national crown.

Listed below are current and former members of Ed's Aluminum team over the past twenty-five years:

Andrews, Johnny	Hepworth, Bill	Pfeiffer, Ronnie, Sr.
Barker, Terry	Horne, Howard	Quinlan, Paul
Block, Ray	Joyner, Kenny	Sansom, "Shake"
Bush, Dave	Jones, Bill	Seely, Vince
Bodley, Howard	Jones, Lonnie	Smith, Clint
Carrick, Larry	Kraznosky, John	Stanhagen, John
Daniels, John	Lemon, Ray	Sunday, Jimmy
DeSorbo, Mike	McLeod, Cecil	Thatcher, Rod
Edgecombe, Robert	Moore, George	Ward, Chris
Falzone, Robert	Mullen, Bob	White, Marco
Faulk, Jimmy	Nelson, Ben	White, Moose
Fraker, Bart	Parker, Lewis	Wood, Jake
Gerwe, Jim	Pierce, Pete	Yates, Wayne

I find it interesting that of the above thirty-nine players, all of whom would have, or did, move up to the "Over 75 Senior" class, only four have died: John Daniels, Bart Fraker, Lewis Parker and John Stanhagen. Eleven are still playing. They are: Dave Bush (plays on an over 80 senior team in South Florida, yet lives in Gulf Breeze), Mike DeSorbo, Bill Hepworth, Kenny Joyner, Ray Lemon, Cecil McLeod, Bob Mullen, Ronnie Pfeiffer, Sr., Jake Wood, Wayne Yates, and "Shake" Sansom.

One lesson I learned while gathering information about Senior Softball is that it's hard as hell to get information from the individual players—they're never home. They must be out practicing or running the streets, which is probably the nature of a senior softballer. They seem to follow the advice Jake Gaither, the legendary coach at Florida A & M University, gave his players: "I want you to be ag-ile, hos-tile, and mo-bile." They are just that, and the ones I talked to were excited about the games, the trips out of town for tournaments, and the fact that wives, kids, and grandkids enjoy the games and activities as much as they do.

Seniors are increasing faster than our younger populations, thus, we no longer have to drive down to St. Pete to watch octogenarians play softball—we can just visit our local ballparks and root for grandpa or grandma.

PENSACOLA 60'S

ED'S ALUMINUM 1990

Kneeling L to R: Ronnie Pfeiffer, Lewis Parker, Bart Fraker, Ed Vignolo, Vince Seely.
Standing: Ken Joyner, Bill Jones, Jimmy Sunday, Ray Block, Marco White, John Stanhagen, Terry Barker, Bobby Mullin

Seniors Softball World Series
Ed's Aluminum

First Row, Left to Right: Bert Foster, Shelton McLeod, John Krasnosky, Robert Falcone, John Daniels, Ed Vigliotti, Lonnie Jones, Moose White. Second Row: Dale Ward, Wayne O. Yates Sr., Jimmie Sanley, Jerry Barton, John Stankagen, Robert Edgecombe, Raymond Block, Ron Jeyton, Bob Mullen.

SENIOR SOFTBALL '97

1996 AAA CHAMPIONS - USSSA
Garland, Texas

Ed's ALUMINUM Buildings
Pensacola, FL

Enter MAY 2009

LOCAL SOFTBALL

Winning is an ageless feeling

Softball
championship
came down
to final out

Sean Smith
@PensacolaNewsJournal.com

A long journey for a bunch of regular guys from Pensacola ended with the Softball Players Association national championship in the 60-65 age group.

But it wasn't until the final out — as Ed's Aluminum whipped the Georgia Peaches twice in the double-elimination tournament last fall in Panama City — that pitcher and Coach Mike DeSorbo let it all sink in.

"It's a real rush," said DeSorbo, 63. "No matter of what level sport you're at. When you know the caliber of the team you're playing

Jim Sands @PensacolaNewsJournal.com

Moose White, left, Wayne Yates, center, and Howard "Hobo" Bodley led Ed's Aluminum softball team in batting during their run at the Senior Softball National Championship in Panama City.

Still going

7/26/2005

Mike DeSorbo, manager and pitcher for Ed's Aluminum Buildings softball team, said some team members have been playing together for more than 20 years.

Photos by Miriam R. Craft/Pensacola News Journal

Members of Ed's Aluminum Buildings softball team are from bottom left: Jimmy Faulk, John Stanhagen, Jake Wood, Ron Pfeiffer, Moose White, Mike DeSorbo, Dave Bush, Wayne Yates and Ray Block.

After almost 20 years, softball team still has the drive and desire to win

Geoff Watts
News Journal correspondent

As the Major League baseball regular season progresses toward its tumultuous conclusion, spirit for America's grand ol' game continues to radiate.

While children of all ages and abilities typically have played out this uniquely American rite of passage on the plentiful Pensacola-area diamonds, another "more mature" version of the national pastime is briskly taking hold.

Softball — in particular senior softball — has been proudly represented in Pensacola by Ed's Aluminum Buildings softball club for nearly two decades.

"Softball's a good, fun sport. It keeps you going and is very much growing," said 67-year-old pitcher/manager Mike DeSorbo, who also

Inside/3D

■ Baby Boomers are taking up the game of softball as more and more leagues pop up for older players.

is a member of the Pensacola City Council. "Ed's (Aluminum Buildings) has sponsored us for 16 years.

"Most of us have been playing together since over-40 ball. A lot of us have been playing together between 20-25 years.

"Everybody (on the team) is at least 68. We've got a couple (players) between 65 and 70."

But don't let the advanced age fool you.

Competitive juices and respect

for the game flow like rapids through every member of this bunch, having previously captured five national softball championships — the most recent being the 2003 World Series in Plano, Texas.

"Well, at the senior level, I guess I'd have to say it's very gentlemanly," DeSorbo said. "The game itself is very competitive, but it's not one of those games that somebody's in there trying maybe to take somebody out or hurt somebody to make a base or throw at somebody or something like that.

"I think people are surprised when they see the caliber of play that we play.

"We've got guys like Jake Wood and Wayne Yates and a couple others that will put the ball out of the ballpark at 300 feet.

See TEAM CHEMISTRY, 3D

403

39

Local Heroes and their Flying Machines

I don't remember the year, but it was probably sometime in the early 1960s. I was driving north on 12th Avenue when a B-17, a four engine, WWII vintage bomber known as the "Flying Fortress," flew low in front of me, its wheels down, preparing to land at the Pensacola Airport. It was surprisingly large and loud as it reached the airport and disappeared from view. I drove faster and headed to the airport, hoping to see up close the type of airplane my brother, W. A. "Bill" Davis, was a waist-gunner in. He completed fifty-five daylight combat missions over Germany during WWII.

W. A. "Bill" Davis, USAAF

When I reached the airport, I drove to the Pensacola Aviation building where private planes are serviced and stored rather than going to the terminal building. As I exited my car, a friend and fellow insurance agent, Walter McLeod, drove up about the same time. After exchanging pleasantries, he asked, "You going flying?"

"No, I came by to see that B-17 that just landed."

"You talking about the P-51?" he said, as we walked toward the small building.

"No, no, I just saw a B-17 Flying Fortress going in to land here at the airport. That's why I stopped by."

"That was a P-51 Mustang. It flew over in a landing pattern while I was in my back yard, so I drove over here to take a look at it," he said.

We reached the building without saying another word to each other. Both of us must have assumed the other didn't know a P-51 from a B-17. As it turned out, we were both right. A P-51 had landed a few minutes before the B-17, and both were taxiing toward us as we arrived. A small group of people had gathered. The Mustang, in the lead, looked so small in comparison to the Flying Fortress. As they drew near, the combined noise from the B-17's four engines plus the P-51's was unbelievable. I wondered how the English, and later the Italians must have reacted to the noise as hundreds of bomb-loaded B-17s and their P-51 escorts took off on their daily missions over Nazi Germany. We watched as both planes parked off the tarmac on the grass as directed by an employee of the aviation company.

Lt. Walter McLeod, USAF, WWII
(Courtesy of Gay Bell)

Lt. Walter McLeod (second row from bottom, second from left) and his squadron
(Courtesy of Gay Bell)

Walter was mesmerized by the Mustang, and for good reasons, as I soon learned. He was a fighter pilot in the U. S. Army Air Corps during WWII and had flown a P-51 Mustang but saw action as the pilot of a P-38 Lightning with the 40th Photo Reconnaissance Squadron in the China Burma India Theater. It was an exciting, and perhaps emotional reunion, of a pilot with one of his flying machines that brought back unbelievable memories of an unbelievable time. After the war, Walter returned home to his Pensacola family and entered the general insurance business. He was one of the founders of the highly successful Hiles-McLeod Insurance Agency.

Both airplanes were privately owned and flew to airports around the country, raising funds for charity groups by charging for tours as well as providing short flights in both planes. Later, I asked Bill if he wouldn't like to take one of the short flights in the B-17 for old time's sake. His quick response was an emphatic, "Hell, no." I hadn't realized at the time how much those fifty-five perilous daylight combat missions over Nazi Germany affected his willingness to ever fly again. A waist-gunner, he was credited with one kill, and on one mission in September 1944, a large section of the left wing of his airplane was blown away by flak, but they made it back

W. A "Bill" Davis, Waist Gunner
WWII

safely to England, reminding us of the popular song at the time, "Coming In On A Wing and A Prayer." The incident, with pictures, was published in the September 22, 1944 issue of Stars And Stripes. Pilots and crew knew the stats were not good for their returning each time they took off on a bombing-run. A Sanitarian with the Escambia County Health Department, and later as a County Commissioner, there were times Bill attended required meetings in distant cities, but his mode of travel was always by car or train. He never flew again.

As I watched and listened to Walter McLeod discuss the attributes of the P-51 Mustang with the pilot, little did I know that someday I would be writing about a father-in-law I would never know, and his love and respect for the P-51.

Above: Bill's plane showing left wing damage
Below: Bill and crew surveying the damage
(Courtesy of *Stars & Stripes*

Lieutenant Colonel William "Bill" Lockney, my wife, Sandra's, father, flew the Mustang in combat in the Pacific Theatre during WWII. He made the transition to jets in the Korean and Vietnam wars. In Korea, his jet was heavily damaged on a mission, causing him to make a "belly landing." A career fighter pilot, he flew every fighter plane the U. S. Air Force had, and earned a drawer full of medals and commendations before his untimely death at age fifty-seven while on active duty. My brother-in-law, Bill Lockney, wrote:

> My father, LTC William J. Lockney, told me about one of his missions over mainland Japan when he was a Second Lieutenant. After escorting U. S. bombers, strafing boats, buildings, and vehicles for 15 minutes his aircraft was hit by enemy ground fire; he was wounded when a hot shell passed through his radio and parachute into his hip. Although in pain, his radio destroyed, and his plane heavily damaged, he successfully flew the eight hour return trip to Iwo Jima with help from his wingman, "My" Starin. When his parachute was removed, it burst into flames.

LTC William J. Lockney
Served in WWII, the
Korean War and the
Vietnam War.

(Courtesy of Bill
Lockney)

409

It seems ironic that only a few years after the B-17s and other Allied bombers literally destroyed Germany, the colonel and his family were stationed in West Germany while the country rebuilt. While living in Germany for several years after the war, where Sandra attended high school and college, and later returned to work in Germany, she said she never met a German who admitted fighting against the Americans. They declared they fought in the Eastern Front against the Russians. Her German friends said they never met an American serviceman who would admit he fought against or bombed Germany.

Jimmy Crooke USAAF
(Courtesy of Teresa Crooke

It's surprising how many local men ended up in B-17s in WWII. One in particular was Jimmy Crooke, who grew up in East Hill. He decided to leave the University of Florida and join the USAAF when his cousin, Gordon Huggins, a cadet in the Army Air Corps at Randolph Field, Texas was killed in a training flight. Jim became a navigator aboard a B-17 Flying Fortress. On September 12, 1944, he and his fellow crewmen took off from Molesworth Airfield, north of London, and joined up with several hundred other B-17s, and their P-51 escorts. Their plane's specific target was the town of Brux on the Czechoslovokian border, an industrial and mining town. Less than fifty miles from Berlin, their plane, the *Lonesome Polecat,* was heavily damaged by Foch Wolf-190 fighter planes. Jimmy and all but three members of his crew bailed out before the plane exploded. They were captured by local citizens, along with a pilot of a P-51 Mustang, whose plane was destroyed about the same time. Jim spent the remainder of the war as a POW at Stalag Luft I, a prisoner-of-war camp near Barth, Germany, for captured Allied airmen.

Jinny Crooke's
German POW
Identification
Card

410

Jimmy Crooke (first row, far right) and his Crew Members
(Courtesy of Teresa Crooke)

Much has been written about, and movies filmed in Stalag Luft I (*e.g. The Great Escape*). Approximately nine-thousand airmen were imprisoned there, about seventy-five hundred Americans, and the rest British and Canadian. The camp was liberated by Russian troops on April 30, 1945. At first, the Russians planned to repatriate the POWs by sea through Odessa in the Soviet Union. Fortunately the Allies balked at the Russian offer, apparently suspicious of their intent, and perhaps rightfully so, because it is well documented that many POWs liberated by Russian troops remain unaccounted for. Eventually, the Russians gave permission for the POWs to be evacuated by air, which became known as "Operation Revival." Thus, between May 13th and 15th, the entire camp was evacuated by American B-17s, including my brother, Bill's, plane, *Pretty Babe's Boys*. I remember him talking about the experience, especially the fact that all the POWs were "eaten alive" with lice and fleas. Even the crew had to be deloused later.

The British POWs were returned directly to England; the American and Canadian POW's were sent to "Camp Lucky Strike," near Le Havre, France, about which Jim Crooke wrote years later:

> . . . a sprawling, hastily erected tent city, with some 40,000 RAMPS (Recovered Allied Military Personnel) in six-man tents. Here I encountered Pensacola friend and fellow Gator, bombardier Philip Beall (prominent Pensacola attorney and future state senator).
> On a clear morning in June 1945 we, along with 5,819 other released prisoners of war, boarded the new 608-foot troop transport USS ADMIRAL H. T. MAYO. Our destination: Boston Harbor, U.S.A.
> In Boston I encountered another friend from Pensacola, Lt. Greenwood Gay, a B-24 pilot who had been badly shot-up while returning from a mission over Nuernberg and had been imprisoned at Stalag I. [1]

Anxious to get home to his family, Jim got a hop on a Navy PBY to Jacksonville, and finally made it to Pensacola on Delta Airlines. Mocking one of his German guards, he wrote: "For us, finally *der var vast truly ofer.*" He returned to the University of Florida's College of Architecture, married Theresa, "the prettiest girl from West Virginia," he wrote, and enjoyed a successful career as a Pensacola architect while raising their three children, Carol Ann, Joey, and Deena.

Jimmy and Teresa pictured on the back cover of Jimmy's book, Berlin to the Gulf of Mexico[1]. (Courtesy of Teresa Crooke).

In the quote above from Jim Crooke's fabulous book, Berlin to the Gulf of Mexico,[1] he refers to fellow Pensacola native, and former attorney, Lt. Philip Beall, Jr., a bombardier, who, like Jim had to bail out of his flaming B-17 while on a bombing raid over Germany. In a June 30, 1945 article in the *Pensacola Herald*, under the heading, "Lt. Philip D. Beall Tells of 15 Months In German Prison Camp," Wesley Chalk wrote:

Lt. Phillip Beall, Jr
(Courtesy of Merry Beall
Brazzelle)

The young officer arrived in Pensacola early Monday morning from Ft. McPherson, Ga., where he was granted a 60-day leave. Lieutenant Beall is here to visit his mother and wife but had little to say of his future military career other than to express a hope of early return to civilian life.

Lieutenant Beall, a bombardier on a Flying fortress was shot down over Germany on February 10, 1944, and was liberated by the Russians from Stalag camp No. 1 in the Baltics on May 1, 1945. 'We were on our ninth mission flying over Brunswick, Germany, when anti-aircraft fire caught us. The big plane caught fire, one member of the crew was blown out over the target and the remaining fellows had to make a jump for it. It was my first occasion to jump and I admit I might have been scared otherwise, but I knew it was the only means of saving my life. I only know that four of the fellows were able to parachute to safety. When I landed, after floating down

Lt. Phillip Beall, Jr, (third from left) and crew members

414

4,000 feet, I got up right in the face of a German farmer armed with a rifle.'

The former attorney, who was associated with his father, the late Sen. Philip D. Beall, Sr., before entry into the service, told of harrowing experiences at the hands of German civilians, transfers from one camp to another, life as a prisoner of war and of final liberation by the Russians.

Lt. Philip Beall's German POW Identification Card
(Courtesy of Merry Beall Brazzelle

Dorothy and Phillip Beall,
Wedding Picture
(Courtesy of Merry Beall
Brazzelle)

Lt. Philip Beall, Jr. wasn't the only family member who took to the air during WWII. His beautiful, young wife, Dorothy Klein Beall, a native of Pender Harbor, British Columbia, Canada, was a former Lieutenant in the Women Airforce Service Pilot program (WASP). It was an organization of women pilots who were trained by the U. S, Air Force to ferry military airplanes from factories and airfields to points of embarkation. In addition, they test-piloted planes, instructed male pilots, and even towed targets for anti-aircraft artillery practice.

Of interest, the WASP program was founded by former Pensacola resident, Jacqueline Cochran, who made aviation history and is in the National Aviation Hall of Fame.

Philip Beall returned to his law practice, and followed in his father's footsteps. Like his father, he was elected State Senator, representing

Escambia County and remained in office for four terms, serving from 1947 to 1962. In the 1950's, Philip, Dorothy and their young children, Philip (Buddy) and Merry Elizabeth lived across the street from my family on Bayou Boulevard, and later moved to Gulf Breeze. Their waterfront home on the sound was among stately oaks that adjoined the National Seashore.

Philip D. Beall, Jr. died April 12, 1988. Dorothy died in 1995. They were preceded in death by their son "Buddy," in an automobile accident in 1974. Pensacola and West Florida benefited from the many laws Senator Beall introduced and helped pass during his years in the Florida Legislature.

Tech Sergeant Charles H. Pohlmann, Jr.
(Courtesy of Chuck Pohlmann)

Pensacolian, Charles H. Pohlmann, Jr., a 1941 graduate of Gulf Coast Military School in Gulfport, Mississippi, like Lt. Greenwood Gay, saw action in the B-24 Liberator. On July 28, 1944, while on a daylight bombing mission over the oil fields and refineries of Ploiesti, Romania, Tech Sergeant Pohlmann's plane suffered heavy damage and several crewmen were wounded. The order to bail out was given, but Pohlmann discovered the tail-gunner, "Mac," was unconscious and seriously injured. Instead of leaving him to a certain death, he dragged him to the escape hatch, squeezed both through the narrow opening, clung to "Mac" as they fell free of the aircraft, and then pulled the unconscious airman's ripcord. To avoid any entanglement he waited a few seconds before pulling his own ripcord.

Both landed safely, and near each other in Yugoslavia, as their crippled B-24 had inadvertently crossed over the border after being hit. Yugoslavian partisans quickly took them to shelter to avoid having them fall into German hands. The partisans administered what medical assistance they could on "Mac," but unfortunately he died of his injuries. The surviving crew members and the pilot, John B. Edwards of Colorado Springs, eventually made contact with each other. Charles' parents at 1413 East Brainard Street received a telegram informing them that he was "missing in action and presumed dead," however, forty-eight days later he and his fellow crewmen reached safety. What a wonderful joy that second telegram must have brought to the Pohlmann family.

The hundreds upon hundreds of Allied daylight bombing missions against the Ploiesti oil fields and refineries by B-17s, B-24s, and P-38s resulted in extremely heavy casualties and loss of hundreds of aircraft. Experts on both sides agree that the destruction of Ploiesti helped shorten the war considerably. Albert Speer, an architect, and Hitler's Minister of Armaments and Industry, wrote in his post-WWII book, Inside The Third Reich what he personally said to Adolph Hitler:

> The enemy has struck us at one of our weakest points. If they persist at it this time, we will soon no longer have any fuel production worth mentioning. Our only hope is that the other side has an air-force general staff as scatterbrained as ours.

Tech Sergeant Charles H. Pohlmann receiving the Silver Star
(Courtesy of Chuck Pohlmann)

I was privileged to know Charles Pohlmann through my older brothers, Bill and Ben, as they were in local schools together, plus for many years my grandmother lived across the street from the Pohlmann family. The truth is, everyone in Pensacola got to know who Charles H. Pohlmann, Jr. was, because of all the publicity about his surviving the war after being presumed dead, and awarded the Silver Star medal for his heroic actions. He was one heck of a nice guy, and he always greeted me with a friendly smile. After returning home, he worked for Sears Roebuck & Company for many years, and was "the man to go to" in the appliance department. In a recent conversation with his son, Chuck, I told him his dad helped me pick out my first new shotgun when I was sixteen years old.

"That was my uncle, he worked in the Sporting Goods department," Chuck said.

"No, I went to your dad first," I said, "and he walked me over to Sporting Goods and told the man there, who was probably your uncle, that I was ready to buy a shotgun, which I did, a sixteen gauge Browning Automatic, known as a 'Sweet Sixteen.' Your dad was excited for me, and made me feel good. That's the way I remember him; he was like that with everybody. "

This chapter on local heroes and the airplanes they flew or worked on would be incomplete without including those in our community who were involved with the Tuskegee Airmen, the name given to a group of African American pilots who fought in WWII. Many books and magazine articles have been written about the heroics of individual Tuskegee Airmen, and their units, the 332nd Fighter Group and the 99th Fighter Group. They were initially equipped with P-39 Air Cobras, P-40 Warhawks, P-47 Thunderbolts, and finally the P-51 Mustangs, with which they became most commonly associated. Early on they painted the tail of each of their airplanes red, so, that's why the nickname "Red Tails" was coined.

I was unable to locate names of other local veterans who were members of the Tuskegee Airmen during WWII, other than General Daniel

General Daniel "Chappie"
James, USAF
(Source: Wikipedia, 3/7/2012)

"Chappie" James, although there were several in years past. General James, a Pensacola native, and the first four-star African American general in the U. S. Air Force, graduated from the Tuskegee Institute in 1942, and received his commission as a second lieutenant. He spent the remainder of the war training pilots for the all-black 99th Pursuit Squadron. He was sent to Korea in 1950, where he flew 101 combat missions in P-51 Mustang and F-80 aircrafts. The local "James Building," a state office building is named in his honor. Of interest is General James was my father-in-law, Lieutenant Colonel "Bill" Lockney's commanding officer at some point during their careers.

Last year, while participating in a book sale in DeFuniak Springs,

Florida, I met Daniel Haulman, a fellow writer in the booth next to the one Sandra and I occupied. He is one of the authors of <u>Tuskegee Airmen, An Illustrated History: 1939 – 1949</u>[2]. Daniel is a highly respected Air Force historian. It's an excellent book, and provides great detail. While reading the chapter on "Chronology of the Tuskegee Airmen," what I discovered on page 177 made me think of Staff Sergeant Charles Pohlmann, above, and his ill-fated mission. The entry read: "July 28, 1944- The 332nd Fighters Group escorted B-24 bombers of the 55th Bombers Wing to, over, and from Ploesti, Romania. Three B-24s were seen to go down in flames." I thought of Charles Pohlmann because July 28, 1944 was the same date his B-24 was heavily damaged over Ploesti, and wondered if perhaps his plane was one of the three, but didn't actually crash until they crossed over the Yugoslavian border.

There are many other "local heroes" to write about, especially the many former U. S. Navy and Marine Corps pilots and crewmen, like fellow writers, Pete Booth, Tex Atkinson, Art Giberson, Leo Murphy, Jim Jowers and others. We're a Navy town, full of heroes, and to write about them would fill the shelves at our local libraries. Maybe someday we'll figure out a way to acknowledge and thank each one of them.

[1] James J. Crooke Jr. <u>Berlin to the Gulf of Mexico, POW 5518 Remembers,</u>. Trafford Publishing. Victoria BC, Canada. 2010.
[2] Caver, Joseph, Ennels, Jerome, and Haulman, Daniel. <u>Tuskegee Airmen, An Illustrated History: 1939-1949.</u> New South Books, Montgomery, ALA. 2011.

B-17 Flying Fortress and the P-51 Mustang , Pensacola International Airport,
Air Show, 2016

Hell's Angels
303rd Bomb Group (H)

(GPR-667-303/10 SEPT 44/LT CLEMENSON E CREW

(Assigned 359BS: 29 August 1944 - Photo: 10 September 1944)
This picture of the crew was taken two days before that fateful day.
Standing:
2Lt Richard L. Clemensen (P)(KIA), 2Lt George S. Burson (CP)
(POW), 2Lt James J. Crooke, Jr. (N)(POW),
2Lt Frank W. Stafford (B)(KIA)
Kneeling:
Sgt Eugene E. McCrory, Jr. (E()(KIA), Sgt Kurt Schubach (R)
(POW), Sgt Lloyd L. Albern (BTG)(POW), Sgt Nick Kriss (WG)
(KIA),Pvt Jack R. Allerton (WG), Sgt John W. Jauernig (TG)(POW)

BERLIN TO THE GULF OF MEXICO
POW 5518 REMEMBERS

James J. Crooke, Jr.

[Germany, 1944]

A

B

C

Caldwell, H. Miller Jr. 271, 273
Calhoun, Jackie   see Saxon, Jackie
Cannon, Charles 99
Cannon, Doris 3, 24, 26,
Cantrell, Homer 258,
Carlan, Charles 271, 272
Caro, Forsyth 224, 226
Carpenter, Josh 219
Carr, Ronald 91
Carr, Virgil, J. SFM3 359
Carrick, Lawrence 99
Carrick, Larry 396
Carter, Charlie 158,
Cary, George 351,
Cary, Lucie Reilly, see Pennewill, Lucie
Cary, Margaret "Molly" Biggs 351,
Cary, Marianne Beckman, 351,
Cassidy, Ted 379
Cassimus, Angelo 246
Castro, Fidel 147, 148,
Catches, George 258, 260, 261,
Catches, Johnny 258,
Chaboudy, Robert B. MM2 359
Chadbourne, Ed 235, 243, 244, 246,
Chadwick, James H. 43, 56, 57,
Chaudron, Ralph 249, 258
Chalk, Wesley 249, 250, 413
Chavers, Bill 249, 258,
Chavers, Foy 91
Chestnut, Vinson 91
Childress, Tommy T. SOG2 359
Chivington, Felecia 269, 270,
Christ, Lee T. BM2 359
Clarke, Clifton 91
Clopton, Agnes 331, 337, 339,
Clopton, Betty 288,
Clopton, Chipley "Chip" 334, 337, 339, 340,
Clopton, David 337, 338, 339, 340,
Clopton, Gail 337, 339,
Clopton, Jeff 334, 337, 338, 339, 340,
Clopton, Jerry 337, 341
Clopton, Johnnie 335, 337, 339, 341
Clopton, Joyce 337, 339,
Clopton, Loice 337, 339,
Clopton, Nathaniel 331,
Clopton, Shane 340,
Clopton, Sheila 337, 339,
Clopton, Sidney Capt. 3, 330, 331, 332, 333, 338, 339
Clopton, Tommy 335, 337, 338, 339,
Cobb, Danny J. 271, 274
Cobb, Rip 238, 246
Cobb, Sherry see Snead, Sherry
Cochran, Jacqueline "Jackie" 415
Cohron, Henry 257,
Colado, Erick 182, 184
Cole, John W. 224, 226
Coleman, Arthur D. RM2 359
Coleman, Dale 91
Coleman, Drew 91

D

427

428

E

F

G

H

431

432

Hull, Jack E. Chief   358
Humphrey, Lucius   246,
Hunter, Charles E. Jr. BT1   359
Hunter, Helen see Gaines, Helen
Hutchings, Nicholas   281, 293
Hutchings, Pat   281, 293,
Hutto, Edward J. BM3   359
Hyer, Em Turner   76, 77, 79,
Hyer, M. T. "Mike"   80, 81,
Hyer, J. Whiting   76, 77, 81, 83,
Hyer, John W. Jr.   77, 80, 83,
Hyer, Margaret Hall   76, 77, 80,

I

Ingram, Duane Jones "Dee"   281, 287, 297
Irwin, Floyd L. SK3   360
Irwin, Joseph R. SN   360, 371

J

Jackson, Gail see Gaines, Gail
Jackson, JoAnn see Gaines, JoAnn
James, Daniel "Chappie" General   418
Jeffords, W. Quintillus Mrs.   377
Jennings, Bud   182
Jennings, Norma   182
Jernigan, Frank "Blackie"   27,
Jernigan, Webb   129
Johnson, Arthur   81
Johnson, Bill Bartender   183
Johnson, Charles, Sr. "Charlie"   44, 57, 58, 59, 66
Johnson, Charles, Jr.   66,
Johnson, Chris   246, 286, 305, 307,
Johnson, Chris Jr.
Johnson, D. L.   135, 342, 343, 344, 345
Johnson, David   307,
Johnson, Doris see Wright, Doris   176, 183,
Johnson, Dorothy   176
Johnson, E. J.   376
Johnson, Ernest W. "Teense"   44,
Johnson, Faye see Schneidewind, Faye
Johnson, Flossie Aliene Davis   44,
Johnson, Ginny Scheidt   307
Johnson, Henry   246
Johnson, Jimmy   60, 65, 66
Johnson, Jimmy, Jr.   65, 66
Johnson, Lois   176
Johnson, Lorraine see Dawson, Lorraine
Johnson, Ola   176
Johnson, Ray   258,
Johnson, Ruby   176
Johnson, Rufus   103
Johnson, Suzy Gavin   307
Johnson, Susan Jane Scheuer,   307,
Johnson, Thomas W. EN2   360
Johnson, Thomas H.   375, 376

K

L

M

436

McLeod, Al   114
McLeod, Cecil   396
McLeod, Dan   280, 281, 289,
McLeod, Don   170, 171, 238, 240, 246
McLeod, Evelyn Thaxton   280, 281, 287, 288, 291, 295, 297
McLeod, Walter   405, 406, 407
McMillan, Alan   3, 10-23,
McMillan, Alan, Jr.   14, 21,
McMillan, Andrew   18, 23
McMillan, Angus   11,
McMillan, Angus Murphy   12, 13, 14,
McMillan, Angus Murphy, Sr.   13
McMillan, Austin   21,
McMillan, Gloria   13, 14, 19, 21, 22
McMillan, Hannah   14
McMillan, Kyle   14
McMillan, Lauren   21
McMillan, Mattie Pou   13
McMillan, Neil   10, 11, 12, 17, 18, 21, 23,
McMillan, Neil, Jr.   18
McMillan, Preston Jr. "P. J."   14,
McMillan, Preston   14
McMillan, Stuart   18
McMillan, Susan Owsley   21
McMillan, Susan   21
McMillan, Van   11, 12
McMillan, Virginia "Ginger"   11, 12, 20
McMillan, Virginia Sheppard   12,
McSwain, "Onionhead"   103
McVoy, Tommy   230, 232, 234, 240, 246
Mead, Dick   235, 236, 241, 246
Mellen, Churchill   255,
Melville, Carlos   23
Melvin, Carlton   258, 260,
Melvin, Jack   257,
Menge, M. J.   127
Menne, Ruth Christina see Rasponi, Ruth
Menschew, Rusty   379
Mercer, Eddie   105, 109,
Merchant, Dot see Gilmore, Dot
Meredith, David   258,
Merrill, Charlie   104,
Merritt, Billy   240, 241, 246
Merritt, Betty Soule   82, 83,
Merritt, Dick   252,
Merritt, Doris   82,
Merritt, Jack   80, 81, 83,
Merritt, John A.   80, 82, 83
Merritt, John A. III   LCDR   356,
Merritt, Mary Turner   80, 82,
Middlebrooks, Gene   96
Miller, Billy   209, 258,
Miller, Butch   107, 109
Miller, Charlie   250,
Miller, Gary   37,
Miller, Gwen   99
Miller, Jeannine see Pritchett, Jeannine
Miller, Jeff   Congressman   173, 378
Miller, Irvin L.   BT2   360
Miller, Lamar   258,
Miller, Margaret   see Davis, Margaret
Mills, Edward R.   271, 272

437

N

O

P

Q

R

S

U

V

Valdez, Linel 261,
Vanderford, Lola see Berry, Lola
VanMatre, George "Junior" 234, 242, 247
VanPelt, George 94, 237, 238, 241, 242, 247, 271, 274, 286, 288, 291,
VanPelt, Jimmy 238, 247
Varnum, J. H. 224, 226
Vickery, Bill "Red" 232, 234, 235, 242, 247, 290
Vickery, Jackie 290
Vignola, Ed 395
Vignola, Joyce 395
Villar, Anita O. 376
Villar, Emanuel II 247

W

Waite, John 379
Walker, Cathleen, 47,
Walker, Dan 235, 239, 241, 242, 247
Walker, Douglas 47,
Walker, Ethel 47,
Walker, George K. LTJG 357, 366
Walker, Lois 47,
Walker, William Wilmer, Sr. 46, 82,
Walker, William Wilmer, Jr. 47, 81,
Walker, Maurice 47,
Walker, Oliver 47, 81,
Wallace, Edwin "Ned" 76, 77, 78
Wallace, Edwin, Sr. 77
Wallace, Jean 76, 77, 78,
Wallace, Em Tucker 77,
Wallace, Rusty 105,
Wallace, Steven 109
Walsh, Teresa see Evans, Teresa
Walters, Lora 140
Waltrip, Darrell 105, 109,
Ward, Ace P. 55,
Ward, Arch 248
Ward, Charlie Coach 391
Ward, Chris 396
Ward, Toby 56,
Ward, Tom 258, 261,
Warren, Jackie see Rush, Jackie
Watson, Jack 32
Watts, Geoff *Pensacola News Journal* 403
Webb, John B. Dr. 271, 272
Webster, Daniel Congressman 387
Weekley, Hugh 238, 247
Weekley, Ken 235, 240, 243, 244, 247
Weekley, Raymond 235, 244, 247, 315, 316,
Weis, Carl A. Mrs. 85,
Weitling, Martha 277
Weldon, C. T. 104,
Weller, Jack 247
Wells, Bobby 243, 247
Wentworth, T. T. Jr. 223, 224, 226, 267, 276, 278
Werhan, Dale 317,
Wessel, Bill 177

X

Y

Z

46834318R00250

Made in the USA
San Bernardino, CA
16 March 2017